MW01235639

STREET CHILDREN:
LIVES OF VALOR & VULNERABILITY

Poonam Sondhi - Garg
(Ph.D)

4831/24, Ansari Road
Darya Ganj
New Delhi-110 002
Phone : 23260807
Fax : 23274173
E-mail: essess@del3vsnl.net.in

© Author

First Published 2004

ISBN : 81-88583-58-8

Price : Rs. 550/-

Published by :
Reference Press
4831/24, Ansari Road, Darya Ganj,
New Delhi - 110 002
Phone : 23260807
Fax : 23274173

Printed at :
Print Line

PREFACE

Many children in most cities of the world, especially in the developing countries, lack adequate family care, protection and supervision. Neglect, ill treatment and abuse of children has always been present in human society. It is only during the late 20th century that some children are now seen as being in need of protection from their families. Many of them are growing in neglectful or abusive families while some have no family at all, or are completely separated from it.

Large numbers of children live and work on the streets in urban area, with or without their families. For many such children the street is their permanent place of abode or home. The awareness regarding the presence of a large number of street children in Indian cities is relatively recent. Child labor has been the subject of attention for past several years. A number of studies are available on working children while data on street children is limited. Compounding the problem is the scarcity of statistics about the number of children working, especially those in hazardous conditions. More data are urgently needed in order to better monitor and prevent child labour violations, particularly since the vast majority of children labour in the informal sector.

During the last two decades (1980-2000) there has been a vast proliferation of literature on street children. More international and national organizations are highlighting the extremely difficult situations of street children. This has led to an increased concern for working street children and a recognition of their problems as a national concern. Street children living alone face varying forms of abuse, neglect, and deprivation. Exposure to excessive physical maltreatment and emotional deprivation, common in the lives of street children, are likely to impinge on their behavior and development. An account of the adverse psychosocial factors in the street child's working and living environment and their critical role in the child's development needs to be ascertained.

This book documents the working and living conditions of street children living without any familial contact or support. In many cities large numbers of street children lack shelter, food, education, and support and are vulnerable to many forms of abuse, despite the best efforts of governments and NGO's. This book explores the phenomenon of street child labor in all its complexity. The contributing factors are multiple and overlapping, including poverty, breakdown of family relations, lack of access to education, etc. In the children's homes, poverty, unemployment, marital instability and alcohol abuse are endemic. The book emphasizes how a family's social, emotional and physical environment influences child's physical and mental health. The risky family environment in which children grow and resultant separation from the primary caregiver during crucial developmental years produce disruptions in physical and psychosocial functioning.

The term street children refers to children for whom the street more than their family has become their real home. It includes children who might not necessarily be homeless or without families, but who live in situations where there is no protection, supervision, or direction from responsible adults. Over 120 million worldwide fight daily for survival. These children's lifestyle exposes them to serious health risks. They also suffer brutal violence, sexual exploitation, abject neglect, chemical addiction, and human rights violations. Children in difficult circumstances, and street children in particular, experience exclusion and precariousness. They were propelled to the streets to find an alternative way of coping with poverty, which is remarkable for its adaptability and resiliency.

Problems faced by street children are overwhelming. In addition to living and working in environments that are generally harmful to their well-being, street children face problems such as hunger, lack of adequate shelter, clothes, and other basic needs, as well as lack of (or limited) educational opportunities, health care, and other social services. As victims of stigma and discrimination, they are more vulnerable than others to various health problems, both at the physical and psychological level. Attention to the problem of street children has been focused largely on the social, economic and health problems of the children - poverty, lack of education, AIDS, prostitution, and substance abuse. They suffer the consequences at two levels: because they are thrown onto the streets and are living on the margins of society, they are ignored and their needs neglected. The public view of street children in many countries is overwhelmingly negative

Children living on the street, without homes or families pose the greatest challenge in terms of rehabilitation often needing long-term one- to- one counseling. Constraints and challenges that add to the difficulty in resolving the problem of street children are listed. The public image of street children acts as a barrier to research and programming, and it is suggested that their relationships to street environments should be analyzed. It also enumerates some of the major programmes and activities undertaken by different government and non-government agencies in their effort to alleviate and eventually eliminate the problem. Because the causes of street child labour are complex, the solution must be comprehensive. The book calls for the immediate end to hazardous child labour and proposes strategies to help eliminate and prevent it including: access to education; wider legal protection, collection of information; and mobilization of the coalition of partners among governments, communities, non-governmental organizations (NGOs). Recommendations especially in the background of legislative actions in India are put forth.

The references in the bibliography are an eclectic mix of academic, nongovernmental organisation (NGO), governmental and news reports. The data is drawn from a wide variety of sources in order to provide the reader with a broad overall picture of the situation.

The book attempts to fill a part in the gap in existing psychological literature which includes extremely few objective descriptions of street children's lives and psychosocial phenomena. It narrates their stories, thoughts, opinions, pains, and hopes from their own points of view. The book is provided for those concerned about protecting and improving the lives of street children including cross-cultural researchers, psychologists, health care professionals, social workers and policy makers in national and international organizations.

17 June 2004   **Poonam Sondhi-Garg**

CONTENTS

CHARTS

TABLES

PART ONE

INTRODUCTION

The problem of working and street children is global one. Children working and living on the street is a phenomenon as old as cities themselves. Although street children is not a specific problem of developing countries and is not a new phenomenon, it is only in recent years that is has become a topic of political and educational attention and a subject matter of worldwide concern. International exposure of their plight goes back many years.

In India, the emergence of innumerable street children or street child labor was never foreseen in any national plan. The issue of children deprived of their most basic rights, their health , denied education and trapped in cycles of poverty with even their lives in jeopardy, is central to humanitarian concern. It is also linked to various other social problems especially faced by the youth population like: violence, drug abuse, delinquency and prostitution. It has begun to receive increasing notice in both the media and academic literature.

The child welfare system has long targeted child workers who work and live with their families. However, homeless children in the sense that they are defined now, as 'children who live without any familial support, living a nomadic, often squalid existence on the streets and in shelters that can never be a substitute for a stable family home', were excluded even till the 1980s (Agnelli, S.1986).

This critical issue is now beginning to get the attention it deserves. Some major initiatives are the formation of the Inter-Non Government Organization (NGO) Program for street children and street youth in Geneva, and a series of international conferences and seminars in various cities all over the world including Marseilles,

New York, Bogota, Sudan and Brazil. The recent ones include: The European Network on Street Children Worldwide Constitutional Conference held in Brussels in April 1997 and Global call for World Bank commitment to street children 2000 in Washington.

United Nations' Children's Fund (UNICEF) has contributed in the creation of dialogue, and focusing on the magnitude and import of the problem. At the national level, with the launching of the scheme by the Ministry of Welfare with assistance from UNICEF for care of street children, India joins countries like Brazil, the Philippines and Sudan that have running programs for street children with assistance from UNICEF.

Increasing awareness about the phenomenon of street children or street child labor has been responsible for three significant conclusions emerging. First, the recognition that the problem may be alarmingly larger than originally thought ; second , the beginning of a practical theoretical structure for model program development for street children; and third, a consciousness of the need for increased publicity for the free exchange of ideas and for effective support on behalf of these children.

Recent commitments of resources have been made by various international agencies supporting joint efforts with certain governments to address this pressing social problem. The need for social action has long been evident and the initiation of these collaborative efforts is indeed welcome.

1.1   THE CONCEPT – DEFINITION AND CATEGORIES

Unlike orphans or disabled children, it is difficult to identify a 'street child' by precise definitional criterion. Aptekar (1994), Lusk (1992), and Ortiz et al (1992) point out the lack of a standard definition of street children. The expression is broad and wide – ranging and covers a number of those previously referred to under different headings such a: juvenile delinquents, child laborers , drop-outs, maladjusted children, abused children and deprived children. Street children who work on the street , irrespective of the fact whether they live with or without their families, constitute street child labor. In contrast with child domestic workers, these children work in the most visible places possible — on the streets of developing world cities and towns. Amongst them, children who work and live on the street without any familial contact, supervision or support are at the greatest risk and the most vulnerable.

'Children without families', 'high risk children', 'abandoned' and 'destitute children', 'children in need of care and protection' and 'children in especially difficult circumstances' are terms commonly used while referring to street children and these terms mostly tend to overlap (Agnelli, S. 1986). Many of them, at various times, spend a significant part of their day in the street, without necessarily sharing any other common characteristic.

Cosgrove (1990) suggests that two factors need to be considered in developing a "working definition" of street children. He defines street child as "any individual under the age of majority whose behavior is predominantly at variance with community norms for behavior and whose primary support...is not a family or family substitute". As Aptekar (1994) notes, however, this definition assumes that degree of family involvement and deviant behavior are the same cross-culturally; yet in India, entire families (the "pavement dwellers") live and work on the streets, and often life on the street may be better for a child than life in an abusive home. Also, the implication of "deviant behavior" is questionable for children who may be forced to commit petty crimes in order to obtain basic necessities (Hemenway, D. 1996).

Little is known and understood about these children. The general or popular perceptions that a society has towards street children reflect the children's image and also society's response, attitudes and degree of tolerance towards them. A striking similarity is observed between the attitude of the society towards street children in the past and the present. Between 1853 and 1890 in the United States, about 90,000 street children were removed from the streets and put in foster homes as farm hands. In a close resemblance to present-day attitudes toward street children, Reverend Charles Brace wrote in 1853: "There are no dangers to the value of property or to the permanency of our institution so great as those from the existence of ....a class of vagabond , ignorant, ungoverned children. This 'dangerous class' has not begun to show itself, as it will in eight or ten years, when these boys and girls are mature. Then let society beware when the outcast, vicious, reckless multitude of New York boys, swarming now in every foul alley and street, come to know their power, and use it!" (quoted in Agnelli, S. 1986).

The street child has been a particular focus for various international bodies since the United Nations International Year of the Child in 1979. Street life, as described by Rapid Situation Assessment report brought out by the United Nations Office for Drug Control and Crime Prevention (UNODCCP), United Nations Children's Fund (UNICEF) and the World Health Organization (WHO) is "scary." It is mostly an unforgiving environment in which children, must survive essentially alone, vulnerable to abuse and exploitation and reliant on their own coping mechanisms (UNICEF, 2001)

Street Child as defined by Myles Ritchie (1999) is "any child under the age of 18, unless otherwise stated, who for a variety of reasons leaves his / her family and community part time or permanently to survive on the streets and is inadequately cared for and protected by reasonable adults". Street children as a group, therefore, are defined under the 'catch-all' phrase *'children in especially difficult circumstances'*. Within this realm they are further categorised as *'homeless children'*, the subcategory being *'children living on the street'*.

"*Street children*" is a term often used to describe both *market children* (who work in the streets and markets of cities selling or begging, and live with their families) and *homeless street children* (who work, live and sleep in the streets, often lacking any contact with their families). The latter group is at the highest risk. On-going abuse, exploitation and inhumane treatment are common for these children, whose ages range from six to 18. They often indulge in petty theft and prostitution for survival. They are extremely vulnerable to sexually transmitted diseases including HIV/AIDS. An estimated 90% of them are addicted to inhalants such as shoe glue and paint thinner, which cause kidney failure, irreversible brain damage and, in some cases, death (Casa Alianza, 1995).

Blanc (1994) presents a "visible-invisible" model: "visible" refers to children who are easily seen occupied in economically gainful occupations on the street in the informal sector of the economy, while "invisible" refers to children in more hidden yet exploitative circumstances, for example as domestic servants, factory workers, and other child laborers; or compelled into prostitution or other illegal trades. Although street children are primarily boys, it is in this second "invisible" category that many street girls are found.

Cockburn (1991) has summarized some of the characteristics of street children identified in the literature: drug abuse (e.g., solvents), high impulsivity, distrust and manipulation of adults, fleeing rather than facing problems, internal locus of control, low self-esteem, high value on personal freedom, adherence to conventional morality, and reluctance to disclose true life story.

In the mid-80's UNICEF coined the category 'children in especially difficulty circumstances'. Within this group are street children, abandoned and neglected children, orphans, children with physical and mental difficulties, working children, children living with HIV/AIDS, children of imprisoned mothers, child mothers, child drug addicts and refugee children (Dunford, 1996).

UNICEF (1996) has proposed a broader definition of a street child as "any minor for whom the street (in the widest sense of the word, i.e. unoccupied dwellings, wasteland, etc.) has become his of her habitual abode, and who is without adequate protection". UNICEF has categorized three types of street children:

* Street-Family,
* Street-Working, and
* Street- living

Street-Family or Children from Street Families: These are children who live on the streets with their families. This group consists primarily of working children who earn a living on the street while still having family contacts of a more or less regular nature. Their focus in life is still the home, some attend school, most return home at the end of each working day and most will have a sense of belonging to the local community in which their home is situated. Making regular contacts with their homes, they circulate, often spending most of their time in the streets.

Street Working Children: children who spend most of their time on the streets, fending for themselves, but returning home on a regular basis. This group of children is smaller but more complex in its characteristics. Children in this group see the street as their home and it is there that they seek shelter, livelihood and companionship. They have occasional or sporadic contacts with their families. They may be away from home for days or months at a time.

Street Living Children : children who run away from their families and live alone on the streets. This group consists of children who exist at an extreme, living on streets without the traditional institutional support of family. These children are entirely on their own, not only for material survival but also psychologically. "This group has two distinguishable subgroups: one comprises of children who have been orphaned or physically abandoned. The second subgroup includes children who are abandoning, not abandoned children. These children appear to have made an active willful departure from home because of varied reasons. "Having broken primary ties with their families, they are essentially responsible for their own physical and emotional survival" (Felsman, J.K. 1981).

For every four street children seen on the streets during the day, three are daytime strollers or *'children on the streets'*, that is they are supplementing parent income and go home at night. The fourth child is of the streets - that is, he will sleep on the streets at night (Ritchie, M. 1999). Easton et al (1994) point out, actual children

Introduction 7

"of the street" are only the "tip of the iceberg", with larger numbers of exploited children and adolescents worldwide who work in situations harmful to their health and well-being.

Street children are often referred to in the literature as 'runaways' or 'throwaways', reinforcing the notion that many are escaping domestic crises (Young et al. 1983; Kufeldt and Nimmo 1987; Janus et al. 1987). In the case of the runaways the child gets to the street without a parent's permission, while the 'throwaways' are overtly rejected by their parents. Street children, therefore, could have been abandoned by their parents, could be orphans, or runaways from neglectful or abusive families. Street children are, however, not a homogeneous group, but are members of smaller subgroups or subcultures. On the basis of choices made while on the street, children can be placed into broad categories for purposes of analysis.

Attempts have long been made to establish categories or typology among street children and identify them on the basis of the availability of shelter to them and also their level of contact with their families. Aptekar, L. (1988) collected data on Colombian male street children in the age group of 7-16 years. He gathered information about street children by using participant observation method. From the data, it was apparent that 'there were two different preadolescent (under 12 years of age) psychological styles that ended at adolescence'.

"The first style was the gamine or the true urchin – children who chose to leave home, having rejected the exchange of childhood protections with family obligations for the freedom from authority with less security. They were abandoners, who survived by cunning and wit. The second style was that of the "chupagrueso", or children who were abandoned (The verb chupar in Spanish means to absorb through sucking and is used idiomatically in certain Andean areas to refer to people who attach themselves to the more powerful) The chupagruesos lacked the arrogant independence of the gamines and they learned to survive by becoming servile to the powerful." (Aptekar, L.1980)

Lusk (1992) in a discussion of street children in Rio de Janeiro uses four categories along this continuum.

1. The first, family-based street workers describes those children who live with their families and work in the street for economic reasons. These children have maximum contact with traditional social structures including their communities and families. They may attend school and have a low level of criminal involvement and drug use.

2. The second, independent street workers, by contrast, have family contacts which are transient in nature. These children have begun to live on the streets occasionally.

3. Children of the Streets are those who have no family contacts (they are often runaways, orphaned, or abandoned). They are alienated from social institutions, such as schools; and may make their living illegally, while also being victims of crimes and sexual abuse and finally,

4. Children of Street families are those whose families are in fact living and/or working in street situations. These are the "pavement dwellers" in India, and many of the "favela" slum residents in Brazil.

Reddy, N. (1992) conducted a study of street and working children in Bangalore city. The study was sponsored by Ministry of Welfare, Government of India and UNICEF. Based on this study, street children were divided into three groups depending on the contact with their families.

The first group consists of children who live with their families, whether it be on the street , in slums, or wasteland, etc. but spend a lot of time working or hanging about on the street. Home and the family still provide the basic framework of their lives. It has been estimated that this is the largest of the three categories.

The second, children who live and work on the street, yet maintain occasional contact with their families who live either in other cities, or, more often, in villages. These children have chosen the street as their home. Some of them sometimes send money home to their families. The most distinguishable characteristic of this group is that their links with families are transient or fleeting in nature.

The last group consists of those children who live and work alone on the street and have no family contact and support whatsoever. These children are either orphaned, or abandoned. They include destitute, runaways, refugees and displaced children. This group of working street children is confronted with a different matrix of constraints and deprivations from that confronted by the first and second group. Children in all the above categories may express varying forms of street child labor. They may be engaged in different kinds of economically gainful activities and many are at risk from hazardous and exploitative child labor. Children in both the second and third categories have much in common: unstable emotional relationships with the adult world, a negative self-image, social stigma, violence, exploitation and uncertain future. The book concentrates on the third and most vulnerable group of street children.

A deeper analytical and comprehensive understanding of these children and their conditions is essential before formulating a universally acceptable definition of street children. At present, there is no precise and objective criterion to define a 'street child' and there is little consensus on it. It is important to establish categories among street children in order to devise specific strategies and planning services for responding to their special and varied needs. The form and nature of these strategies will be determined by factors like: age group, gender and the degree or extent and duration of isolation from family and home, the kind of deprivations faced by the child in both his living and working environment.

1.2. MAGNITUDE AND EXTENT - A GLOBAL PERSPECTIVE

Most of the figures on street child labor are open to challenge. Depending on how the street child is defined, estimates of their number vary. Figures tend to be contentious as street children are not easy to count, numbers depend on the definition used and criteria chosen, on which there is little consensus. The definition or concept of street child, as it exists today, is ill defined and ambiguous and thus an objective statistical calculation of the total number of street children does not exist (Agnelli, S. 1986). The criteria for defining street children vary from country to country and with time, making it difficult to arrive at any precise global estimates. It is also difficult to ascertain statistical records either in terms of absolute numbers or proportion of children who consider the street as their home to children who maintain contact with their families but spend most of their time on the street.

Ten years ago, UNICEF estimated that over 30 million children worldwide (Agnelli, 1986) work and/or live in the streets, for circumstances usually beyond their control, and often without family support. Current estimates of street children worldwide number in the hundreds of millions. Estimates reported by the WHO Project on Street Children and Substance Abuse put the number of street children between 10 and 100 million worldwide (WHO, 2002). The United Nations has estimated the population of street children worldwide at 150 million, with the number rising daily. These young people are known as 'community children' as they are the offspring of our communal world. Ranging in age from three to eighteen, about 40 percent of those are homeless (Human Rights Watch, 1997) A common feature of all the existing numerical estimates of street children is that the basis on which they are derived is seldom specified

While Latin America represents only 10% of the world's children, it has more than 50% of the world's street children. The numbers involved in this estimate are: 20 million abandoned in Asia , 10 million in Africa and the Middle –East and 30-40 million in Latin America (Inter American Parliamentary Group on Population in Development, 1984, cited in Ennew J.& Milne, B. 1989). In parts of the former Soviet Union the increase in poverty from economic collapse has contributed to the conditions that give rise to the emergence of street children (PANGAEA, 1996).

None of the above estimates explains what constitutes abandonment, the criteria used to define street children and identify them. A report published by the Association of Children's Court Judges of Brazil in July, 1984 states that more than 30 million children live in the streets of Brazil alone (cited in Ideas Forum, 1984). The number of street children in Latin America and the Caribbean, which includes children up to 18 years, exceeds 50 million. There are an estimated one million street and working children in South Africa according to the University of Pretoria (Child Hope, 1991)

Recent figures show that nearly 20,000 children in Colombia are abandoned by their poverty – stricken families annually. About 5,000 of them live on city streets, roam together in gangs during daytime and take refuge in the warmth of the sewers during the chilly Andean nights (Castellanos, A. 1991). China is reported to have very few street children. It's strict family planning ('one-child' policy), and the 'street committees' closely linked to the formal police structure, are presumably the responsible factors. Ethiopia, in contrast, has a high number of street children mainly because of natural and man- made disasters (Agnelli, S. 1986).

Ennew, J. and Milne, B. (1989) attempt to give a global estimate of the number of street children by using data from the 1984 UNICEF Report on 'State of the World's Children', along with some other world demographic indicators and figures.(Chart 1). The estimate relates Infant mortality rate and child welfare in general and countries are categorized in groups of high, low and medium rates of infant mortality, according to the scheme used in UNICEF report, 1984. The figures for socialist countries are excluded from this as number of street children living on the street in these countries is reported to be comparatively low.

Chart 1.
ESTIMATED NUMBER OF STREET CHILDREN (MILLION)

IMR (Infant Mortality Rate) Per 1000	Total Population 1981	%of Population Urbanised (1981)	Urban population	Urban child Population aged 5-15 yrs	Economically active urban chidren	Children on the street	Children of the street
Over 100	1,301.9	21	273.4	90.2 (33%)	29.8	9.8	3.2
60 – 100	657.1	41	269.4	89.9 (33%)	29.3	9.7	3.2
26 – 50 (excluding socialist countries)	322.3	51	164.4	36.2 (22%)	11.9	3.9	1.3
Under 25 (excluding socialist countries)	741.0	76	563.2	61.9 (11%)	–	–	–
TOTAL	–	–	–	–	71.0	23.4	7.7

Source : Ennew, J. & Miline, B. (1988) The Next Generation- Lives of Third World Chidren, Zed Books Ltd... Lindon (Based on Unicef Report- State of the World's Chidren. 1984).

The variables taken into account are:

(a) Total population;

(b) Percentage of population urbanized;

(c) Urban population: Using the figures given by UNICEF for the mean of population urbanised in each group, the urban population is derived;

(d) Urban child population in the age group of 5-15 years: As street children are usually found in the 5-15 age group, total urban child population in this age group is derived

(e) Economically active urban child population: This number in each group is taken to be about one-third of the urban child population as this tends to accord with most known studies of child labor;

(f) Children on the street: It is estimated that one –third of the total number of economically active children will be children on the street, i.e. children who are working on the street and also have familial contact and a relatively permanent dwelling place. This figure is likely to vary;

(g) Children of the street : The number of children living on the street without any family or shelter is estimated to be one – third of the total number of children living on the street but maintaining links with their families.

Although this estimate employs a few criteria used in the definition of a street child and conceptual structures that need to be used while arriving at this kind of an estimate, it still has its own limitations. The figures for the total urban child population in the age group of 5 to 15 years, the number of working or economically active children; children of the street and children on the street are likely to be areas of error. (Ennew, J. & Milne, B. 1989).

Approximately 75 percent of all street children live at home, but the remaining 25 percent spend all or most of their time on the street. These latter children, in addition to suffering from problems such as hunger, lack of adequate shelter, clothes, and other basic needs, as well as lack of (or limited) educational opportunities, health care, and other social services. , are also victims of drug addiction, general exploitation, criminal acts, sexual abuse, and sometimes frighteningly high levels of violence (Street Children, 1992; Oliveira et al, 1992).

Peter Tacon, the founder and director of CHILDHOPE (an organization for street children) who has worked with street children in Latin America for a number of years has given a pyramid diagram to estimate the incidence of street children (Chart 2)

Chart 2
INCIDENCE OF STREET CHILDREN

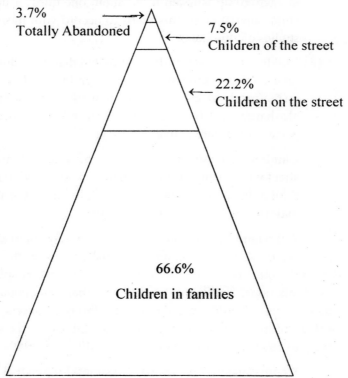

3.7%
Totally Abandoned

7.5%
Children of the street

22.2%
Children on the street

66.6%
Children in families

Source : Ennew, J. & Milne, B. 1989. The Next Generation- Lives of Third World Children

1.3. THE PROBLEM OF WORKING CHILDREN

Child labor is recognized today as a problem that affects countries around the world. The International Labor Organization (ILO) estimated that there were some 211 million children between the ages of 5 and 14 in economic activity in the world in 2000 (ILO , 2002)

Statistics on the number of children in labor force activity are often reported as a single estimate, and are not disaggregated for work that is exploitative or harmful to children. It is important to note that statistics presented do not necessarily reflect that the work performed by children is considered child labor. Work that is considered "child labor" prevents children from attending and participating effectively in school, interferes with his recreation or rest or is performed by children under hazardous conditions that place their healthy physical, intellectual or moral development at risk and at times forces the child to leave home and fend for himself. Such work is palpably exploitative and destructive. Some work performed by children, however, is not considered to be harmful or exploitative. Such work need not impact negatively on the child's development. This could include performing light work after school, household chores, or lawful apprenticeship programs.

The impact of work on a child's development is the key to determining when such work becomes a problem. Work that is harmless to adults can prove to be extremely damaging to children. Among the features of a child's development that can be endangered by work are: physical development — including overall health, coordination, strength, vision and hearing; cognitive development — including literacy, numeric learning and the acquisition of knowledge necessary to normal life; emotional development — including adequate self-esteem, family attachment, feelings of love and acceptance; social and moral development —including a sense of group identity, the ability to cooperate with others and the capacity to distinguish right from wrong (UNICEF,1997).

There is no internationally endorsed definition on working children, or universally prescribed methodology for collecting data on child labor. The lack of concepts and methods for collecting child labor data makes it difficult to obtain comparable and reliable statistics across countries on working children. Therefore, statistics on the incidence of working children in the individual country profiles vary by age ranges and the criteria used to measure child labor.

Child labour is usually defined as participation in economically gainful activity by children (between the ages of 5-14 years). Most of the street children are also working and are school drop-outs also. In this context their situation is related to issue of child labour and education. However, neither of these sectors has demonstrated any interest in dealing with this particularly disadvantaged group. At times street children are not considered as working, and yet child work is defined as 'the involvement of children in work for the purpose of earning livelihood for themselves or their families'. This is one of the major reasons why street children are on the street. Furthermore, many children who have been working as domestic helpers or on farms have become street children after they suffered abuse and maltreatment from their employers. Hence it is advocated that the two groups closely overlap; majority of the street children being working children, and many working children becoming street children.

To a certain extent, the basis for child labour lies in child-rearing norms, which permit the participation of children in domestic activities. Traditionally, such activities were believed to prepare the child for his future role as an adult. Thus, children of all ages took part in productive and economic activities central to the life of the family. The International Labor Organization (1986) also seems to support work by children as is evident by this statement, "when work by children is truly a part of the socialization process, and a means of transmitting skills from parent to child, it is hardly meaningful to speak of child labor". This cultural provision has been misused very often and child labor in the form of systematic exploitation of children by employers is widespread.

A great majority of children work in the unorganized sector including agriculture, animal husbandry, and household industries. Rural child labor is believed to effect urban child labor in a significant manner. "Often these, urban trades and occupations depend for their very survival on rural-migrant child labour indicating that rural areas are the major source of urban child labour' (Kanbargi, R. 1991). The situation of children who have migrated with their families to the cities or children who have left their families and are working on the streets provides ample evidence to this effect. Because of social and economic changes poor rural families and in some cases children alone have left their villages to seek work in cities.

In many developing countries, working children are especially visible on urban streets mainly in unorganized economic activities. Most are between 7-17 years of age and although quite a few of them have homes to which they can return, many end up essentially working and living on the street. Street children work in circumstances that put their physical, mental, moral and social development at risk. They work in conditions where they are exploited and denied their basic right to education and development. These children miss out on school entirely. There are more children under the age of fourteen in India than the entire population of the United States. The great challenge of India, as a developing country, is to provide nutrition, education and health care to these children. (www.indianembassy.org)

Children under fourteen constitute around 3.6% of the total labor force in India. In 1998, the International Labor Organization (ILO) estimated that 13 percent of children between the ages of 10 and 14 in India were working (*World Development Indicators 2000)*. India's 1991 national census reported that 11.3 million out of the country's 210 million children between the ages of 5 and 14 were working. Some speculate that the number of working children is much higher than official statistics indicate, since one-half of all children ages 5 to 14 (105 million) were not enrolled in school. (Chaudhri, D.P. 1996). The Law Minister said that the country has 20 million child labourers. (Indian Express, 5 February 2000)

Unofficial estimates from non governmental organizations (NGOs) and international organizations find that the number of working children ranges between 44 million to 55 million (US Dept of State, Human Rights Report, 1998). India's Country Report states that the number of working children was estimated to be 17 million. The present figure is estimated to be around 20 million. However, this is without including employment in the unorganized sector of the economy such as domestic workers, agricultural workers and so on (Campaign Against Child Labour CACL, "An Alternative Report on the Status of Child Labour in India", submission to the UN CRC, September-October 1999). Based on the number of non-school going children and families living in destitution, CACL estimates that there are between 70 and 80 million child laborers in India (CACL, "An Alternative Report on the Status of Child Labor in India", submission to the UN CRC, September-October 1999). Unofficial child labor estimates are as high as 111 million, which is slightly equivalent to the number of 'out-of-school' children. (US Dept of Labor, Sweat and Toil of Children: Efforts to Eliminate Child Labour, 1998)

Interpolation of census figures by the National Labor Institute indicates that out of 203 million children between the ages of 5 and 14, 116 million are in school, 12.6 million are in full-time employment, and the status of 74 million is unknown. Most, if not all, of the 87 million children, not in school, do housework, work on family farms, work alongside their parents as paid agricultural laborers, work as domestic servants, or are otherwise employed (US Dept of State, Country Reports on Human Rights Practices - 1999, 25 February 2000). The 2001 Census of India will update figures from the 1991 national census, including estimates of the number of children who are economically active in the country.

Evidence from a number of developing countries shows that

many children are reported to work under particularly hazardous conditions. International Labor Organization (ILO) Convention No. 182 identifies and places emphasis on the worst forms of child labor. The "worst forms of child labor" is understood to be those types of work for children described in Article 3 of ILO Convention 182. The full text of this article is:

(a) All forms of slavery or practices similar to slavery, such as the sale and trafficking of children, debt bondage and serfdom and forced or compulsory labor, including forced or compulsory recruitment of children for use in armed conflict;

(b) The use, procuring or offering of a child for prostitution, for the production of pornography or for pornographic performances;

(c) The use, procuring or offering of a child for illicit activities, in particular for the production and trafficking of drugs as defined in the relevant international treaties;

(d) Work which, by its nature or the circumstances in which it is carried out, is likely to harm the health, safety or morals of children.

Article 4 of the Convention requires that in determining what is hazardous child labor, governments must consider Paragraph 3 of Recommendation 190, which state:

In determining the types of work referred to under Article 3(d) of the Convention, and in identifying where they exist, consideration should be given, inter alia, to:

(a) work which exposes children to physical, psychological or sexual abuse;

(b) work underground, under water, at dangerous heights or in confined spaces;

(c) work with dangerous machinery, equipment and tools, or **which involves the manual handling or transport of heavy loads;**

(d) work in an unhealthy environment which may, for example, expose children to hazardous substances, agents or processes, or to temperatures, noise levels, or vibrations damaging to their health;

(e) work under particularly difficult conditions such as work for long hours or during the night or work where the child is unreasonably confined to the premises of the employer.

Article 32 of this convention establishes the right of a child to be protected from economic exploitation and from performing any work that is likely to be hazardous, interferes with his or her education, or is harmful to his or her health or physical, mental, spiritual, moral, or social development.

Of the estimated 250 million children between the ages of 5 and 14 who are economically active, some 50 million to 60 million between the ages of 5 and 11 are engaged in such intolerable forms of labor. (The Progress of Nations 2000 , The United Nations Children's Fund (UNICEF), New York, 2000). The ILO estimated that 250 million children between 5 and 14 worked for a living, and that over 50 million children under age twelve worked in hazardous circumstances (ILO, Child Labor, Targeting the Intolerable, ILO Geneva, November 1996).

P. Sondhi (1994) in her study on street child porters found that the Children in the study were engaged in working on the railway station carrying heavy loads in and out of the station, often traveling a distance of half to a kilometer with load on their heads and under constant fear of being caught by the police. In such a situation, the physical harm caused to the child's growing body is, of course, quite obvious and the easiest to see (Poonam Sondhi, 1994). There is evidence that carrying heavy loads or sitting for long periods in unnatural positions can permanently disable growing bodies. Hard physical labor over a period of years can stunt children's physical stature by up to 30 per cent of their biological potential, as they expend stores of stamina that should last into adulthood (UNICEF. 1997). Children are also vulnerable psychologically:

they can suffer devastating psychological damage from being in an environment in which they are demeaned or oppressed. Street children are often seen as social rejects and this inhibits the development of a positive sense of esteem or self-worth.

Using the standards set forth in the International Labor Organization (ILO) Convention No. 182, these children were engaged in hazardous or worst forms of child labor. Following significant facts emerge about the work these children were occupied in:

1. The work by its nature or the circumstances, in which it was carried out, is damaging to the health, safety or morals of the children;

2. The children worked in dangerous, insecure situations which involved the manual handling or transport of heavy loads while under constant fear of being apprehended by the police;

3. Children's working environment exposed them to physical, psychological and sexual abuse.

While the global campaign to end child labor has gained considerable momentum over the past decade, some governments still lack the kinds of policies and initiatives needed to protect children from being exploited in the workplace and from suffering the worst forms of child labor.

1.4. REASONS WHY CHILDREN WORK

Child labor is most common in rural areas and in the informal sector. It is generally the result of a combination of factors. The most frequently cited cause, however, is poverty. Children often work to provide for themselves or to help their families meet basic needs such as food and shelter. Families may suffer financial hardship because of adult unemployment, underemployment, low prevailing adult wages, or the death, illness, or injury of a parent or guardian. Child labor perpetuates poverty since children who work in lieu of going to school are generally more likely to earn a lower income in the future. (U.S. Department of Labor, 2000)

Many children also work because they lack alternatives. Globally, an estimated 113 million children do not have access to primary education (www.unesco.org/education). Some lack access because schools are not available or are located too far from their homes. Costs of schooling that have to be paid by the family— such as school fees or the cost of textbooks or required uniforms— can also place education beyond the reach of children from poor families. While child labor occurs in both urban and rural areas, evidence suggests that work participation rates for children are much higher in rural areas, where most children work in agriculture. Survey evidence suggests that, on average, children in rural areas are twice as likely to participate in economic activities than children in urban areas. (*Statistics on Working Children* , Section II, ILO 2001)

Most children work in the unregulated "informal sector," which is generally beyond the reach of the protection afforded by national laws on child labor. Child labor does not affect all children uniformly. Certain children may also face greater risks than others. Working children under the age of 12 years and working girls as being among the most vulnerable.

1.5.   COMBATING CHILD LABOR -INTERNATIONAL ACTION

Support for initiatives to combat the exploitation of children has grown significantly in the past decade. To eliminate child labor, governments have developed national plans of action and taken steps to promote the collection of child labor data, passed child labor laws, increased access for children to schooling, and implemented targeted interventions to remove children from exploitative work. In 1992, the International Labor Organization launched the International Program on the Elimination of Child Labor (ILO-IPEC) with the aim of working towards the progressive elimination of child labor through strengthening countries' capacity to address the problem and supporting a movement to address child labor worldwide. The United States has also funded child labor programs through the United States Agency for International Development (USAID). These programs include activities intended to remove children from abusive child labor and to develop educational alternatives for these children and others at risk of abusive child labor.

The global campaign to address child labor has also involved the adoption of new international instruments that seek to address the most serious forms of child exploitation. Among other things, the declaration calls for the elimination of all forms of forced or compulsory labor and the effective abolition of child labor. In June 1999, delegates to the ILO's 87 th International Labor Conference unanimously adopted ILO Convention No. 182 on the Worst Forms of Child Labor. The convention calls on ratifying countries to take immediate and effective measures to secure the prohibition and elimination of the worst forms of child labor as a matter of urgency. Article 7 of the convention further calls upon ratifying countries , including India to take time-bound steps to ensure that children removed from the worst forms of child labor have access to basic education, and where appropriate, vocational training. Convention No. 182, which formally came into force on November 19, 2000, has become the most rapidly ratified convention in the ILO history.

Child Labor Laws and Enforcement – The Indian Context

The passage and effective implementation of child labor laws represents an important landmark toward combating the problem. Laws prescribe at what age and under what conditions children may work or ban children's involvement in certain types of work altogether. ILO Convention No. 182 calls upon ratifying countries to establish that some forms of work are not appropriate for any children, under any circumstances. It is also important that child labor laws and basic education requirements be complementary. Minimum work age laws and education requirements that complement each other become mutually reinforcing.

However, child labor laws and regulations apply and tend to be enforced primarily if not solely in the formal sector. In India, most children engage in child labor in unregulated sectors of the economy. In such instances, laws are not sufficient to address the immediate needs of children facing abuse and exploitation Regardless of how well conceived child labor laws are however, to have an impact, they must be properly implemented and enforced. In India, this remains a challenge since enforcement requires political will and the commitment of often scarce financial and personnel resources.

India has laws restricting work by children and limiting the sectors and activities in which children may legally work. The Child Labor (Prohibition and Regulation) Act of 1986, which was extended in 1999 to encompass more employment activities, prohibits the employment of children under 14 years old in 13 occupations and 51 work processes. In 1996, India's Supreme Court directed national and state governments to identify and withdraw children from hazardous work and provide them with education(*Country Reports 2000—India,* IPEC, India Briefing Note). The enforcement of child labor laws falls under the jurisdiction of state-level labor ministries, but implementation of the law is limited.

In August 1987, the government established National Child Labor Projects (NCLPs) in 12 states with a high proportion of working children, along with a national policy on child labor(*Economic Survey 2000-2001,* India: Ministry of Finance, February 2001). In 1994, then-Prime Minister Mr. Narsimha Rao announced a national program to combat child labor. These projects provide children with non formal education, health care, nutrition, and vocational skills training. The projects are implemented by NGOs, with the government covering up to 75 percent of the project costs.

Two core conventions of ILO on child labor—ILO Convention No. 182 on the Worst Forms of Child Labor and ILO Convention No. 138 on Minimum Age for Employment Ratification have been ratified by India. India became a member of the International Labor Organization's International Program on the Elimination of Child

Labor (ILO-IPEC) supported by the U.S. Department of Labor in 1992. In August 2000, the United States and India signed a Joint Statement committing both countries to support new ILO-IPEC projects aimed at reducing the incidence of child labor in 10 selected hazardous industries(ILO-IPEC, September 2001).

The passage and enforcement of child labor laws and the promotion of schooling for children are key strategies for reducing child labor. Eliminating child labor, however, may also require more targeted and urgent action. This is especially true in the case of children who are working in particularly dangerous circumstances, as in the case of children engaged in the worst forms of child labor

1.6. STREET CHILDREN IN INDIA - INCREASING NUMBERS

In India there is no firm or reliable statistics available on the number of street children including street child labor. No accurate information is provided by the Government on the number of street children living and working on the streets. The nature of the group of street children is such that they are excluded from official records. While child labor, for example, has often been the subject of attention for the government and researchers, street children and street child labor have, till recently, not been systematically studied as they are highly mobile and are likely to drift in and out of different places and occupations. Until 1993, the term "street child" had no place in the "Official Vocabulary" of Indian Government and they did not exist as a separate category but as a sub- group of 'neglected children'.

India reportedly has the largest population of street children in the world. At least eighteen million children live and / or work on the streets of urban India, laboring as porters at bus or railway terminals; as mechanics in informal auto-repair shops; as vendors of food, tea, or handmade articles; as street tailors; or as rag pickers, picking through garbage and selling usable materials to local buyers. (United Nations Development Program, Human Development Report,

1996,) Child welfare organizations estimate that there are 500,000 street children nation-wide. (US Dept of State, Country Reports on Human Rights Practices - 1999, 25 February 2000)

The number of street children continues to rise with urbanization. It has been clearly established by various surveys, studies and professional observation that with the growth of urban centers and industrialization , the problem of working and street children is assuming an alarming scale.

It is estimated that there are 314,700 street children in Bombay, Calcutta, Madras, Kanpur, Bangalore and Hyderabad combined and about 100,000 in Delhi (Claire O'Kane, 2003) One of the early reports on the magnitude of the problem includes a situational analysis of 11,864 street children in seven major cities of India: Bombay, Calcutta, Madras, Delhi, Bangalore, Hyderabad and Indore. It attempts to give an idea about the complexity of the problem. According to this study there are 3,14,700 street children in these seven cities. In Bangalore, unofficial estimates put the number of street children at about 45,000 out of which, approximately 25,000 are said to be homeless. It has also been estimated that Bangalore gets an average of 12 children every day coming to city (Molake, Concerned for Working Children, 1989).

According to the studies conducted in these cities, 47% of street children spend their night on the open streets except in Calcutta where almost every street child (99%) spends night on the street. The percentage of such children is also quite high in Bombay (61%) because a large number of families live on pavements. Majority of street children (58%) in the study were found working, 46% of them self- employed as porters, vendors, shoe-shiners, newspaper hawker or parking attendants. About 32% are employed in shops and establishments. Though the law prohibits children working for more than 5 hours a day, 60% of them work for 7 -12 hours day. Nearly 70% of them earn just Rs. 100/- per month (The Hindustan Times, Sept.19, 1992).

Among the sample of 2,169 street children in Bombay, 71% were working for a living (street child labor), Half of them were self- employed working as ragpickers and petty traders of edible and non- edible items; 14% working in shops and servicing centers and 32% as a casual labour carrying loads, cleaning and washing utensils at marriage parties and doing other such manual works. Most of the children worked for 10-12 hours a day, some for 7-9 hours. 48% of Bombay's street kids earn less than Rs. 400/- a month. Those who worked as apprentices to tailors earned a stipend ranging from Rs. 50 to Rs. 300 per month depending on their years of training and experience. Those engaged in ragpicking were able to earn Rs. 50 a day. But for this they had to put in 10-12 hours of work every day. In Hyderabad there were 5,000 street children in 1983 which increased to 25,000 by 1988 and at present the figure is believed to be 40,000 Bombay which attracts runaways from all the over the country, has over 2 lakhs of street children (Ifthekar, J.S. in the Indian Express , Dec.6, 1992).

In Bombay, a United Nation's Educational , Social & Cultural Organization (UNESCO) sponsored census has revealed that six out of every ten street children in the city are engaged in ragpicking (Census conducted by social organizations in Bombay with the Department of Social Welfare, Govt. of Maharashtra, 1986). A study by the College of Social Work, Bombay focused on street children working as ragpickers. It reported that 75% of the children were between 12 to15 years of age. 65% of them had runaway because of the ill treatment meted out to them at home while 35% left home because of constant quarrels and fights in the home. Most children ran away to the closest railway station. They later came to Bombay. Children in the 12-13 age groups had spent between 3-4 years away from home. Over half the children included in the study had at one time or another been remanded to judicial custody and had run away from the institutional care.

The Missing Persons Bureau, Bombay stated that on an average 2,00,000 persons leave their home annually. 50% of the cases do not get reported, but of the 50,000 who are registered as missing, 45% are minors below the age of 16 years (cited in Waiting for Tomorrow (1991), Society for Promotion of Area Resources Centers, Bombay).

Whatever the figures are, three significant findings emerge from the data that is available: one, the number of street child labor (including children living alone and working on the street) is increasing at an disturbing rate; second, the phenomenon of street children is largely one of the urban areas and third, being a street child is predominantly a male condition. For children who work, including those who have families, it appears that boys are more likely to be involved in activities which put them on the streets, for example, street vending, running messages, providing street entertainment, washing cars, collecting scrap, pick-pocketing, shoe shining, pulling rickshaws, and involved in drug dealing. Whereas girls, often are employed or earn an income off the streets, for example working in factories, making crafts, employed in domestic services, involved in commercial sex and vending. It is also reported that often girls who work on the streets are not entirely on their own. They are usually under the supervision of an adult, mostly a female. For example, while the mother stays in the background, a young girl may sit on the roadside selling small goods or may approach passing cars or pedestrians begging for money.

Attempts have been made to identify and categorize children in especially difficult circumstances in various groups. They include: children living in families in extreme poverty; working children especially in the unorganized sectors; orphans, destitute and abandoned children; abused children; illegitimate children and street children. These categories are not mutually exclusive and often tend to overlap.

It may be noted that the list is not exhaustive and should not be considered complete as other categories of children e.g. child beggars, child prostitutes, bonded children, etc. can also be included in this classification. However, the focus of this study is to highlight the plight of urban, homeless, working street children and describe and analyze the especially difficult circumstances in which they exist.

Also, the category of street children is in itself a complex one. It also comprises of children belonging to extremely poor families, destitute or orphan children, working children and abused children. Thus, while discussing the phenomenon of street children it is essential to establish linkages between these varied but related aspects of this phenomenon. The categorization is done primarily to illustrate the multi-dimensional nature of the phenomenon.

In the following sections, attempts have been made to encompass links between the phenomenon of street children and diverse yet interrelated areas like: child abuse, working children/ child labor, neglected children and juvenile delinquency. This has been done to present an adequate explanatory account for the phenomenon of street children and thereby gain a comprehensive understanding, which has seldom been achieved.

PART II

HISTORY AND ETIOLOGY

2.1. HISTORICAL BACKGROUND

Street children are not unique to any country. Major cities in Brazil, Mexico, Turkey, Colombia, Sudan, and other countries face similar problems on an identical scale.

Historically, accounts of street children can be traced in literary works like Charles Dicken's 'Oliver Twist', Victor Hugo's 'Les Miserables', Stephen Crane's 'Maggie: A Girl of the streets' and famous R.K. Narayan's 'Malgudi Days' . More recently, street children have been portrayed in such films as Luis Bunuel's (1950) 'Los Olvidadas' (The Forgotten One), Hector Babenco's (1981) 'Pixote' (Peewee) and Mira Nair's (1989) 'Salaam Bombay' (Agnelli, S. 1986) .Another street child ten-year old Raju, a shoeshine boy on the streets of Delhi, played a reincarnated Lama in Bernado Bertolucci's magnum opus Little Buddha. The child belonged to a nomadic family and worked on the street to add to his family income (Pioneer, Feb. 1993).

Current street children scenario can be traced to the Industrial Revolution in Europe and North America in the 19th Century. These countries were still developing during that time and presence of street children was a common sight in urban areas of these countries (Agnelli, S. 1986). Descriptive historical accounts of street children include Jacob Rii's observations of the "street arabs" and "gutter snipes" of the turn –of- the century New York city in "How the other half lives" (Hill & Wang, cited in Felsmen, J.K., 1984).

In 1852 in New York, police records estimated there were 10,000 vagrant children in New York city, and similar problem existed in Boston and Chicago. Father Borrelli's 'A Street Lamp and the Stars' (Mecann, C. cited in Felsman, J.K., 1984) and Morris West's 'Children of the Sun ' (Double day, cited in Felsman, J.K.,

1984) are accounts of the street children of Naples after World War II . Some of the most abundant historical records of street children in late 19th and early 20th century England are contained in accounts of the Barnardo Homes that took in such children and also placed many abroad in adoptive homes in Canada & Australia (Bready, J., 1935).

With regard to the present day phenomenon , accounts of 'gamines' of present day Colombia (Felsman, J.K., 1981; Aptekar, L., 1988; Hodge, W.1980; and MacPherson, H.1979), the ' garrots' of Brazil and the street boys of Istanbul all exemplify the existence of a large number of street children . In Nobody's Child, Christina Noble (1994) describes how her life as a street child in mid-twentieth century Ireland led to her work with street children in Vietnam. The public image of street children is distressingly negative. Often names for street children display the contempt in which they are often held by the public. In Vietnam, street children are known as "bui doi", the dust of life (Noble, 1994). In Rwanda, they are "saligoman", nasty/dirty kid (Agnelli, 1986,). In India, they are often called " sadak chaap", stamp of street.

2.2. CAUSES OF THE PROBLEM

This section examines why children leave home, how they survive on the street and the importance of other elements within their environment. Despite the fact that the phenomenon of street children has been widespread for many years, and children, social workers, educators and others are struggling with the problem, a relatively insignificant amount of objective, scientific research has been done on the subject in India. Causal factors contributing to the emergence of street children are as diverse and as interdependent as definitions and classifications.

A careful review of literature in educational, psychological, social work and psychiatric journals of the past reveals that little has been published regarding the dynamics and nature of the problem of street children. The processes of factors that separate children from their families have so far attracted little attention. Speculation about the root causes of the problem rapidly leads onto shifting ground. There is a host of precipitating factors that leave the child unprotected ranging from economic, social, political, environmental, intra-familial and psychological factors (Agnelli, S. 1986). The interweaving political, economic, and psychological conditions that drive children to the streets are too complex to give a simple explanation for this worldwide phenomenon.

The traditional literature on the etiology of runaway behaviour is focused on the psychology of the individual child or social structure, the environment in which the child lives. Clinical literature has blamed the "troubled child", often citing factors of impulsivity, lack of superego development, poor self-esteem and friendlessness. Few psychologists have suggested that some hereditary predisposition, irrespective of the family conditions, actively pushes some children to take to the streets on their own initiative and make an early bid for independence. Psychologists have looked at the motivational factors of the individual child. The theory assumes that children are driven by a complex motivation which seeks out a greater autonomy and an active involvement with the social environment (Agnelli, S. 1986).

However, Bernstein and Gray (1991) propose "individual pathology cannot be the only explanatory factor for children taking to the streets. In all countries, street children must be seen as a social problem resulting from social causes". The socio-political scenario places tremendous pressure on disadvantaged families.

A large number of studies have held the environment primarily responsible and running away from home is viewed as an effort at self- rescue from an ongoing situation of abuse and neglect. Social policy literature (Tacon, P. 1981; Hollnsteiner & Tacon, 1983) regarding street children indicates external or environmental circumstances as the sole etiology of their condition. Without much debate, factors such as poverty, rural –to-urban migration, civil strife, and family crisis play a central role in the genesis of the phenomenon of street children (Tacon, P. 1981). It is believed that environmental stressors may be a necessary cause, but they are not sufficient to help understand why these children take to the streets

Another theory emphasizes the interaction of environment and personality attributes. Proponents of this view suggest that by understanding the interplay between the environmental or sociological factors and the psychological or personality characteristics one can get a full understanding of the causes or the origin of the phenomenon of street children.

Felsman, J.K. (1981) suggests that an interaction of factors, including physiology, temperament, intelligence and character play a major role in these children's running away from home and the nature and pattern of their daily street life is also affected by these factors. It needs to be emphasized that an appreciation of the situation of street children necessitates a 'contextual integrationist approach', a social-psychological analysis which accounts for particular children who depart from home in a particular situation at certain stages in their own social and developmental histories. However, it is difficult to verify this hypothesis in such an unstructured and changing environment, and to separate the psychological factors from the environmental factors (Agnelli, S. 1986).

Repetti, R. L., Taylor, S. E. & Seeman, T. E.(2001) proposed an 'integrated bio-behavioral profile', focusing on the processes by which certain families may not only hinder healthy development in childhood, but also influence physical and mental health into adolescence and adulthood (Chart 3). Such 'risky' families are characterized by conflict and aggression and by relationships that are cold, unsupportive, and neglectful These family characteristics create vulnerabilities and/or interact with genetically-based vulnerabilities in children which leave their children vulnerable to a wide array of mental and physical health disorders. These families are precarious in multiple ways. First, experiences of physical abuse and neglect which are characteristic of such families, represent

Chart 3

RISKY FAMILY ENVIRONMENT AND STREET CHILDREN PHENOMENON

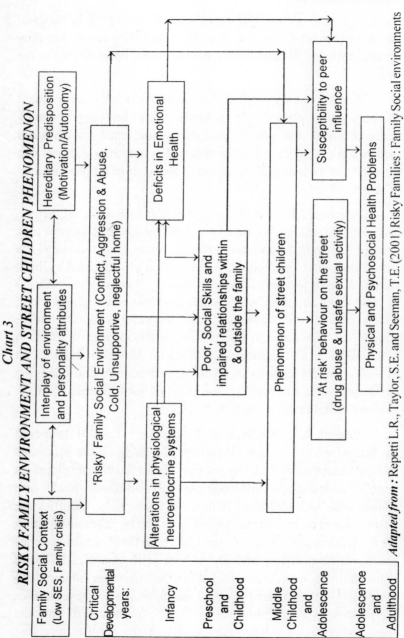

Adapted from : Repetti L.R., Taylor, S.E. and Seeman, T.E. (2001) Risky Families : Family Social environments and the Mental and Physical Health of Offspring, Psychological Bulletin, 128(2).

immediate threats to the lives and safety of children. Second, children's developing physiological and neuroendocrine systems are adversely effected by the threatening and stressful circumstances created by these family environments which enhances vulnerability to chronic disease and to early mortality in adulthood (McEwen & Stellar, 1993; Seeman et al., 1997).

Third, growing body of literature points to the negative effects that lack of warmth and nurturance in a family can have on the ability to form and maintain social relationships. With respect to mental health outcomes, evidence indicates that exposure to family violence during childhood can lead to chronic interpersonal stress in adulthood (Kessler and Magee, 1994). Finally, risky families increase children's vulnerability to behavior problems and substance abuse, including smoking, alcohol, drugs, and promiscuous sexual activity. Researchers suggest that these risks are multiple and pervasive, and they are related to each other through common biological and psychosocial pathways.

This integrated bio- behavioral explanation places significant emphasis on childhood family environments and its repercussions on children's mental and physical health across the lifespan. In the context of the street children phenomenon, majority of the street children's families can be termed 'risky' since they portray the above characteristics. Separately and in concert, such families place a child at risk and under such circumstances children leave home and end up living on the streets.

The gene-environment model depicted in chart 3 is a relationship between growing up in a risky family environment and the street children phenomenon. It also links the adverse effects of living in such risky families and later on the street to the child's mental and physical health. The critical developmental years represent the time when such effects are observed. The social context of the family and genetic factors may directly and indirectly influence all of the variables in the model. The consequences of exposure to these sources of family stress early in childhood may be potentially irreversible interactions between genetic predispositions and these environmental factors that can lead to physical and mental disorders.

Kaime-Atterhog (1996) has proposed a conceptual framework for understanding the street children phenomenon (Chart 4). It incorporates factors at the individual, familial and structural (cultural, social and political) level which account for the phenomenon of street children. The framework suggests that street children phenomenon can be viewed as 'a product of both individual and collective vulnerability' (Anarfi, J.K. 1997).

At the individual level, it is assumed that the child's personality plays a crucial role in determining whether he will take to the street or not. Keeping in mind the changes at the societal level, poverty, structural changes in the family and dysfunctional homes all contribute as causal factors. The framework presents the phenomenon as a kind of continuum. At one end are causal factors, that is, complex and interlinked factors that push children to the street. Among the causal factors the child's own personality attributes and motivational factors play a major role in whether or not he will run away to the street. However, the social context of the child's family is also important. Indian society is undergoing rapid social and economic change. The consequences of such change include increased stress on adults and the isolation of nuclear families.

Throughout the world there is a gradual transformation of the family from the extended to the nuclear. Where extended families or other support networks are strong, abuse of children is far rarer (UNICEF 1986). Where the nuclear family predominates, there are apparently fewer relatives to provide support in times of crisis (Kalu 1986). The nuclear families are also increasingly facing problems of marital disharmony, rising divorce rates and increasing number of single parent households. At the cultural level, in many Indian families, particularly poverty-stricken rural families, the child is seen not just as a mouth to be fed but also as another pair of hands to help with income generating activities. In such circumstances the difference between what constitutes child work that is acceptable and child labour which is harmful becomes blurred and it threatens the physical, emotional and social development of the child.

Chart 4

FRAMEWORK FOR UNDERSTANDING STREET CHILDREN PHENOMENON

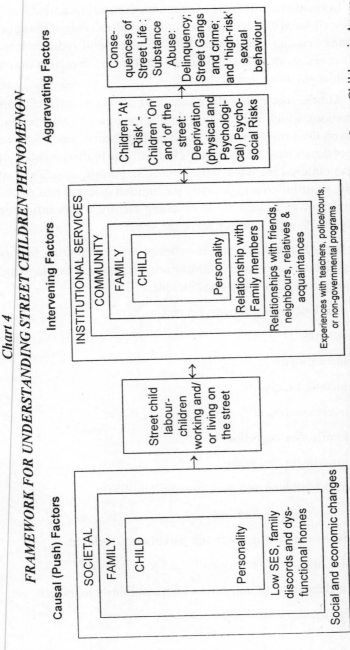

Adapted from: Anarfi, J.K. (1997) 'Vulnerability to Sexually Transmitted disease; Street Children in Accra-Health Transition Review, Supplement to Volume 7.

In situations when due to economic constraints parents have put their children to work outside home, the attractions of the street existence that can range from drugs to a sense of independence from the restraints of an unpleasant family life have also drawn the child away from home.

At the other end of the continuum, are aggravating factors or situations which are the high-risk behaviour of children who remain on the street. These factors manifest themselves in various forms of deprivations faced by the children. The high–risk behavior of street children includes: delinquency and drugs, unsafe sexual activity, prostitution and sexually transmitted diseases and AIDS. Linking the two factors are intervening factors which influence the children to either stay or leave the streets.

Broadly speaking, across cultures, the contributing factors to the phenomenon of street children are multiple and overlapping. The most commonly cited ones include:

- a lack of family support services

- poverty

- unemployment

- income inequality

- overcrowding

- family disintegration

- inadequate child care

- over burdened and over stressed families

- irresponsible parenting

- poor relationships between parents and children

- absent parents (emotionally and physically)

- inadequate communication between family members

- family and community violence

- child abuse and neglect
- alcohol and drug abuse
- lack of community resources (health, welfare and legal services) and:
- an education system which fails the child

(Draft document on policy issues and strategic guidelines on street children in South Africa, National Department of Welfare and Population Development, 1998).

At the macro or societal level, a host of factors relating to social environment have given rise to the phenomenon of street children namely: increasing pressures generated by developmental imbalance; unequal distribution of wealth and lopsided development policies of the government, massive poverty, unemployment, overcrowded homes, urban dislocation and inappropriate education system.

Poverty and global economic imbalance contribute to the phenomenon of street children. Many leaders of non-governmental international development and child welfare organizations view the problem of street children as a symptom of a gross imbalance in the distribution of resources globally. The late Executive Director of UNICEF, James Grant, stated: "Lines of causality can even be drawn connecting the street child to an international economic system that has accelerated impoverishment and stalled development in much of the Third World." In most developing countries, poverty is the most commonly cited leading cause of this crisis.

According to the UNDP, 49 percent of India's rural population live at or below the poverty line (United Nations Development Programme, *Human Development Report, 1996).* Some of these unemployed or underemployed people are forced to go to cities in search of economic opportunities. Cities provide a slightly better opportunity for these people. However, since the UNDP estimates that 38 percent of India's urban population is at or below the poverty line, this accounts for more than eighty-nine million people. A 1992 UNICEF study of street children in Bombay observed that ' large-scale migration of families from rural to urban areas... has resulted in severe overcrowding, degrading work conditions, homelessness, deprivation of basic services and appalling living conditions in the city. Yet, to return to the village means starvation; to remain in the city means possible survival at least physically' (Hazel D'Lima and Rima Gosalia, 1992). Many other factors stem from (and are often consequences of) poverty, such as rural-to-urban labor migration, family crises and breakdown, maltreatment and abuse.

Poverty is no longer an exclusively rural phenomenon, but an increasing urban problem. Rapid industrialization and urbanization have lured a large number of rural poor to migrate to cities and towns. India's population has increased from 238 million in 1901 to 846 million in 2001. During this period the share of urban population has gone up from 11% (25 million) to 23% (160 million). In India, the number of urban poor is growing at such an alarming rate that policies on urban development need to be reviewed. The Indian government's five-year plan for 1992-1997 reported: There has been a marked acceleration in urbanization over the past two decades. If the present trends continue, urban population may account for about one-third of the total population by the turn of the century (Government of India, *8th Five Year Plan (1992-1997)*.

Urban population statistics for India reflect this observation. According to the United Nations Development Programme (UNDP), in 1960, 18 percent of India's population lived in cities. In 1992, this number had risen to 26 percent of the population. Figures from The State of the World's Children, 2002 (UNICEF) state, in India of the total 1025 million population, 28% live in the urban areas.

A major factor that contributes to rapid urbanization is the increased migration from rural areas to India's urban areas. Many of these migrants are landless agricultural laborers whose traditional occupations no longer exist or do not provide sufficient income.

and who have come to the cities in search of employment. The World Bank in its report on 'Urban Policy and Economic Development: An agenda for 1990's,' which was released in 1991, has warned that Indian urban poverty will become increasingly serious in future. Referring to the rate of urban population growth rate in India, the report states that it would reach 3.96% flanked by 1995 to 2000 A.D., which is higher than 1980-85 periods when it was 3.91% (The Hindustan Times, June 8, 1990).

The number of urban poor is rising. According to a study conducted as a part of an inter—country research project on "Critical issues and policy measures to address urban poverty" sponsored by the Asian Development Bank, between one-fifth and a little under two-fifth (291.6 and 237.6 million) of the total urban population do not have the level of income for the daily nutritional intake. They do not get stable and productive jobs or houses or other services (The Hindustan Times, July 30, 1993). The root cause of this urban crisis is poverty, whether it is poverty of rural areas that drives people to the cities, or the poverty of underemployment. Poverty in India had decreased between the 1992 survey and 1999-2000 survey from 40.9% to 26.1%. Using the international poverty line (below $1/day), however, the proportion of population below the poverty line in India in 1997 was 44.2% (**Source:** World Bank, *The World Development Report 2000/2001*).

Large scale migration from rural areas to urban settlements will continue at a fast rate in the coming years. The slum dwellers, footpath dwellers, unskilled and casual workers, workers in unorganized sectors and street children constitute a major proportion of urban poor population and this segment of society has not been paid adequate attention. Global consensus on the need to reduce and eventually eliminate poverty was emphasized in the Plan of Action emerging from the 1995 World Summit for Social Development held in Copenhagen. In order to reduce the number of poor, it is imperative to take steps to increase economic and social development. The Summit emphasized the need for policies that lead to labour-intensive economic growth, increase poor people's access to productive resources and basic services and ensure adequate economic and social protection of all people (Report of the World Summit for Social Development, 1995).

Street children are primarily an urban phenomenon linked to the tremendous rural- to – urban migration. Agnelli,S. (1986) describes street children in developing countries as " products of rural-to- urban migration, unemployment, poverty and broken families", in industrialized nations they are considered as "victims of alienation and systematic exclusion". In Colombia this phenomenon of massive rural –to-urban migration has been termed 'Gaminismo' (Felsman, J.K. 1984).

Industrialization has not kept pace with this population shift, which has brought the poverty of rural areas to urban centers. The 20th century can be called as the age of urbanization. The urban population of the world, which was estimated as 1983 million in 1985 has reached around 2,854 million by the year 2000-an increase of 44%. The population of cities is also becoming younger. Half of the world's population is under 25 years. In the age group of 5-19 years, there are 247 million more urban children than in 1990. Of these, 233 million are in developing countries, where 25% of the total population is less than 14 years of age. The number of street children living in complete or partial abandonment is thus growing on a large scale (Agnelli, S. 1986)

Within this population are children, who may become street children when they arrive in the cities. This process was described in a study of street children by UNICEF in 1992 in Calcutta: ' In India due to the increasing pressures of population rise, urbanization, and unemployment along with the rapid collapse of the traditional social structure of joint families and close –knit neighborhoods, the number of street children is growing at a fast rate. Throughout the world there is a gradual transformation of the family from the extended to the nuclear. Where the nuclear family predominates, there are apparently fewer relatives to provide support in times of crisis (Kalu 1986). The nuclear family itself appears to be in danger of collapsing with rising divorce rates and increasing numbers of one-parent families. The incidence of child maltreatment is reportedly higher in urban than rural communities and is particularly widespread in societies undergoing rapid social and economic change (Korbin 1983). The consequences of such change include increased stress on adults and the isolation of nuclear families. Where extended families or other support networks are strong, abuse is far rarer (UNICEF, 1986).

The rising number of street children can be linked to India's burgeoning population growth: eighteen million children are added to the population every year, a rate that will result in India's mid-1993 population of approximately 902 million people doubling to 1.8 billion by about 2043.(United Nations Human Development Report, 1996).

The United Nations Research Institute for Social Development has attempted to define and measure level of living at the international scale by giving certain criteria of social well being. They have identified the following nine components of the basic needs, which are: nutrition, health, shelter, education, leisure, security, social stability, physical environment, and surplus income. Using this scale of measurement, more than three-fourth of the child population of India would be living in difficult circumstances (cited in Nangia, S. 1990).

Most children of poor families do not attend school or are forced to drop-out of school and instead go to the streets to earn. Access to educational facilities is limited for some children in rural areas. The need to purchase uniforms and textbooks, as well as other associated costs, discourages many children from attending school (Ministry of Human Resources Development, Education for All (EFA) 2000 [online], Country Report, India, Section 2). Large concentrations of the estimated 32 million children who have never attended school come from the impoverished states of Bihar, Madhya Pradesh, Rajasthan and Uttar Pradesh.

Research has indicated that economic deprivation is most likely to lead to crime and delinquency when it is coupled with marked inequality in the distribution of society's resources. However, in a large number of other poor families or even in very poor families, many children do not leave home and become street children. The answer seems to lie in the fact that family and peer relationships, together with other social and psychological influences, appear to play a far more crucial role. A study of Observation Homes for boys in Delhi conducted by Sharda, N. (1985) revealed that 'majority of the cases for both delinquent and non-delinquent children, had runaway from their homes because of poverty, inadequate care by the parents, broken families, overcrowding in the house and peer influences'. Beyond poverty, lack of employment opportunities and lack of access to basic community services and education, the breakdown of traditional family and community values serves as a major factor in the increase in the number of children on the streets.

RISKY FAMILY ENVIRONMENT

Childhood family environments characterized by certain qualities have damaging outcomes on mental and physical health across the lifespan. These 'risky families' show characteristics which include: overt family conflict, manifested in recurrent episodes of anger and aggression, and deficient nurturing, especially family relationships that are cold, unsupportive, and neglectful(Repetti, R. L., Taylor, S. E. & Seeman, T. E.,2001). Research literature in developmental psychology, sociology, and public health relate the characteristics of risky families to a wide range of adverse adult outcomes that cluster with low SES, including illiteracy, high rates of school drop-out or low school achievement, low educational attainment, poor adult income, high likelihood of family disharmony, low occupational status, and poor status on other indicators of life success (Power & Hertzman, 1997).

Poverty engenders a host of problems in the family such as the breakdown in communication between parents, the stress of financial hardships and the inevitable result: the child losing out.

In many poor families, economic deprivation, endemic unemployment or disease lead to frustration, depression, alcoholism, drug abuse and a vicious cycle of overwhelming stress and strain. At the micro- level, the child is on the street typically, because his family in crisis. The child on the street is the end product of a chain of events beginning in the home. Poor children are at heightened risk for physical mistreatment or abuse (McLoyd, 1998; Reid, Macchetto, & Foster, 1999) and exposure to family violence (Emery & Laumann-Billings, 1998; Garbarino & Sherman, 1980), and are also more likely to be in family relationships lacking in warmth and support (McLeod & Shanahan, 1996).

Both sustained poverty and descent into poverty appear to move parenting in more harsh, punitive, irritable, inconsistent, and coercive directions. McLoyd (1998) reviews evidence that poverty precipitates marital and parent-child conflict which, in turn, alters parental behavior in a hostile and coercive direction. These parenting characteristics may be a result of deficient coping strategies needed for managing the stressors associated with low socio-economic status(SES). However, low SES is not inevitably associated with risky family environments. Just as parenting characteristics may be an important mediator of the effects of low SES on children's mental and physical health, effective parenting may safeguard children from the adverse effects of low SES.

Among other environmental factors, the home conditions which make the child into a runaway are varied but all point to a near unanimous answer i.e. family crisis and the breakdown of the family and home due to deteriorating human relations or factors linked to social environment. Such a breakdown manifests itself in various forms like: the neglect and abuse of children, dysfunctional parents who do not adequately care for their children, lack of support from the traditional extended family system, abuse of psychoactive substances by the parents or by other members of the family, domestic violence, deterioration of values permitting maltreatment of children, and finally, break-up of families. Such families are characterized by conflict and aggression and by relationships that are cold, unsupportive, and neglectful. A United Nations study on youth maladjustment reveals, 'If one conclusion has to be drawn from the data it would be that increase in juvenile delinquency is not the inevitable result of poverty and rapid urbanization. The key intervening variable is the strength of adult-child relationships, most notably family relationship', (cited in Agnelli, S. 1986).

Typically, street children come from families which are in crisis or on the point of breaking down. In some cases accidents or illness can leave children unprotected and without families. Violence is reportedly the common method of settling interpersonal problems between the parents themselves or between parents and children. Under the pressure of physical, psychological and emotional overload, familial relationships decline, bonds of family life weaken and beyond a certain threshold, the child steps out of the home or is deserted by the parents or other family member (Agnelli, S. 1986). Rane, A. & Shroff, N. (1992) estimate that one in every sixteen street children is deserted by his parents.

Studies indicate that children whose parents were less responsive, warm, and sensitive were less likely to initiate social interactions and were more aggressive and critical (Brody & Flor, 1998; Kerns et al., 1996; Landry et al., 1998). In addition, families in which parents were cold, unsupportive, or neglectful, their children's social relationships throughout life were more problematic and less supportive (Bost et al., 1998; Graves, Wang, Mead, Johnson, & Klag, 1998; Kerns et al., 1996).

Data suggest that the development of social competence and supportive relationships outside of the family are compromised by growing up in a risky family environment. Early family environments which are unsupportive, unaccepting, and conflictual contribute to the development of hostility (Houston & Vavak, 1991; Woodall & Matthews, 1989). Parents and siblings in risky families are poor models of pro-social behavior, and they do not provide appropriate socialization opportunities that would facilitate the early development of complex social skills. There is also a long-term association between childhood social competence and adult mental health; rejected children are at an increased risk for adult psychopathology (Bagwell, Newcomb, & Bukowski, 1998; Parker & Asher, 1987).

"The loosening of the family bond, not to mention the actual breakup, may be a source of psychic stress and heightened conflict. A separation from the family….. not only brings a sense of insecurity in worldly social sense, it also means a loss of significant others who guarantee the sense of sameness and affirm the inner continuity of self" (Kakar, S. 1978). According to UNICEF (1987), "children on the street face the unhappy reality of increasing separation from their natural families and become at risk for losing their limited access to basic facilities, such as health, education, and recreation. Once this process is underway, it is very difficult to hold in check, with the result that the child may end up abandoning the family or being abandoned by it".

The emotional environment of the family is significant to the child's development of self-esteem and self-image. Donald and Swart-Kruger (1994) have noted that, in terms of emotional health, the lack or loss of a satisfactory relationship with an adult caregiver poses the greatest problem for most street children. They cited Bowlby's (1988) theory of attachment and its effects on the development of emotional security and trust, as well as its function in psychological nurturance and the identification process has profound implications for street children. In the emotionally healthy family, the child feels loved and wanted, as the parents' approval and acceptance encourages the child to bond and form a secure attachment with each parent. As a result of the parents' loving and positive interactions with the child, they convey their belief to the child that he/she is a "valued" member of the family. Consequently, the child develops positive self-esteem, as one who has "worth," and a positive self-image.

In the emotionally abusive family, the child feels unloved and unwanted. The parents or caretakers consistently reject the child and the child's behavior. They might also encourage others to reject and ridicule the child. The emotional family environment is "cold." as the parents do not express nor show any affection.

support or guidance toward the child. Families which show high levels of negative affect are less likely to engage in conversations about children's feelings (Dunn & Brown, 1994). Many street children report feeling lonely and more talk about feeling states in the home is associated with better emotion understanding in children (Dunn, Brown, Slomkowski, Tesla, & Youngblade, 1991)

The child is deprived of the psychological nurturing necessary for a child's psychological growth and development. Emotional abuse in the form of a continuous, on-going behavior reduces a child's self-concept and makes the child feels unworthy of respect, friendship, love and affection.

Ironically, it is the inadequacy or lack of such a caring relationship that usually precipitates the choice, or forced acceptance, of street life. A survey conducted on street children in Delhi revealed that about one-fifth of them had runaway from their homes after abandoning their families. They had suffered a miserable experience of child abuse mostly by their step parents (Nangia, P. 1988). Children who become street children invariably encounter varoius forms of child abuse in their homes, schools and/or communities. This abuse is, in some cases, so severe that it becomes the central causal factor for the children to leave their homes and communities and seek refuge on the streets.

The physical environment of the family also aggravates the process. Poor housing or overcrowded houses create tensions, conflicts and stress among their inmates. Socio- economic conditions of the family are also contributing factors for the child leaving his home. Most street children are reported to come from homes where they faced not only physical but also psychological deprivation. The child is very often denied warmth, love, affection and security. Increased stress on parents in the context of poverty and poor environmental conditions is believed to be associated with the phenomenon of street children.

Cultural differences have also been identified in the characteristics of the families of street children. Aptekar, L. (1990)

in his study of Colombian street children collected data about their families. The matrifocal family structure in Latin America constitutes families headed by females who were maltreated by their male partners. In such families, children's step fathers ('padrastros' as they are called in Colombia) were often found abusive and the mothers tolerated the abuse because of economic compulsions. As a result of being placed between the demands of the 'padrastros' and the love for her children, there was severe tension in the home. Thus, children were mostly neglected, abandoned, or otherwise forced to leave. This created a large number of children who left home at an early age.

Many research workers have come to regard the concept of maternal deprivation as being of primary etiological importance in the field of delinquency. This seems to have been especially so since the publication of Bowlby's (1952) well-known book, 'Maternal care & Mental Health'. The concept, despite its usefulness, fails to take adequate cognizance of the important complementary role, which is played by fathers. The significance of the role of the father, especially in relation to male children, is an important feature of family life across cultures. For a considerable time as a result of investigations highlighting the maternal role, fathers were thought of mainly in terms of the support they provided to the mother rather than their direct emotional involvement in the upbringing of their children.

The role of father has been exemplified in the psychoanalytical approach of Sigmund Freud and sociological analysis by Talcott Parsons. Describing the role of the father, Freud, regarded the father as the parent who influences children, especially boys, to incorporate the prohibitions, rules, principles and values of society. Identification with the father means that the father becomes the boy's model and the boy strives to be like him (Freud, S. cited in Lynn, D.B. 1974).

Talcott Parsons has also elaborated on the role of the father as society's representative within the family and the family's representative within the society. He differentiates the father's "instrumental" role from the mother's "expressive" role (Parsons,

T. & Bales, 1955). Parsons, T. (cited in Lynn, D.B. 1974) refers to the father's efforts to relate the family to society as the instrumental function. The father is considered as the primary family executive who provides authority, discipline and neutral and objective judgment. While the mother plays the expressive, integrative, supportive role, the father must perform these crucial instrumental operations to enable the family to function well in society and to help children grow as effective, independent adults.

The mother's role as caretaker enables her to carry out the expressive functions. The expressive role involves keeping intact the internal affairs of the family by coping with it's stress and strain. The mother is required to maintain smooth relations between family members by regulating the tensions among them, give emotional support, and operate as a mediator of father-child relationship (Lynn, D.B. 1974). She must sometimes serve as a buffer between father and child or control rivalry between siblings. These activities enhance family solidarity and sustain the children's emotional security.

The father is also seen to have an important role to play in the development of sex-appropriate identification. Identification can be defined as, "the process by which the child incorporates in him his parent's strength, adequacy, personal attributes, characteristics, and motives (Mussen, Conger, & Kagan, 1974). Identification with the father is possible only when the father is constantly available and allows himself to be idealized. He should provide emotional access to the child making possible a masculine identification.

It has been stressed that the absence of the father has consequences on the supervision, education, recreation and finances available for the child. Fathers who stay away from home most of the time are less-accessible, inadequate and ambiguous role models for their sons. If the father is extremely detached or excessively punitive, the boy may become so alienated that he will not wish to model after him or accept his concept of sex-role for males (Lynn, D.B., 1974).

During the last few decades, the family in India has undergone phenomenal transformations. In the traditional family, the role of the primary disciplinarian was that of the father or other male members. The father in traditional Indian society has been the figure of authority and power amongst other male members of an extended family network.

Kakar, S. (1981) while describing the role of the father in Indian childhood states, "the son's identification with his father can take place only if the father allows his son emotional access to him, this is, if he allows himself to be idealized at the same time that he encourages and supports the boy's own efforts to grow up .... Identification is a process; however, it requires that over the years the father be constantly available to his son in a psychological sense. In autobiographical accounts, fathers, whether strict or indulgent, cold or affectionate, are invariably distant".

Father's affection has also been reported to be the most important parental influence on a boy's relationship with others in society and the leadership qualities (Bronfenbenner, U. cited in Pilling & Pringle, 1978). Street children, mostly boys, do not have cordial or affectionate relations with their fathers and most of these relations are on the verge of breaking down. For most of these children there is no positive father-figure or role model with whom the child can identify. This is likely to have long-term repercussions on the child's personality, social and emotional development.

Apart from parents and stepparents, street children have also been reportedly abused and ill treated by their siblings relatives, caregivers, teachers and others. Violence against these children or physical abuse is probably the commonest form of maltreatment faced by them in the home.

PART III

STREET LIFE

3.1   LIVING AND WORKING CONDITIONS OF STREET CHILDREN

Street children vary with respect to their family backgrounds, contact and support, the occupations they are engaged in, circumstances in which they live and the kinds of problems they have. However, all of them present major needs arising from their particular and especially difficult circumstances. "What particularly characterizes this diverse group of children is that they live outside the parameters that their society has allocated to childhood" (Aptekar, L. 1988).

Street children cope with street life in different ways which depends on several factors. These factors include the experiences they had at their homes, relationship with their family members, the kind of work they do on the street, the quality of their peer life on the street, their self-concept and future aspirations, the kind of support they get from peers, benefactors, or institutions and societal reactions to them (Aptekar, L. 1988). It is only by understanding the interplay between the physical, sociological and psychological realities that the children live in, can one get a comprehensive understanding of the lives of street children.

Working street children are mostly engaged in activities in the unorganized or informal sector in cities offering cheap labour and catering to the various needs of city population. Since they do unskilled and repetitive work, they get little or no training on the job. "Their long work experience as children, especially if it precluded education, leaves them unprepared for their future. They are at a greater risk of lifelong marginalization. These children work in a variety of street jobs and many of them grow up prematurely. They become proto-adults adept at surviving in the midst of poverty and unemployment" (Ennew, J. & Young, P. 1981),

Street children are found to be engaged in various activities like: selling newspaper, serving tea or working in roadside hotels and restaurants, shining shoes, working in small factories or automobile workshops, rag picking and parking attendants (The State of the World's Children, UNICEF, 1997). Many of them are found to earn their livelihood in a variety of clever ways and they are often portrayed as heroic survivors against enormous odds. This also demonstrates a developmental maturity beyond their years. Aptekar, L. (1988) examined the emotional and social lives of Colombian street children in the age group of 7-16 years. In his sample several eight-year-old children collected popsicle sticks left over from a vendor, washed them, and sold them back to be reused.

In another instance, "a group of boys in a national cemetery rented ladders to the bereaved so that the mourners could get a closer look at their loved ones stored in coffins six feet above the ground. Two 12 years old street boys, pretending that they were starving, were able to get leftover food daily from a restaurant owner. After sorting out the food and eating the sweets, they traded the rest to a street vendor in exchange of cigarettes. Irrespective of their family situations, street children were also found to sing songs in buses and public places and seek alms and the songs had reference to their sick mothers and abusing factors" (Aptekar, L. 1988).

The Status Report on street children by the Social Welfare Directorate, Government of West Bengal, 1992, describes the life on the street. It reads, "On arrival on the street, street child's immediate needs are food and shelter. The commercial centres, public places, railway stations and bus stands provide them not only shelter but also opportunities to work in a wide range of occupations. Many prefer to go in for self-employment such as vending, shoe shining, rag picking and carrying luggage while a few others survive by begging" (cited in Mukherjee, S. 1992). Contrary to the popular belief that street children are vagrant or generally beggars, almost all of them work for survival. Since most them are not literate and are unskilled without any experience, they mostly find menial skill jobs, which need minimum skill. Street children, who work, constantly fear arrest since all their income-generating activities are illegal.

In a situational analysis of street children in Bangalore, nearly 95% of the 1,750 street children sampled in the study were working. Rag picking, vending and coolie work were the major occupations of street children in that city. Only 10% of the working street children in the sample were skilled workers such as garage mechanics, tailors and apprentices in small factories. 16% of them were semi-skilled (Stone- cutters, cart/cycle-rickshaw drivers, bangle or agarbatti or beedi or cardboard box makers) while nearly three-fourth of them were manual labourers (ragpickers, coolies, construction workers, cart pullers, vendors, egg or milk suppliers on day-to-day basis) (Reddy, N. 1992).

Working street children are also highly mobile and move from one place to another or shift from one occupation to another very frequently. They often work under abominable conditions for very low returns. Children are vulnerable, less likely to organize in unions , easier to exploit and therefore are employed in large numbers(N, Burra; 1995)

They are also subjected to prolonged working hours and face other problems like low or nil wages, insufficient rest intervals, night work, exposure to hazardous machinery or chemical products and exploitation by the employers. They are abused, punished or humiliated by their employers and this is one of the reasons which accounts for high mobility and instability in the paid jobs they engage in and also these children's reported strong preference for self-employment.

A great variation is found in the working hours of street child labour particularly self-employed street children. The working

Chart 6
LIST OF ACTIVITIES STREET CHILDREN ARE ENGAGED IN:

The following is a list of occupations commonly undertaken by street children:

(a) collecting & selling waste paper, plastic, glass, scrap metal etc.

(b) carry luggage or load on the station and in market places:

(c) cleaning cars or other vehicles on roads or in garages:

(d) hawking or vending:

(e) selling newspaper magazines etc. at road junctions:

(f) selling popcorn, balloons, peanuts, etc. on the station:

(g) working in tea stalls, restaurants or hotels:

(h) working as parking attendants.

Street children are also found engaged in : begging, prostitution, drug-peddling and pick pocketing.

Sources:

1. Helen Rahman, 'Situation of the street children and girl domestics (Preliminary Report), 1992 cited in Ahmadullah M. (1992) 'Working and Street Children' – A challenge to, and potentials of social work, Paper presented at the South Asian Workshop on Street Children, organized by Tata Institute of Social Sciences (TISS) in Collaboration with International Association of Schools of Social Work, Austria April, 1992, TISS, Bombay.

2. Report of NGO workshop on Working and Street Children in U.T. of Delhi 16-17 July, 1987 organized by ICCW and UNICEF's mid-north India zone office, New Delhi, Unicef, 1987.

hours vary from 1 - 2 hours to 18 hours a day. The duration of working hours depends on the kind of work the child is engaged in and whᵥther he has any familial support. Domestic helpers and children working in restaurants or hotels work for 17-18 hours a day. In such cases, since a child has the provision of free meals and space to sleep at night act, these act as incentives for children choosing to work in such places.

A wide variation also exists in the wages earned by these children in different occupations and also within the same occupation. According to Nangia, P. (1988) children working as porters, rickshaw pullers, shoe-blacks and ragpickers can easily earn between Rs.500-600 per month by working for eight to ten hours every day. For the same duration of work, vendors earned between Rs.300-500 per month. In small industrial units and offices in the private sector, street children were paid Rs.150-300 per month for their work. The domestic helpers and shop attendants were found to be paid between Rs.50 to 250 per month.

In street child labour, low wages, irregular payment and job insecurity were too common. In some particular occupations e.g. work in 'dhabas' or tea stalls, domestic helpers and mechanics in repair shops, there was no time for the children to rest during daytime and no holidays also. Street children are also engaged in tasks that are too strenuous for them e.g. working in factories or carrying heavy loads and they often work in unhygienic and unsanitary conditions. Besides having to do uninteresting and monotonous jobs devoid of intellectual or creative stimuli, the child at this crucial developmental stage is denied the possibility of normal social and emotional development.

3.2.   HEALTH AND NUTRITIONAL STATUS

Growing up in stressful and abusive families creates a cascade of risk, beginning early in life, which puts a child not only at immediate risk, but also at long-term and lifelong risk for a wide variety of physical and mental health ailments. While on the street, children experience serious health risks and physical danger. Street children, particularly those living alone without families, are now an integral part of the urban scenario and they lead harsh, precarious and hazardous lives. They have specific problems like deprivation of basic needs of health, nutrition, education and recreation, physical and sexual abuse, harassment and coercion by authority and by other people involved in anti-social activities. They are exposed to high levels of violence, victimization, sexual exploitation by pedophiles and pimps, and to the use of harmful substances. Many suffer from psychiatric symptoms and mental health problems.

Literature shows that repeated social challenges in a child's environment can disrupt basic homeostatic processes that are central to the maintenance of health. Children who grow up in families at-risk or in crisis often suffer stress-related physical health problems, such as cancer, heart disease, hypertension, diabetes, obesity, depression and anxiety disorders. Large numbers of studies reveal a pattern of serious long-term health consequences for children who grow up in homes marked by conflict, anger and aggression; that are emotionally cold, unsupportive; and where children's needs are neglected(Repetti, R. L., Taylor, S. E. & Seeman, T. E.,2001).

Street children may be also be exposed to specific health risks associated with untreated illnesses and injuries, pedestrian traffic accidents, physical abuse from older street youth, criminal elements and occasionally the police. In addition, a perception exists that there is a high incidence of infectious diseases, HIV/AIDS, Sexually Transmitted Diseases (STD's), respiratory problems, parasitic infections (e.g. worms, scabies and lice), skin infections, malnutrition (undernourishment and malnourishment), oral and dental problems, skeletal and soft tissue injuries, diarrhoea and constipation among these children (Draft document on policy issues and strategic guidelines on street children in South Africa, 1998). Due to their lack of trust in adults, children living on the street tend not to seek medical attention for health conditions until complications set in. Self-diagnosis and self-treatment thus complicates health problems in the long term.

Some children, unsupervised by adults, spend their days on the street but are able to return home at night. Others have no home to return to and they sleep anywhere they can find shelter. They do not have access to basic amenities like toilet facilities or a place to bathe. Lack of hygiene in their lives increases the chances that wounds or infections picked up in the streets, where accidents and assaults are all too common, will become worse. It is difficult for street children to go to medical dispensaries partly because of their own fear about requiring to reveal their identities and also because of lack of awareness about available medical facilities.

Apart from physical and sexual exploitation, undernourishment, poor health conditions and a high prevalence of diseases and infections are features common in the lives of street children. Because of the vulnerable and precarious situations in which they live, the incidence among them of under nutrition and other health problems seems particularly high. Poor, inadequate shelter arrangements available to homeless street children, inadequate and poor-quality diet, at times starvation, lack of access to medical facilities, respiratory infections, skin ailments, and high environmental risks due to their hazardous working and living conditions have all been found to contribute to the ill- health of street children (Shah, P.M; 1987 Heredia, C.R. & Kaul, K., 1987; Nangia, P., 1988 and Sondhi, P., 1989).

Homeless children are assumed to be in poorer health than children who are not homeless. Lack of on-going health care and the problems of growing up in unhygienic, dangerous and unprotected setting are primary factors that negatively affect the child's health. Although street children are more in need of health services than other children because of the 'high-risk' environment, in which they constantly work and live, their access to health care is limited. This is primarily due to frequent moves, the chaotic state of their lives and lack of adequate services for the poor in urban centres. This also implies that problems that may be observed and given appropriate medical attention in non-homeless children are very often overlooked among homeless children.

According to situational analysis of street children carried out in Bombay, Bangalore, Calcutta, Delhi, Hyderabad, Indore and Madras by the Ministry of Welfare, Government of India and UNICEF in 1988-89, health of most of the street children sampled in the studies was found to be in a poor state. A test of the degree of nourishment showed that 90% of the total of 2,301 street children sampled in the city of Calcutta was undernourished while 3% of them were severely undernourished. Of these, 65% of them have been reported to suffer from excessive lack of protein and essential vitamins. The data were based on the study of quantity and quality of food usually taken by the street children (Ghosh, A. 1992).

In Indore, an analysis of the height-weight ratio of the 300 street children included in the study showed that 86% of the boys were below the normal ratio of height and weight. Only 20% of the street children included in the sample in Madras were found to be adequately nourished, while in Bangalore 87% were found to be undernourished (Arimpoor, J. 1992). In Bombay, it was observed that though 60% of the children had two meals a day, the nutritional value of the food was poor. As a result of under nutrition, intake of nutritionally poor diet and unhygienic living conditions, children often suffered from diseases like: gastroenteritis, ringworm infections, anemia, vitamin A deficiency and rickets (Philips, W.S.K., 1992).

In another situational analysis of street children of Bangalore, of the total sample of 1,750 street children, 87% of them were stated to be undernourished and 7% severely undernourished. Moderate or excessive protein and vitamin deficiency was found in over 95% of the sampled children. However, the age-height ratio as assessed by the field workers was found to be satisfactory for 72% of the children. The study also revealed that children constantly suffered from scabies, tuberculosis, amoebic dysentery, rickets, sores, ringworm infections and ear, and throat infections (Reddy, N. 1992).

Millions of children and adolescents who live or work on the street sell sex to make a living, increasing their exposure to sexually transmitted diseases. The predisposition of street children and youth to drug abuse increases their susceptibility to sexually transmitted infection as they lose the power to take rational decisions (Barker 1993; Fieldman 1994; Ruiz 1994; Raffaelli et al. 1995).Young street children are particularly vulnerable to sexually transmitted diseases. A study by the Child in Need Institute, Kolkata, 1990, revealed that child prostitution at Sealdah Railway station was widely prevalent. The number of runaway children found on the platform was around 250 children. Out of these, fifteen children in the age group of five to fourteen had been found to be sexually exploited for periods ranging from one to two years. Sexual exploitation of very young street children, in lure of some money or the promise of shelter during the night, was common at the platform or on the streets (Mohan, S. 1990).

STREET CHILDREN AND HIV/ AIDS:

The incidence of HIV infection among street children is increasing. At least half of the people infected with HIV are younger than age 25 (Population Reference Bureau 1994).

In the Indian context , data about HIV infection or prevalence among street children is very limited and more research is required in the area. National AIDS Control Organization (NACO) has listed street children as one of the "at-risk" groups of HIV infection (1999). The vulnerability of street children to HIV/AIDS is linked to their way of life and to a host of other factors, such as:

➢ Precocious sexuality

➢ Exposure to unprotected sexual activity (in particular for food, protection or money)

➢ Drug use, which lowers inhibitions and increases the taking of risks

➢ High prevalence of sexually-transmitted diseases which go untreated

➢ Exclusion from the school system

> Lack of information on sexuality and false beliefs about HIV/ AIDS

> Low self-esteem and general disrespect for both the body and life

(Supplement to Health Transition Review Volume 7, 1997)

When one considers the holistic (emotional, physical, mental and social) nature of health care to street children it is obvious that no one department, be it government or non-governmental, could possibly cater for all the health needs of street children. Appropriate health care intervention must, therefore, be co-ordinated with different role-players providing different services at different levels.

3.3. SPECIAL PSYCHOSOCIAL RISKS OR PROBLEMS FACED BY STREET CHILDREN

It is now being increasingly recognized that street children are deprived of adequate care and protection and therefore, are in especially difficult situation. These children who need substantial protection beyond what their families now offer are termed by UNICEF as "Children in especially difficult circumstances" (UNICEF, 1988). All these children who are neglected, deprived and abused, irrespective of the fact whether they live with or without their families, are in vulnerable conditions and require special assistance and protection.

Street children living without families lack adequate shelter, food, education, guidance and support. These children living in unhygienic and infected conditions are much more likely to suffer serious and long-term consequences from illness, particularly when they are also under nourished. Clearly, then, the basic physical needs of most of the street children are not met but they have many other important requirements if they have to grow up and realize their full potential. Until recently, little attention has been paid to adverse psychosocial factors in the street child's living and working environment .The improvements in conditions of physical health will not suffice. Better physical conditions will not necessarily reduce the incidence of psychosocial problems faced by these children (MachPherson, S. 1987).

Child welfare issues with special reference to street children should focus on the concept of psychosocial development of the street child and the associated risk factors. The intellectual, social and emotional handicaps normally associated with the social and material circumstances in which street children live need to be ascertained.

The World Health Organization (WHO) has proposed a fourfold classification of psychosocial needs of children (WHO, 1982). These include the need for love and security, for new experience, for praise and recognition and for responsibility. Pringle (1974) has grouped the psychosocial needs of children into four main areas: the need for love and security; the need for new experiences; the need for praise and recognition; and the need for responsibility. If these needs are not met or are thwarted, children may be at risk for emotional and behavioral problems, and fulfillment sought elsewhere (away from the family unit). Street children are very likely to fall into this category.

According to WHO report (1979) 'Psychosocial problems have a basic etiology which is psychosocial, that is, they are inappropriate psychosocial reactions of the individual to something (or things) in the environment. Psychosocial problems may have some intrinsic or internal cause; for e.g., the individual may react inappropriately to the rapid physical, sexual and psychological changes of childhood and adolescence; or they may be due to extrinsic factors, e.g., features of the micro social and/or macro social environment. Whatever the factors involved, they invariably cause stress in the individual in the face of rising insecurity, alienation and anomy'.

The micro social factors involved in the etiology of psychosocial problems, according to the report, often include the family. Many of the stabilizing forces of more traditional family life have been eroded. Family instability increases the risk of stress and inappropriate psychosocial reactions.

Macro social factors, which have been found to be frequently associated with increased risk of psychosocial problems, include urbanization and non-optimal socioeconomic conditions. Increasing urbanization is a phenomenon common to all developing countries. For a number of reasons, socio-economically deprived children and adolescents are at higher risk of falling victim to psychosocial problems. 'The families of such children are more often forced to migrate, and more likely to be disrupted or broken than the average family. Children and adolescents living in suboptimal social and economic conditions are less well prepared for school, more likely never to attend school and more likely to leave school early' (WHO, 1979).

A child, who has a stable affectionate, consistent and dependable relationship with his parents or care giver, feels loved and secure. Affection and security are among the most important inputs for personality development in childhood. The absence of affectionate behaviors and affiliate contact with adults during early childhood is likely to lead to deviant behaviors in children. Children who grow up in risky families are also more likely as teenagers and adults to engage in drug and alcohol abuse, smoking, risky sexual behavior, and aggressive, anti-social behavior. Many studies provide evidence that children and teenagers who abuse drugs and engage in risky sex are more likely to have hostile, unsatisfying and non-supportive relationships with their parents (Repetti, R. L., Taylor, S. E. & Seeman, T. E.,2001).

Parental neglect has been quite consistently indicated as an antecedent of weak development of affection system in young children. Research is quite clear in showing that street children who have experienced lack of appropriate security and emotional support with their parents have had less affective and emotionally close relations with them (Agnelli, S. 1986; Sondhi, P. 1994). It can be inferred, then, that conditions of neglect and abuse (recognized as aspects of psychosocial deprivation) in all likelihood interfere with formation of emotional bonds by street children. These affectional inadequacies experienced by street children in early childhood may well be linked with their poor emotional health. Both Berger and Bundy (cited by Duncan & Rock, 1994) have stated that these children, who experienced stress, turmoil, and violence, especially at the family level, are at risk for a range of psychological problems and deviant behavior. Setiloane (1991) has confirmed that the emotional stress accompanying violence negatively affects relationships with family, peers, teachers, and others.

Coupled with the need for love and security, is the need to develop a positive self-image or self-esteem. When the parents are concerned about their children and offer guidance and direction, such conditions enhance the child's self-concept and foster development of self-esteem. There is abundant evidence that children who live in conditions of family disorganization, financial instability, and social rejection are likely to be lower in esteem. They lack trust in their capacities and are overwhelmed with feelings of helplessness and hopelessness (Diggory, 1966; Rosenbery, 1965).

Perhaps the most common observation regarding the families of disadvantaged and destitute children is the consistent absence of conditions, which favor development of high self-esteem. These families are very often headed by parents who are absent, apathetic, or rejecting and incapable of responding to the needs of children. For a street child, both the absence of conditions that contribute to the formation of positive self-esteem and the presence of insensitive, rejecting and abusive conditions reduce the feelings of worthiness and competence. This, in turn, has serious consequences on the child's social and emotional development.

The need for opportunities for new experiences which are potentially maturing is also a key prerequisite for the child's cognitive, social and emotional development. Impoverished early childhood experiences lead to deficits in the child's emotional, social and intellectual learning. It may be assumed that exposing the child to a breadth and variety of experiences and opportunities to relate to, facilitates social role development (MacPherson, S. 1987). When socializing agents neglect the child's physical and / or psychological needs, as observed in the case of street children, the child will often try to fulfill these needs by himself in whatever way he can. Such premature efforts to be independent of others both at the physical and psychological level, can have dysfunctional consequences (Ausbel, D. 1952). This includes the development of attitudes of mistrust towards socializing agents and adoption of deviant role behaviors, particularly delinquency.

The daily lives of many street children are unstructured and unstable. Kennedy (1987) has stated that, "in the long run, this sense that nothing is stable can produce distortions of the mind. Many young people on the streets lose track of time and do not know how long they have been wandering around with no structure or specific purpose. They are unable to describe clearly their activity on a given day.

Because street children are constantly en route from one place to another, moving about makes it difficult for them to form stable relationships with their peers or adults in their environment. They are unable to form intimate, mutually supportive and enduring personal relationships with people in their environment. It is quite possible that they may be emotionally and psychologically isolated from others and have only superficial social contacts. Further, these children perceive the streets as productive or barren, friendly or unfriendly, at different times of the day or night (Kennedy, 1987). Physical danger is all too pervasive, real and visibility signifies not protection but vulnerability (Peacock, 1994).

The child copes with harsh, violent, competitive and risky environment of the street by forming street gangs or being a part of them. Street gangs are mechanisms to ensure survival and they provide protection, security and comradeship (Agnelli, S. 1986). It also meets the needs, in particular, for a sense of identity. Aptekar, L. (1988) has suggested that by observing street children in their peer groups, attempt can be made to look into their psychological functioning. While collecting data on street children in Bogota, Latin America, he found that two groups exists, the 'galladas' (from 'gallo', rooster, which is used idiomatically to mean aggressive and bossy) and the camadas (a litter of little pups, as they are called).

"The gallada was described as a close-knit and formidably efficient platoon of five to twenty-five children who associated together principally for monetary reasons. The galladas were first described in their present day form in 1860 in Latin America. Each member of the gallada has some kind of obligation to every other child. Children who had passed pubertal stage (above 14 years of age) had the responsibility to run the gallada, while prepubertal children were their underlings. The ultimate power and authority of the gallada rested with 'jefe' – the boss. He maintained his power and position in the gallada by his qualities like physical prowess, intelligence and ability to protect or 'fence' the products, which the group had collectively gained. Members of the gallada rarely associated outside of work" (Aptekar, L. 1988).

The gallada had its own customs and rites to ensure it's members were obedient and loyal which was also instrumental for their survival. While operating in the street, the entire group was often divided into tactical units of two or three members. It's members often specialized in particular tasks like snatching bags or jewellery, stealing bicycles, guarding territory etc.

The second form of peer groups described by Aptekar, L. (1988) is the camadas. "They were composed of two or three 'preadolescent' boys (9-12 years of age) who shared the intimacies and camaraderie of being together. These groups were different than the galladas in several ways: they were more like family and friends than business partners, and they were formed by fewer children all of whom had not reached adolescence. The internal dynamics of the camadas were also found to be different than those within the galladas. They were able to get food for themselves by posing as young, innocent kids and therefore, were able to meet their basic needs. Children in the çamadas played together and ate together. Because these children associated with each other more for personal than for business reasons, their relationships to each other were more intimate, which also resulted in less hierarchy and formal organization in the camada" (Aptekar, L. 1988).

Children in the gangs devise their own special languages, by rearranging words or by a secret vocabulary or gestures, cries, whistle or signal. They give each other aliases so that they won't be recognized (The UNESCO Courier, Oct., 1991). They very often conceal their real identities, their names for the fear of being caught by the police.

The public view of street children in many countries is overpoweringly negative and results in children engaging in anti-social activities. They are lured into pick-pocketing, stealing, gambling, drug peddling and prostitution. A common diversion in the life of street children is gambling, which can take the form of playing cards, pitching small coins or bottle caps or even empty plastic glasses which can be sold later. In order to cope with disturbing thoughts of low self-esteem and feelings of rejection or alienation, the street child resorts to substance abuse. The percentage of substance abusers among street children varies greatly. Studies in different parts of the world indicate that among 25% to 90% of street children abuse psychoactive and harmful substances. Street children have been found to sniff glue, shoe polish, paint-thinner or cleaning fluid (Agnelli, S. 1986).

Drug abuse is one of the means the children cope with the demands of the lifestyle. The World Health Organization has documented a link between status of children as members of "children and youth in especially difficult circumstances" [CYEDC] and vulnerability to substance abuse disorders, particularly chronic inhalant abuse. Even among the CYEDC population, however, street children are the group most vulnerable to inhalant addiction.

Many studies have found increased rates of substance abuse or risky sexual behaviors among children of families lacking in cohesion or families in which parents were neglectful and unsupportive. There is a large body of corroborating cross-sectional data suggesting that teens who abuse substances or engage in risky sexual behavior are more likely to live in homes in which interpersonal relationships, particularly with parents, tend to be hostile, distant, unsatisfying, nonsupportive, or lacking in cohesion (Barrera, Chassin, & Rogosch, 1993; Campo & Rohner, 1992; Denton & Kampfe, 1994). The direct impact of neglectful parents on opportunities for alcohol and drug use may be compounded through a concomitant increase in the influence exerted by peers, especially true in case of street children.

In one report carried out by various UN organizations, children interviewed cited "peer pressure," "the need to sleep easily" and "relief from fear pain and hunger" as reasons that they took drugs. Other social workers are keen to point out the bonding effect of sharing the rituals of drug, a process that serves to separate the children from society around them and at the same time bringing them together. The use of drugs by street children, because of peer pressure, emotional disturbances, and societal rejection or to escape from pressures of life, is widely reported. These children, living in misery and daily hopelessness, easily fall in the trap of drugs and become their unfortunate victims.

Like drugs and gambling, violence is also common in the lives of street children. Living without any adult guidance, control and supervision, these children are more likely than others to turn to violence as a way of living. Most of them have experienced or observed physical abuse or violence at home. On the street, the danger and fear of beatings and brutality at the hands of employer, older street boys, peers, police and other hostile people in the child's immediate social environment is always present.

Street life most often denies the child the pleasures of childhood and opportunities for play and recreation. As for games, sports and leisure activities, the child's basic needs are not adequately met. Almost all street children seek refuge in the cinema. Movies are perhaps the all-time favorite pastime and also a source of entertainment. They provide easy, cheap and temporary escape from boredom, tension and stress associated with living on the street.

Many street children are emotionally immature and show strong psychosocial needs. They exhibit strong and desperate need for affection and love. They have a strong need to, but experience difficulty in gaining intimacy or relating to other people in their environment. In a street child's life, psychosocial deprivation may manifest itself in the form of feelings of rootlessness, a decreased sense of purpose and direction in life, and a diffused sense of self. Street children have reportedly expressed strong feelings of insecurity, uncertainty, stress and tension of living on the street (Sondhi, P. 1989).

Keen (1990) has stated that a small but significant proportion of street children has severe emotional and behavioral problems. Richter (1988) without attributing psychopathological traits to street children, has distinguished between three types of boys: the first group which showed no signs of psychological disorder; the second group that displayed moderate to severe symptoms; and the third group fell somewhere in-between. Richter (1988) found that boys with a strong internal locus of control demonstrated less psychopathology. Those with a strong external locus of control had spent a longer time on the street and had "less positive relationships with peers and showed more signs of psychopathology, particularly in the form of depression and psychosomatic symptoms". Yet, in spite of the hardships to which they had been subjected, some of the boys in Richter's sample displayed tremendous resilience and capabilities beyond their years.

However, there is evidence in the research literature that adverse life conditions breed a host of maladaptive behaviours and, it is in this context that the book aims to stress on the long-term psychosocial repercussions of the state of homelessness and living without any familial support.

VULNERABILITY AND RESILIENCE

In the area of psychosocial health of street children, the concept of vulnerability and resilience is gaining increasing attention. Resiliency is defined as the capacity of individuals to face up to an adverse event, withstand considerable hardship, and not only overcome it but also be made stronger by it. The concept of resiliency has been discussed in past studies as involving both the idea of stressors and an innate capacity of children to respond, endure, and develop normally in spite of the presence of stressors (Richmond & Beardslee,1988). The concept offers an encouraging insight because adverse life events during childhood have been associated with child and adolescent depression (Freidrich,et al,1982), substance abuse (Biafora,et al,1994; Duncan,1977), and other forms of deviant behavior.

The concept of resiliency started a recent paradigm shift in the field of child development. This shift has moved from focusing on decreasing the environmental risk factors that make individuals susceptible to the development of maladaptive behavior and psychiatric disorders to the highlighting of resiliency and its promotion. In this paradigm, it is essential to identify protective factors in the child's environment that can serve as a defense against the damaging effects of risk factors, as well as the individual's vulnerabilities that can threaten his resiliency. Resiliency, therefore, is viewed as a product of interaction between individual (nature) and environmental (nurture) factors, something that can be promoted through the developmental years of childhood and adolescence. It can be developed by strengthening the protective elements in a child's environment while simultaneously promoting the child's life skills and other personal strengths.

The importance of the macro environment in fostering resiliency cannot be exaggerated. The hardships associated with poverty and unemployment is great and at times puts the family at-risk. These adversities can lead to marital disharmony, domestic violence, maternal depression, parental discord, coercive and abusive parenting, and child neglect and maltreatment. On the other hand, some studies suggest that these same adversities may serve to strengthen the resiliency of children. Turner, Norman, and Zunz (1993) synthesized various studies on resiliency factors that serve to promote positive psychological growth and development.

Many of studies on resiliency have been done with children and youth living with families under various circumstances of adversity and these studies have identified critical factors associated with the resiliency of some children. However, there is very limited data on the resiliency of children living without any contact, support or guidance from their families.

The especially difficult circumstances in which street children live have been studied for eliciting evidence showing developmental risk and vulnerability in physical, social, emotional and cognitive areas on the one hand, and on the other, evidence of the adaptability, resourcefulness ,coping ability and streetwise attitude of street children. Swart (1988) has stated that, contrary to popular belief, street children are not necessarily society's dropouts, and that "they should be recognized for the exceptional fortitude, creativity, and astute knowledge of human nature that they must possess to survive on the streets". Gordon (1979) has noted that running away from a physically abusive situation may indeed be a positive experience for some children. Agnelli (1986) suggests that a predisposition to seek greater autonomy and freedom from adult control may motivate some children to run away, and has pointed to the lack of psychopathology in street children and their successful coping strategies. For many street children, freedom from adult control is the most important attribute of their adopted way of life (Scharf et al., 1986). However, a number of studies indicate negative traits including low self-esteem, apathy, and fatalism among street children (Richter & Swart-Kruger, 1995; Cronje et al., 1976; Sondhi, P. 1994).

In a critical review of resiliency literature and its relevance to homeless children, Neiman (1988) identified certain factors associated with resiliency among street children. She grouped these factors into individual (constitutional factors, gender, and temperament) and environmental factors (bonding, mother-child relationship, family relationships, and extra familial factors). In the context of present study of street children living without families, these factors include: external supports and resources available to a child, mainly peers and adults in his living and working environment and institutions, personal strengths that the child develops (like development of autonomy, self-esteem, self reliance, confidence), and social skills the child acquires (such as conflict resolution and communication skills).

O'Sullivan (1991) showed that the presence of one caring and nurturing adult in the family can have a clear positive effect on the child's later life as an adult, even in the presence of a dysfunctional parent. It is obvious that the development of resilience is dependent on the child's living conditions, in the context of the family and the community in which he works or lives.

Research conducted on the resilience potential that exists in children living under stressful or abusive conditions suggests that young people are resilient and that the damaging psychological repercussions will reduce if they are provided appropriate nurturing environment. At present, resources for providing psychosocial assistance and support to street children, both at the governmental and non-governmental level are highly inadequate or minimal. This support includes interventions of supportive counseling, empathic listening, and knowledge of normal stress-related symptoms, or specialized psychiatric services for serious cases of severe depression or psychosis.

There are large numbers of children who would benefit from psychosocial interventions that encourage positive coping techniques, recognition and handling of stress and its management, and a supportive adult to listen to worries, in general. Addressing these effects within the framework of very limited psychological resources existing in the programs for street children, especially government-run programs will be a challenge, and training of personnel will be needed. General stereotypes about street children, created by politicians, media, police, and the public at large effect the nature of interventions designed for them.

PART IV

CHILD ABUSE AND MALTREATMENT

4.1. STREET CHILDREN AND CHILD ABUSE

Street children suffer an ongoing situation of abuse and neglect. There is evidence that abuse and neglect have several long-term psychological effects on behavior. Exposure to excessive physical aggression and emotional deprivation, which is common in the lives of street children, is likely to have impact on their personality development and can manifest itself in several varieties of antisocial and violent behavior.

The Convention on the Rights of the Child recognizes the problems of child abuse and neglect and refers to the need for protection of children against all forms of physical or mental injury or abuse, neglect, maltreatment or exploitation (UNICEF, 1988). In 1999, the Convention ratified by all countries globally except the United States and Somali stood as the single most widely ratified treaty that ever existed. However despite this, the objectives of the convention are still unfulfilled. Child abuse and neglect continues in violation of the rights guaranteed to them under the Convention and government's efforts have failed miserably to establish and implement the prohibitions essential to end the phenomenon of abuse of working children.

Review of literature on child abuse in India reveals a dearth of information on the subject. Information on abuse of street children is even scantier. Since 1980s the existence of child maltreatment, neglect and abuse of children within the family has gained attention and started being recognized as a problem. The first National Seminar on Child Abuse in India was held in New Delhi in 1988 under the auspices of the National Institute of Public Cooperation and Child

Development (NIPCCD), Delhi. Certain forms of child abuse occurring at the societal level have been identified as major social problems. Most common among these are: child labor, child prostitution, child marriage and the phenomenon of street children (Segal, U. 1991)

Child abusing practices have been present in the society since long. Mistreatment of children by adults and institutions charged with their protection is increasing. Children thus become most vulnerable when the people responsible for their care and safety betray that function, becoming instead direct threats to their health, development or even their life (UNICEF 1986). Female feoticide, infanticide, physical battering, sexual exploitation and abandonment are forms of child abuse, which have been reported in ancient times and can still be found in varying degrees. Thus, while the phenomenon of child abuse and neglect can be found in all human societies, what acts or behaviors are classified as abusive are culturally determined.

Child abuse must be viewed within the socio-cultural context of a society as what may be regarded abusive in one culture may not be so in another (Giovannoni, J.M. & Becerra, R.M., 1979). The problem of child abuse needs to be viewed from the total societal context within which it evolves (Gil, D. 1975). As Cantwell, N. (1979) has put it, "apart from physical violence, there are other manifestations of maltreatment such as abandonment and exploitation, both within and outside the family, which, according to the country concerned, may require more immediate response and priority".

Abuse of children may be direct and more visible, as in the case of physical and sexual abuse, or indirect, as with child labor or street children. Street children all around the world are harassed, exploited and abused. They have no access to education and they continue to live and work for long hours in risky and hazardous conditions. While working and living on the streets, they face inhumane conditions and daily physical assaults along with severe psychological and emotional deprivations (Human Rights Watch,

World Report 2000). Emotional abuse consists of "internal" injuries and is more difficult to identify. This form of abuse can be devastatingly dangerous to the child's development than other forms of abuse, as it negatively affects the child's self-esteem and self-image, causing distressing, life-long consequences. The behavioral indicators of physical/sexual abuse and neglect are external and easily visible injuries. However, the behavioral indicators of emotional abuse are more difficult to identify and assess.

It is difficult to operationally define the concept of child abuse because firstly, almost all research on child abuse and neglect has been in industrialized countries and thus available literature on the topic is based on it. Kempe, H.C. and Helfer, R.E. (1980) state, "our understanding of this perplexing social problem is limited due to the fact that it is based almost entirely on studies in western nations".

The second issue concerns the lack of clarity and specificity while using concepts and terms to indicate child abuse. Very often terms such as "child abuse", "child neglect", "child battering", "child maltreatment", have been used to refer to the same phenomenon (Cantwell, N. 1979; Sweet, J.J & Resick, P.A; 1979; Kempe & Helfer, 1980; Braden, A. 1981). This lack of consensus on the definition of child abuse and its related concepts can be attributed to the multidisciplinary nature of the subject. Just as there are no universally accepted norms or standards for child rearing, there exists a wide variation across cultures, over time and in forms or kinds of acts regarded as abusive.

The National Centre on Child Abuse and Neglect (1981) in the United States defines child abuse or battering as "purposefully mistreating children by physically, emotionally or sexually injuring them", and neglect as, "not providing for their basic physical, emotional or educational needs" (cited in Kameran, S. 1975). The U.S., Canada and Great Britain have elaborate and specialized programs to identify abused children.

Giovannoni, J.M. (1971) defines child abuse as "parental acts that constitute a misuse (or abuse) or exploitation of the rights of parents and other guardians to control and discipline children under their care. It occurs when a parent or guardian knowingly misuses a privileged position over the child to commit acts which are not in tune with the societal norms and which are detrimental to the child's health and well being".

According to Norgard, K.E. (1983), "child abuse or the purposeful maltreatment of children by physically, emotionally or sexually harming them often occurs within the family, and is the result of a variety of combinations of child related factors, parent related factors and situational factors".

The 1988 National Seminar on Child Abuse in India adopted the following definition of child abuse, "Child abuse and neglect is the intentional, non-accidental injury, maltreatment of children by parents, caretakers, employers or others including those individuals representing governmental or non-governmental bodies which may lead to temporary or permanent impairment of their physical, mental and psycho-social development, disability or death" (NIPCCD, 1988).

This explanation of child abuse highlights two significant aspects:

(a) Child abuse occurs both within and outside the family, i.e. at the familial and societal level. This also implies that very often it is difficult to differentiate between familial and societal abuse; and

(b) A common definition has been suggested for both child abuse and neglect and it includes all forms of child abuse and neglect. However, it would be difficult to specify and operationally describe these forms and manifestations.

Child abuse within the family is of significant importance and can take various forms. Generally speaking, in India, abuse of children by parents, guardians or caretakers can be considered as result of two related factors:

(a) the widespread acceptance and use of corporal punishment as a disciplinary technique in child rearing; and

(b) the belief that it is the right of the parents to discipline their children as they want (NIPCCD, 1988).

The family is the most important primary group to which an individual belongs and identifies with. The family should be the immediate protective and supportive environment of the child. However, many children belong to families which are in crisis due to poverty, family disintegration or other causes and such families are unable to meet the child's basic needs. Still others are in neglectful or abusive families that have become threats to, instead of protective of their children's welfare.

Children are also subject to abuse by other adults unrelated to them, outside the environment of the family. The following discussion focuses on the abuse and neglect which street children suffer at the hands of their parents, step parents, guardians or caregivers within the family environment. Attempts are also made to identify abuse of street children by adults in their immediate environment, that is, while they live unprotected on the streets.

4.2. CAUSES OR EXPLANATIONS OF CHILD ABUSE AND NEGLECT

Different models have been proposed by various investigators in order to identify and delineate causative factors of child abuse and neglect and also the influence of these on children's development. The development and expression of the phenomenon of child abuse and neglect can be related to various factors – social, cultural and psychological. Broadly speaking, three models can be identified to explain child abuse: cultural, sociological and psychopathological models (Freeman, M.D.A., 1979).

These models should not be considered as mutually exclusive or contradictory. They describe the phenomenon of child abuse and neglect from different perspectives and adopt diverse though usually overlapping approaches to the same problem. Taken together, these models provide a holistic understanding of the link between the functioning of an individual in his family and the society and the incidence of child abuse and neglect.

The first, the cultural model stresses that the cultural value of children has an impact on the incidence of child abuse and neglect. Mead, M.. (1949) described the effects of culturally different types of child rearing practices observed in two tribes in New Guinea. The Arapesh tribe is extremely kind to children, responding to all the needs of infants and young children. The care of children is shared among many extended family members. These early childhood experiences influence later development. Members of this tribe were found to feel quite secure and were peaceful when they grew up into adults.

An almost opposite kind of childrearing is adopted by people of Mundugumor tribe. In this culture, infants are brought up in ways which result in repeated frustration and anger. While growing up, children are encouraged to show anger and violence freely in their daily interactions with peers and adults. Children of this tribe were seen to grow up into adults who tend to be angry, violent and aggressive in their behaviour (Mead, M. 1949).

Sociologists have observed that the experience of growing up in the violent atmosphere of city slums can lead to aggressive and violent behaviour in children and adults. This provides evidence of the effects of early experience particularly abuse, aggression and violence on later behaviour (Freeman, M.D.A., 1979).

Sociological models also stress upon the link between environmental stress and incidence of child abuse. Sociological theories of child abuse stress upon the role of interaction between parents and child and interplay between the family and it's social context with regard to child abuse. Poverty and poor socio-economic conditions of living result in an increased stress on parents and this is seen to be associated with an increase in the incidence of neglect and abuse of children (Gil, D. 1971; Freeman, M.D.A. 1979).

Gil, D. (1971) has been one of the leading advocates of environmental stress as the causative factor of child abuse. According to him a major cause of child abuse is stress and frustration which are the result of 'multi-faceted deprivations of poverty' and it's correlates namely: over-crowded, dilapidated surroundings, large number of children in the family and lack of or poor education''. Statistics, mostly from Western literature, have revealed a significantly higher incidence of child abuse and neglect from lower income groups. This has led some sociologists to assume that the primary causes of abusive parental behaviour are poverty and poor education. Gil, D. (1975) does not suggest that "poverty per se should be treated as a main cause of child abuse. It seems to operate through the intervening variable of psychological stress and frustration experienced by individuals in the context of culturally sanctioned use of physical force in child rearing".

Abuse and neglect of children is likely to be precipitated when parents become overwhelmed by financial problems. Unemployment is a common cause of financial crisis in poor families. It also produces psychological stress and frustration within the family. The adult experiences a sense of failure and loss of self-esteem and confidence. Anger and frustration, in such situations, are directed toward spouse or children. Family stress as a result of father's joblessness or job loss has been found to be closely associated with child abuse (Helfer E.R. & Kempe, H. 1980).

Levine, S. and Levine, R. (1981) studied child abuse and neglect in sub-Saharan Africa and emphasized the preventive role of the constraints of traditional social system. They argue that, "it is when that social system starts to fall apart that we begin to come upon instances of abuse and neglect which the old system largely prohibited. As a result of increasing social disparity and disorganization, parents are more vulnerable than in the past to physical and emotional stress, and thus incidence of child abuse and neglect is on the rise". Similar arguments are put forth by Mumba, F. (1981) while discussing child abuse in Zambia and by Okeahialam, T. (1984) in relation to Nigeria. Okeahialam, T. (1984) stresses the role played by rural-urban migration and the stress associated with urban poverty. Ritchie, J.W. and Ritchie, J. (1981) in their discussion of child abuse in Polynesia suggest that 'large families, poor living conditions, marital instability, stress and alcoholism all creates the preconditions for child abuse'.

The psychopathological models for explaining child abuse see the problem as located within the deviant parent. According to this model, child abuse is solely due to a single causal variable i.e. a parent who has been abused as a child expresses this experience in child abuse. Evidence in psychopathological literature suggests that abusive parents were themselves abused during their childhood. However, this model is too narrow to explain the prevalence of child abuse. It also does not clearly specify the personality traits, which characterize the pathology of child abuse.

A common observation made by proponents of the sociological and psychopathological models is that abusive parent themselves was abused during their childhood. It is suggested that this can be attributed to the techniques of child rearing and socialization. A child who grows up in a family where parents use aggression and violence to deal with life's problems and to discipline the child is likely to use similar techniques when he grows up. Steele, B. & Pollock, C. (1986) found that neglect and abuse of children by parents has its roots in the very earliest period of their parent's life. They found that most often these parents were significantly deprived or neglected, with or without physical abuse, during their childhood. They suggest that 'this one finding is more nearly universal in the population of parents who maltreat their children than any other single variable such as socio-economic status, living conditions, race, religion, education, psychiatric state, cultural milieu, or family structure'.

Whatever theoretical framework is used to understand the causes of child abuse, there is ample evidence that neglect and abuse of street children manifests itself on three different levels. It is manifested in the home by parents and caregivers; in the especially difficult environment and circumstances in which they live; and in institutions particularly the residential, closed-door settings.

To facilitate a systematic and comprehensive understanding of child abuse, Obikeze, D.S. (1984) has proposed an analytical model (Refer to Chart 5). The model attempts to explain the problem of child maltreatment and abuse as it exists in non-industrialized

Chart 5
CHILD MALTREATMENT (WITH SPECIAL REFERENCE TO STREET CHILDREN)

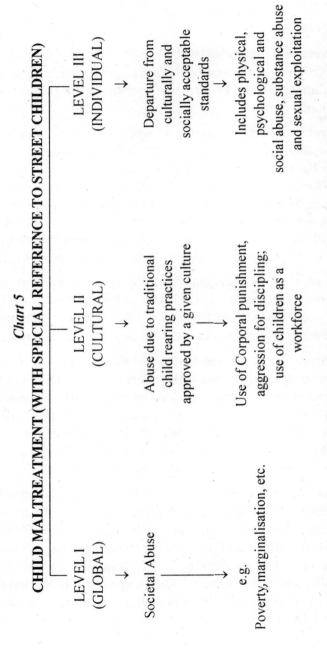

LEVEL I (GLOBAL)	LEVEL II (CULTURAL)	LEVEL III (INDIVIDUAL)
Societal Abuse	Abuse due to traditional child rearing practices approved by a given culture	Departure from culturally and socially acceptable standards
e.g. Poverty, marginalisation, etc.	Use of Corporal punishment, aggression for discipling; use of children as a workforce	Includes physical, psychological and social abuse, substance abuse and sexual exploitation

Based on : Obikeze, D.S. (1984) Perspectives on Child Abuse in Nigeria, International Child Welfare Review, 63.

countries. While analyzing this problem he suggests that it operates at three levels.

Level one, or the global level, where it is related to the socio-economic conditions in the world and where it's eradication is possible only by radical change of structural conditions in the world socioeconomic order.

Level two, or the cultural level where maltreatment refers to "child-rearing practices that may be viewed as acceptable by one group but as unacceptable or even abusive and neglectful by another" (Kempe, C.H. and Helfer, R. 1980). The child is a victim of harsh disciplinary or other customary practices approved by societal norms but, detrimental to the child's well being and development. To deal with maltreatment at this level, Obikeze suggests that efforts should be directed towards changing societal norms and child-rearing.

At level three, the individual level, maltreatment is "idiosyncratic departure from culturally and socially acceptable standards" (Kempe, C.H. and Helfer, R. (1980). Efforts to eradicate child maltreatment at this level must focus on parents or caregivers.

In order to describe and analyse the various dimensions of the phenomenon of abuse and maltreatment as is evident in the case of street children, the analytical model developed by Obikeze, D.S. (1984) can be explored further and used as the framework. Considering the characteristics of street children and the conditions in which they live, provide ample evidence that most of them suffer abuse and maltreatment at all the three levels described above.

Level one or the global level - This level deals with societal abuse of children which is engendered by economic conditions of the society such as underdevelopment, poverty, inequality, ignorance, etc. Child maltreatment and abuse caused by poor socio-economic conditions manifest themselves in the forms of starvation, malnutrition, and child mortality. Recent economic trends have lead to deterioration in the living conditions of the poor people and their children. Conditions of deprivation, poverty and underdevelopment have resulted in scarcity of vital resources. In poor countries basic resources essential for survival are minimal and children of these countries are thus at a greater risk.

The World Bank data attempts to estimate the incidence of poverty on a global scale and also give some indication of the scale of absolute poverty. It is estimated that around 1,299 million people are living below the most rigorously defined of poverty lines – essentially a starvation level of poverty. A significant finding has also emerged: "poverty is concentrated in the most economically weak countries. Most of the World's poor people are believed to live in Asia and especially in the countries of Southern Asia with Bangladesh, India, Indonesia and Pakistan together having the greatest number of poor population. These four countries contain almost two-thirds of the World's poorest people". (MacPherson, S.1987).

Changes in economic and social conditions have put communities and families under stress. Unemployment or underemployment along with urbanization have put tremendous pressures on poor families particularly those in rural areas. The neglect of rural areas, the marginalization of traditional occupations, advances in technology involved in agricultural practices and unemployment has all resulted in massive rural poverty. This, in turn, has led to large-scale migration of rural population to the cities in search of employment opportunities. Under such circumstances, children are neglected and often abused within the family.

It has been suggested that increased stress on parents in the context of poverty and poor environmental conditions is associated with an increase in neglect of children with regard to nutrition, health, clothing and education, etc. Along with the material conditions necessary for survival, the child's psychosocial needs like need for love, security and a stable, loving relationship with parents or caregivers are not frequently met. Due to these circumstances, many children abandon their families and some are left to fend for themselves. The incidence and consequence of exploitation and abuse are worst for street children living without families. Conditions of economic deprivation, exploitation, and neglect have profound effects on the physical and psychosocial development of these children.

At the second or cultural level, child maltreatment and abuse result due to traditional child-rearing practices which are acceptable and approved by a given culture but these practices adversely affect the child's development. Schmitt, D. (1980) describes punitive maltreatment or punishment as "disciplining children in painful ways or corporal punishment". In most countries, including India, child-rearing norms and values permit physical punishment as a method to enforce discipline. The intentional use of physical punishment of children has found legitimacy since centuries. It's basis lies in the belief that physical punishment is necessary for achieving discipline both at home and in school. Physical abuse manifests itself in various forms like: spanking, beating, caning, miaming, chaining and exposure to heat or cold.

The Report of the Joint Commission on Mental Health of Children (1970), U.S. Deptt. Of Health, Education and Welfare, discussed the child rearing patterns more prevalent among the very poor including harsh and inconsistent punishment, and a push for premature child independence (Kessler, J. 1988). There is evidence that abuse of street children within the family can be related to the relationships the child has with his parents. Street children have reported being brutally punished and harshly treated by their parents (Agnelli, S. 1986; Sondhi, P. 1994).

At level three or individual level of child maltreatment are included those behaviours and omissions of parents and other individuals which do not conform to their communities' child-rearing norms. Beliefs about particular groups of children perpetuate idiosyncratic abuse and neglect of these children by others in their environment (Korbin, 1981). Illegitimate children, orphaned children, children with impairments and street children can be categorized as groups of children who do not measure to normal expectations and so do not receive the same quality of care given to children in general.

Street children suffer various kinds of social discrimination and alienation because of the negative attitudes towards them. The social and psychological implications of such stigmatizing conditions need attention. The personal and social characteristics of street children are negatively valued by the society in general. Interactions of street children with individuals who care for them are relatively infrequent events. There is also considerable evidence suggesting that the stigmatized individual may experience outcome from his environment which have potentially negative implications for his subsequent development (Kleck, R. 1968). This lack of social acceptance is likely to interfere with street child's optimal social-emotional development. Being shelter less, street children are also prime candidates for sexual exploitation. The harmful effects to such kind of abuse are too obvious to need recounting; the most important of them being it's serious effect on the emotional health of these children.

In India, majority of the children living in difficult situations, particularly street children are victims of child exploitation and abuse at each of the three levels described above. These levels are not mutually exclusive and they tend to overlap. At a given point of time a child may suffer abuse and neglect at more than one of these levels. This can be illustrated by taking the case of a typical street child. At a given point of time, a street child may be found to suffer economic destitution and deprivation (i.e. Level one) and also face physical abuse in his family which includes corporal punishment which mostly occurs due to culturally approved child rearing norms (Level two). Being a street child, he also suffers social ostracism and alienation because of the pejorative attitudes of the society towards him (Level three) and he is denied his right to health, education, and a better future (level one).

Obikeze's (1984) model allows for a comprehensive understanding of child maltreatment and abuse and can be applied to the situation of working and street children. Exploitation of children for economic gains is also a very common form of child abuse. This kind of maltreatment can be ranked as one of the highest among the various forms of child maltreatment in India where according to the Asian Labour Monitor (1991) every third household in India has a working child (Indian Express, April 23, 1991). There is thus a growing urgent need for the recognition of child labour as a major form of child abuse and neglect.

For majority of street children, street existence is not easy. "Very young street children are often pitied and are successful at begging for alms. But as they approach puberty, they come to be perceived as thugs and were treated accordingly" (Aptekar, L. 1988). For the very reason that a street child is without any familial support and protection, he is also more vulnerable to exploitation during work as compared to other working children who work in a family setting, be it agriculture, commerce or handicrafts.

Street children often work in noisy, unhealthy premises, in unhygienic and overcrowded surroundings, without special resting areas, without medical facilities, adequate means of security. Many of them are also engaged in occupations listed as hazardous by the law for e.g. children working in glass factories in Firozabad or in match factories in Sivakasi. Children who lift heavy loads either on railway stations or in market places are also working in violation of the principles laid down in the International Labour Organization (ILO) standards and also the Child Labour (Prohibition & Regulation) Act, 1986.

There exists practically no facility for recreation and play within the reach of a working street child. Spare time is usually given over to resting, gambling, going to cinema or just loitering around. The duration of working hours vary considerably for street children according to the availability of work and the child's need to work. A street child who is self-employed can vary his working hours according to his own needs and capabilities.

During work the child is also faced with the risk of occupational accident/diseases, and this risk is heightened in case of children (Mendelievich, E. 1979). At work, the street child faces potential accident situations and often works in dirty conditions, with increased dangers of infection. Street children are also exposed to the vagaries of weather, to traffic hazards and violence of urban areas.

Apart from occupational problems, the street child experiences difficulties when he has to compete with more experienced adults in his work environment. The child has to adapt himself to this new and complex situation. Lack of adequate education and vocational training reduce his chances of improving his conditions. The normal, developmental needs and interests of childhood and early adolescence are not fulfilled in the case of working street children. This is sure to have a limiting and disturbing effect on the psychological development of the child.

In addition to this, the fact that street child is in a disadvantaged position in the society can have deleterious consequences for his social and emotional development. The stigmatizing conditions in his environment and the lack of social acceptance have negative implications for his subsequent development. "There are clear reasons to expect that those persons who are characterized as stigmatized may elicit from their non-stigmatized socials environment patterns of behavior and reaction which are very likely to interfere with their psycho-social and emotional development" (Goffman, 1963). It is suggested that studies are necessary to ascertain the relationship between the stigma conditions and its social and psychological implications for the street child.

PART V

INITIATIVES AT THE NATIONAL LEVEL

5.1. GOVERNMENT'S RESPONSE TO THE PROBLEM OF STREET CHILDREN

Concern about, and support for, the rights of the child has been growing steadily both at national and international level. Many millions of children are no longer able to count on their families for all the support and protection they need. 'To support families, or to compensate for their failings, there is a need for a broader social and legislative consensus on what is and what is not acceptable in the treatment of the young'. (UNICEF, 1987). Street Children have received much attention in the media, both national and international, in the recent years. The awareness and sensitization efforts have led to several initiatives involving numerous groups working with street children, launching of specific schemes and programs at the local, state and national level and initiation of numerous studies on street children.

In India, the post-independence era has experienced an unequivocal expression of the commitment of the government to the cause of children through constitutional provisions, policies, programmes and legislation.. The Constitution of India in Article 39 of the Directive Principles of State Policy pledges that "the State shall, in particular, direct its policy towards securing .... that the health and strength of workers, men and women, and the tender age of children are not abused, and that citizens are not forced by economic necessity to enter vocations unsuited to their age or strength, that children are given opportunities and facilities to develop in a healthy manner, and in conditions of freedom and dignity, and that childhood and youth are protected against exploitation, and against moral and material abandonment."

India adopted the National Policy on Children in 1974. The policy reaffirmed the constitutional provisions and stated that "it shall be the policy of the State to provide adequate services to children, both before and after birth and through the period of growth to ensure their full physical, mental and social development. The State shall progressively increase the scope of such services so that within a reasonable time all children in the country enjoy optimum conditions for their balanced growth.." Children's programmes have occupied a prominent place in the national plans for human resource development. Successive Five Year Plans have aimed to deal with these issues.

India is also a signatory to the World Declaration on the Survival, Protection and Development of Children. Most of the recommendations of the World Summit Action Plan are reflected in India's National Plan of Action. The National Plan of Action has been formulated keeping in mind the needs, rights and aspirations of 300 million children in the country and sets out quantifiable time limits for India's Charter of Action for Children by 2000 AD. The priority areas in the Plan are health, nutrition, education, water, sanitation and environment. The Plan gives special consideration to children in difficult circumstances and aims at providing a framework, for actualisation of the objectives of the Convention in the Indian context. The National Plan of Action also lists out activities to achieve these goals. To make the aims and activities of the plan more need-based and area-specific, the Central Government has urged the State governments to prepare a Plan of Action for Children for their States, taking into account the regional disparities that may exist.

The world's largest child labor elimination program is being implemented at the grass roots level in India, with primary education targeted for nearly 250 million. The International Program on Elimination of Child Labor (IPEC) has the world's largest international initiative on child labor in India. With the setting up of the National Authority for the Elimination of Child Labor (NAECL) under the Chairmanship of the Labor Minister, Government of India, a convergence of services and schemes for eliminating child labor is being achieved. The NAECL, comprising representatives from the Central Ministries, meets the need for an umbrella organization to coordinate the efforts of the different arms of the Government for the progressive elimination of child labor. So far 76 child labor projects have been sanctioned under the National Child Labor Project.

Though the problem of homeless street children is not new to India, the Government has been slow to respond to the problem. Till very recently, street children as a separate category of children in need of care and protection were not included in any of the welfare or development programs. However, there have been efforts to provide statutory framework for the welfare of destitute and neglected children. This has found expression in the form of services provided to children in difficult circumstances and the laws passed by the government for the welfare of children. The Constitution of India, the National Policy for Children, many other policies and legislation accord priority to children's needs. The Government of India ratified the Convention on the Rights of the Child on 2nd December, 1992. Accordingly, the government is taking action to review the national and state legislation and bring it in line with the provisions of the Convention.

Different laws and schemes have been formulated and various institutions have been set up to provide services for care and rehabilitation of working children, destitute, neglected and delinquent children. For the purpose of analyzing these services, they have been classified in two broad categories: institutional and non-institutional. Existing governmental services in India are predominantly institutional in nature.

Institutional care is perhaps the oldest form of childcare service. It usually refers to closed-door, residential facility for a group of children. These institutions may be statutory i.e. under the laws enacted for the welfare of children e.g. Observation or Remand Homes set up under the provisions of Juvenile Justice Act (2000) or non-statutory being run by voluntary agencies (Rane, A; Naidu & Kapadia, 1986). The statutory institutions set up under the purview of Juvenile Justice Act are of various kinds (Refer to Chart 7).

Following are the Authorities and Institutions set up for Juveniles at the statutory level:

1. Juvenile Welfare Boards- For exercising the powers and discharging the duties conferred or imposed on such Board in relation to neglected juveniles under the Juvenile Justice Act.

2. Juvenile Courts-For exercising the powers and discharging the duties conferred or imposed on such court in relation to delinquent juveniles.

3. Juvenile homes-For the reception of neglected juveniles

4. Special homes-For the reception of delinquent juveniles.

5. Observation homes-For the temporary reception of juveniles during the pendency of any inquiry regarding them.

6. After-care organisations-The State Government may, by rules made under this Act, provide-

(a) for the establishment or recognition of after-care organisations and the powers that may be exercised by them for effectively carrying out their functions under this Act;

(b) for a scheme of after-care programme to be followed by such after-care organisations for the purpose of taking care of juveniles after they leave juvenile homes or special homes and for the purpose of enabling them to lead an honest, industrious and useful life (Juvenile Justice Act, 2000).

Chart 7
Services for Children in Difficult Circumstances in India

Neglected Juveniles & Juvenile Delinquent:

SERVICES

Institutional Services

Statutory	Non-Statutory	Non-Institutional Service
1. Remand Homes/ Observation Homes	1. Orphanages run by	1. Foster care
2. Certified Schools, Approved Schools, Special Schools.	a) State or UT Govt.	2. Sponsorship
3. Classifying centres,	b) under Grant-in-aid of Central Social Welfare Board)	3. Adoption
4. Children's Homes	c) under Grant-in-aid financial	4. Programs of State Govt., assistance to voluntary organizations.
5. Industrial Schools,	d) Privately run orphanages (unaided)	5. Day care services.
6. Reformatory Schools,	2. Children's Homes under the Centrally Sponsored Scheme.	6. Programs for working children.
7. Borstal Schools	3. SOS Children's villages	
8. After-care Homes	4. After-care Homes	

Source: Rane, A.,; Naidu, U. & Kapadia (1986) Children in Difficult Situations in India, Bombay, Tata Institute of Social Sciences.

To protect and promote the interests of children, Juvenile Justice emerged as a special form of legal justice (Singh, S. & Chauhan, B., 1970). Earlier laws were formulated and implemented without giving due attention to the special needs and problems faced by children who were maladjusted in the society. The concept of juvenile justice has led to the development of new legislation and more appropriate procedures for dealing with juveniles.

The Juvenile Justice System is based on two concepts: the legal principle of 'parents patriae' and the clinical approach. The Latin maxim of 'Parents patriae' refers to the state as a parent. It is assumed that juvenile justice system is a substitute for parents or family and it would always work in the best interests of delinquents. It is believed that it's both the state's right and duty to take care of those who are in need of protection. As a result, the laws framed for juveniles attempt to benefit not only juvenile delinquents but others who are categorized as pre-delinquents' or 'non-delinquents'.

The concept of clinical approach assumes that delinquent children possess characteristics of physical or mental sub normality or have deviant personality characteristics. The focus is on 'correction' through diagnostic and therapeutic methods and institutionalization is believed to be the only alternative and to be used as a guiding principle. The clinical approach is highly controversial and it's underlying assumptions are no longer held valid.

5.2. LEGISLATION ON NEGLECTED AND DELINQUENT JUVENILES

There is absolutely no legislature that specifies the term "Street Children" in the judiciary of India. One of the earliest legislative efforts to provide a statutory framework for the welfare of children was the Apprentices Act of 1850. It provided children, especially orphans and destitute, who were convicted by the court, with vocational training for their rehabilitation.

The first law dealing with delinquency was the Reformatory School Act, 1897, which provided that a child below 15 years of age, found guilty of any offence might, at the discretion of the court, be ordered to be detained in a reformatory school for a period of three to seven years. In India, it was the Jail Committee Report (1919) that recommended the need for separate trail and treatment of juvenile offenders. As a result of the recommendations of this Committee, number of States passed the Children's Act which provided protection, care, custody, trial, maintenance, training and rehabilitation not only for juvenile delinquents but also for neglected and destitute (Batra, M. 1990).

In 1920, the first Children's Act was passed in Madras and this was followed by the Bengal Children's Act of 1922 and the Bombay Children's Act of 1924. A few other States also passed similar acts. In 1960, the Parliament passed Central Children's Act which was intended to be model legislation for all states. During this time the Children's Acts which were passed in different states were not uniform and they had wide discrepancies, for e.g. the age limit of child in order to be called a juvenile varied from one state to another (Batra, M. 1990).

It was in 1986 when the Parliament passed the Juvenile Justice Act which became effective from 2nd Oct., 1987. This act is uniformly applicable throughout India and has replaced the Children's Act of 1960 and other related state enactments. The Act aims to provide for the care, protection, treatment, development and rehabilitation of neglected and delinquent juveniles and 'for the adjudication of certain matter relating to, and disposition of delinquent children' (Singh, H. 1990).

The constitution has in it's several provisions, including clause (3) of Article 15, clauses (e) & (f) of Articles 39, 45 & 47 imposed on the State a primary responsibility of ensuring that all the needs of children are met and that their basic human rights are fulfilled. The Convention on the Rights of the Child emphasizes social reintegration of child victims, to the extent possible, without resorting to judicial proceedings. The Government of India has ratified the Convention on 11 December, 1992 and it has become expedient to re-enact the existing laws relating to juveniles.

Keeping in view the above objective, the parliament enacted The Juvenile Justice (Care & Protection of Children) Act, 2000 on 30 December 2000. It aims to consolidate and amend the laws relating to juveniles in conflict with and children in need of care & protection, by providing for proper care, protection and treatment, by catering to their developmental needs and by adopting a child-friendly approach in the adjudication & disposition of matters in the best interest of children and for their rehabilitation through various institutions established under this enactment. The provisions of the Act came in force on 1 April, 2001(Gazette of India, Extraordinary, Part II, Sec.3 No. 88, 1March, 2001)

The Juvenile Justice Act (JJ Act) provides two different machineries for dealing with neglected and juvenile delinquents. The Juvenile Justice Board is constituted to deal with juveniles in conflict with law under this Act while Child Welfare Committees are formed for helping children in need of care & protection .The Act also lays down the procedures to be followed by the police, the Juvenile Justice Board and Child Welfare Committees while dealing with these children. The Act envisages a comprehensive approach towards justice for children in situations of abuse, exploitation and social maladjustment. The Act empowers any state government to establish observation homes & special homes for the temporary reception and rehabilitation of juveniles in conflict with law. Children's Homes are established for the reception of children in need of care & protection including homeless, destitute, abandoned or abused children. These institutions aim at the child's education, development, and rehabilitation. Children's Shelter Homes are also set up which function as drop-in centers for children in need of urgent support.

The salient features of the Act are:

a) To provide uniform legal framework for juvenile justice in India and to ensure that no child under any circumstances is lodged in a police station or detained in a jail pending inquiry against him;

b) To establish norms and standards for the administration of juvenile justice during processing of cases of the juveniles by the Juvenile Justice Board ;

c) To provide for the establishment of long-term and short-term institutions for care, protection, development and rehabilitation of neglected and delinquent juveniles. The Act contemplates the constitution of three types of institutions: the Juvenile Homes for the neglected and runaway juveniles; Special Homes for delinquent juveniles and Observation Homes for under-trial juvenile delinquents (Singh, S & Chauhan, B. 1990).

The Juvenile Justice Act prohibits the detention of juveniles in police station or jails for periods longer than twenty-four hours. In situations where juveniles are detained, a complete and secure record of the relevant information on the personal situation and circumstances of each juvenile should be drawn up and submitted to the administration. The Act states that as soon as possible after the moment of admission, each juvenile should be interviewed, and a psychological and social report identifying any factors relevant to the specific type and level of care and programme required by the juvenile should be prepared.

The Act empowers a police officer, or any individual or organization authorized by the State Government to bring a neglected child before the Juvenile Justice Board. Attempts are then made to ascertain the whereabouts of child's parents or guardians and to persuade them to take the child home. It is stated that juveniles be sent back to their parents or guardians or to a remand home immediately following either their identification as a "neglected juvenile" or their arrest as a "delinquent juvenile." Thus the Act makes the police responsible for identifying neglected juveniles and apprehending delinquent juveniles. Only on being satisfied that the child is a neglect child, is the Board empowered to send him to a juvenile home for that period till he is a child (Batra, M. 1990).

The police actively abuse their authority, resulting in a pattern of arbitrary arrest, detention, extortion, and beatings of street children, and a practice known as the "round-up," in which children are detained in large groups and either sent to remand homes or disciplined in the police station. There are several reasons for the round-up. The Act views children working in railway stations as "delinquent juveniles;" such children are frequently victims of the round-up. Because police generally view street children as criminals, a round-up is an easy way to catch and interrogate them.

A distinct feature of the Juvenile Justice Act ,2000 is the setting up of special juvenile police units. In order to enable the police officers who frequently or exclusively deal with juveniles or are primarily engaged in the prevention of juvenile crime or handling of the juveniles under this Act , they shall be specially instructed and trained to perform their functions in a more child-friendly manner. In every police unit at least one officer with aptitude, appropriate training and orientation can be designated as the ' juvenile or child welfare officer' who will handle the juvenile while coordinating with the police. The Act thereby contemplates the constitution of special juvenile police unit to coordinate and upgrade the treatment of the juvenile by the police.

The police normally have the first contact with the street child. The street child is either apprehended by the police as an offender or a victim found to be in need of care. Once apprehended, the police have to investigate. As soon as a juvenile is apprehended or arrested, the officer-in-charge of the police station or of the special juvenile unit to which the juvenile is brought , shall intimate the parent or guardian of the juvenile regarding his detention and direct him to be present at the Board before which the juvenile will appear. The officer shall also intimate the probation officer regarding the child to enable him to obtain information regarding the antecedents and family background of the juvenile.

Any child in need of care and protection can also be produced before the Child Welfare Committee and sent to Children's Home pending inquiry. After the completion of the inquiry if the Committee is of the opinion that the said child has no family or ostensible support , it may allow the child to remain in the Chilren's Home or Shelter Home till suitable rehabilitation is found for him or till he attains the age of 18 years. Restoration of and protection of a child deprived of a family environment shall be the prime objective of any Children's Home or Shelter Home. However, the implementation of Juvenile Justice Act, 2000 and setting up of special juvenile police units needs to be reviewed.

According to NGOs, lawyers, and human rights activists working with street children, juvenile crime has been increasing, largely due to an increasing population of children and worsening economic conditions. The Swedish Childrens' aid agency, Rädda Barnen, a member of a coalition of agencies affiliated with Save the Children, wrote in October 1995 that:

Limited data reveals that, in 1991, 29,591 juveniles were apprehended for various crimes in India. Most of them were charged with theft, burglary and riot. Of those, 20% were children aged between 7 and 12 and 64% were between 12 and 16. Over 60% were from families earning less than Rs.500 a month Very little information is available on what happens to these children. Legal representation is rare and there are few facilities existing for the detention of children separately from adults. Little is known about the effectiveness of any rehabilitation centre that may exist. Again, in India, juvenile crime rates are exploding (Flynn, T. 1995).

The number of children falling under the 'neglected juveniles' category has been increasing consistently in Delhi. A large majority from them come from places outside Delhi. Street children who have run away from their homes or are abandoned by their families and live on the streets without a settled place of abode come under the category of neglected juveniles. They may also be apprehended as delinquent juveniles if they are found to have committed an offence. Street children are, in many cases, sent to remand in adult jails where they are abused, both physically and sexually, for indefinite periods of time. There is little or no provision made for these young children to contact their parents or obtain proper guidance or legal representation. There are reports of children eventually escaping from these "Homes" just as they run away from their real home.

On being caught by the police, the children may be sent before a juvenile board, or a juvenile court, headed by a magistrate with jurisdiction over juveniles who have been arrested on a criminal charge. Both the court and the juvenile board have the authority to send children to institutions known variously as observation, remand, special, or juvenile homes. Thus, regardless of their status as juvenile offenders, abandoned or orphaned children, or children awaiting trial, all children are remanded to the same institutions. The homes are poorly maintained, inadequately staffed, and are not rehabilitative. In addition to the appalling conditions, NGO representatives, lawyers, and children themselves consistently allege physical abuse and sexual exploitation.

The Juvenile Justice Board, despite its authority, has done little to improve the deplorable conditions of the homes. The Juvenile Justice Act strongly advocates that children should not be kept in lock-ups as juvenile justice is distinguished from criminal justice. Most children arrested are non-offenders but the two categories-neglected children and juvenile delinquents are wrongly clubbed together (Reeta D. Gupta, 1996). The uninformed and arbitrary nature of detention in observation homes has been documented in several studies on street children.

The joint reports of studies done on street children by the government of India's Ministry of Labour and UNICEF list some of the reasons children had been sent to remand homes. In Bangalore, majority (81.5 percent) of children were sent to remand homes on charges of theft, the second largest group (11.3 percent) were sent to the institution on "doubt" that the police had regarding these children. This means that 11.3 percent of children were sent to remand homes without having been informed of the reasons and without any explanations what so ever (Reddy, N. 1992). The Bombay study reported that the majority of children (74.6 percent) were sent to remand homes on charges of vagrancy or suspicion. In other words, they were arrested because the police considered them vagrants or suspected they might commit crimes or may have committed a crime. But these children were never formally charged with any offense.

5.3. THE ROLE OF POLICE

There is no denying the fact that the police has an important role in the prevention and control of delinquency especially juvenile delinquency. The police being the first agency in whose contact a neglected juvenile comes, it must understand its role while dealing with these children. The JJ Act requires the police to ascertain before taking charge whether the neglected juvenile has a parent or caregiver. More importantly, the police must also ensure that the child does not suffer any kind of physical or mental trauma.

Human Rights Watch has reported that in countries like India, Bulgaria, Guatemala, and Kenya police violence against street children is pervasive. Human Rights Watch Children's Rights Project (2000) conducted a research on the abuse of street children by the police in selected Indian cities. This report documents police abuse of Indian street children and deaths of children in police custody. It is based on investigations conducted in India during February and March 1995 and December and January 1995-96. The failure of law enforcement bodies to promptly and effectively investigate and prosecute cases of maltreatment and abuse of street children allows the violence to continue. The threat of police reprisals against them serves as a serious deterrent to any child coming forward to testify or make a complaint against any officer (HRW, World Report, 2000).

Indian street children are routinely detained illegally, beaten and tortured by the police. Torture, usually in the form of severe beatings with fists, lathis, or other instruments, and kicking is a common feature of police treatment of street children (Human Rights

Watch, 1995). Beatings themselves are used extensively as a means of investigation, punishment, and reprisal.

Several factors give rise to this phenomenon: police perceptions of street children, widespread corruption and a culture of police violence, the inadequacy and non-implementation of legal safeguards, and the level of impunity that law enforcement officials enjoy. The police generally view street children as vagrants and criminals. While it is true that street children are sometimes involved in petty theft, drug-trafficking, prostitution and other criminal activities, the police tend to assume that whenever a crime is committed on the street, street children are either involved themselves or know the culprit. Their proximity to a crime is considered reason enough to detain them. This perception and consequent abuse violates both Indian domestic law and international human rights standards.

Street children are also easy targets. They are young, small, poor and ignorant of their rights and often have no family members or any other adult who will come to their defense. Thus, they are often detained for short durations and beaten to extract a confession, and the children are unlikely to register formal complaints.

Reports of exploitation and extortion by the police have been frequently reported. Policemen on the beat often take away the child's earnings on the grounds that the money was obtained through unlawful ways or it is also taken away as a form of 'protection money' to let the child work and sleep in a particular area on the street (Human Rights Watch, 1996). With street children, extortion by police is an integral part of the processes that perpetuate illegal detention and custodial violence Police have financial incentives to resort to violence against children. Children are either beaten on the street or brought to the police station and beaten; they are told that they must pay the police otherwise they will face beatings.

Children are also required to pay 'Hafta' (a form of extortion money) when they are involved in illegal activities. Children working on the street as ragpickers, porters, shop vendors, or shoe shiners have all reported the payment of *hafta* (protection or kickback money) to the police. Failure or inability to pay usually results in a child being beaten, detained, or arrested by police. In some cases, payment does not necessarily guarantee no further extortion by the police. Children who sell "black" movie tickets told Human Rights Watch that they had to pay about 25 to 50 percent of their earnings to the police, otherwise they would be beaten, arrested or both. At railway stations, children pay 'hafta' in order to get around the minimum age requirements for obtaining a porter's license and to avoid being arrested under laws which make it a criminal offense for a child to work in railway stations.

Many children report that they were beaten on the street because the police wanted their money. The prospect of being sent to a remand home, the police station or jail, coupled with the threat of brutal treatment, creates a level of fear and intimidation that forces children or in some cases, their families, to pay the police or suffer the consequences. Establishing police accountability is further hindered by the fact that street children often have no alternative but to complain directly to police about abuses they have suffered at the hands of other policemen . The threat of police reprisals against them serves as a serious deterrent to any child coming forward to testify or make a complaint against any law enforcing official.

Hundreds of street and working children held a march on 30th April, 1993 in New Delhi and they protested against the harsh treatment meted out to them by the police. They staged a skit which depicted policemen using lathis mercilessly on children (The Hindustan Times, May 1, 1993). The police needs to be oriented on issues of street children and the especially difficult situations in which they survive in order to sensitize them about street children's problems and how to deal with them.

A long-term approach to curb police abuses against street children began in 1994 when Indian government's Ministry of Home and Welfare, UNICEF and a Bangalore-based NGO working with street children initiated a "Police Training Curriculum." The curriculum is designed to sensitize police to the special problems that street children face and educate police about the provisions and implementation of the Juvenile Justice Act. UNICEF eventually expects this curriculum to be implemented at the national level, but the program for implementation has not yet been finalized. A more positive, preventive and empathetic role of the police needs to be stressed.

5.4. LIMITATIONS OF THE JUVENILE JUSTICE ACT

1. Inadequate infrastructure: It is essential to establish institutions for effective implementation of the Act. The Juvenile Justice System has proved to be ineffective in coping with the problem under its present structure. For example, In Mumbai, in 1989, 3,301 cases were brought before Juvenile Court whereas the number of street children is around 50,000. There are many States in India where there exists no Juvenile Board or Juvenile Court system. The number of juvenile homes in Delhi and the capacity of these homes is insufficient keeping in mind the number of street children in Delhi. Also many states of the country have not even set up separate institutions for neglected children and juvenile delinquents.

2. Whatever machinery and infrastructure exists which is set up for rehabilitating children coming within the purview of JJ Act, are characterized by an abysmal lack of or inadequate facilities. Under ideal situations, personnel in these institutions should be qualified and include a sufficient number of specialists such as educators, vocational instructors, counselors, social workers, psychiatrists and psychologists. These and other specialist staff should normally be employed on a permanent basis. However, very few of these institutions have services of these personnel. Thus, the relevance and efficacy of services provided through these institutions is a matter of concern. The functioning of these institutions has much scope for improvement and programs need to be more innovative and child centered.

The JJ Act provides country-wide uniform legislation incorporating provisions for rehabilitation of neglected and delinquent juveniles.. The laws applicable under the Juvenile Justice Act relate quite strongly to the care of and rights of street children in general, without explicitly mentioning them in any term. However, these norms and standards established for the administration of juvenile justice in terms of investigation, adjudication, disposition and care, treatment and rehabilitation of these children are not implemented efficiently. In effect, police officers who frequently deal with juveniles are not cognizant of the details of the Act.

Though the amended JJ Act clearly outlines the need for appropriate training and orientation of police officers towards the problems of juveniles, such training or sensitization facilities are absent or highly inadequate. It has been noted that there is very little awareness about the provisions of the JJ Act among the lawyers and courts as well. Most often juveniles are treated like hardened criminals. Soli Sorabjee, The Attorney General in 2000 admitted that there are many deficiencies in the amended Juvenile Justice Act, 2000 (The Times of India , 17 May, 2000).

There is an urgent need for making the law more effective by providing suitable training to the concerned agencies which are associated with implementation of the Act, establishing coordination among these agencies and developing necessary infrastructure for achieving the legislatively prescribed objectives of rehabilitation of neglected children.

For survival, most of the neglected, homeless children work. They are engaged in different kinds of occupations mainly in the unorganized sector. By virtue of the fact that they are working, i.e. engaged in economically gainful activity, they are also included in the category of working children or child labour.

UNICEF (1988) has delineated certain well-defined indices of exploitation of working children. These apply to street children also and include:

a) Work and life of the streets in unhealthy and dangerous situations;

b) Starting full time work at too early an age;

c) Children not being able to attend school;

d) Work in dangerous situations which causes damage to the health and safety of the child; and

e) Work that does not facilitate the social and psychological development of the child (cited in The Lawyers, 1988).

In India, a wide gamut of legislation has been enacted prohibiting child labour. Article 24 of our Constitution states that, "No child shall be employed to work in any factory or mine or engaged in any hazardous employment". Yet a large number of children are working in various hazardous occupations like glass factories in Firozabad, match factories in Sivakasi, slate quarries of Mandsaur, M.P. and lock industry in Aligarh.

Article 39 (e) and (f) and Article 45 of the Directive principles of State Policy enunciate:

39 (e) : "The tender age of children should not be abused and citizens should not be forced by economic necessity to enter occupations unsuited to their age and strength".

39 (f) : "Children should be given opportunities and facilities to develop in a healthy manner and in conditions of freedom and dignity and they childhood and youth are protected against exploitation and against moral and material abandonment".

Art. 45 : "The State shall endeavour to provide within a period of ten years from the commencement of this Constitution, for free and compulsory education for all children until they complete the age of 14 years".

In 1986, the Child Labor (Prohibition & Regulation) Act was enacted which prohibits employment of children in some occupations and aims to regulate conditions of work in some other occupations. But despite a host of constitutional provisions and a plethora of legislation prohibiting child labour, a great number of children work in various industrial and non-industrial occupations. Street children are found engaged in certain occupations which have been listed as hazardous for children, for e.g. according to the Child Labour (Prohibition & Regulation) Act, 1986 and its schedule, Part A, 'no child under 14 years shall be employed or permitted to work in any occupation connected with transport of passengers, goods or mails by railway, but street children have been found to work as porters at railway stations carrying heavy loads (Sondhi, P. 1994).

At work, street children are comparatively more disadvantaged since they not only suffer the ill-effects of work which are also common to other working children but they are also victims of separation from the family. This makes these working street children different from other working children. They are therefore highly vulnerable to abuse and exploitation and are highly 'at risk'. The problems faced by them are more acute and complex and these children are more susceptible to neglect and exploitation.

The problem of working, homeless street children is therefore very complex. A working street child should not be viewed either only as a worker or as a street child. He needs to be considered as a child in difficult situation and one who is both working and living in especially complex conditions. Therefore, the approach adopted in our social policy, welfare measures and legislative efforts, which are designed to facilitate interventions for street children, should be multi-dimensional and comprehensive.

5.5. GOVERNMENT POLICIES AND PROGRAMS FOR STREET CHILDREN

Sensitivity to the subject of street children is very limited among the various departments of the government concerned with welfare of children. Till very recently, street children did not enjoy any explicit attention of the development programs. Since 1980s, a number of seminars and workshops have been organized by the government in collaboration with various other agencies and organizations focusing exclusively on destitute children and more specifically on street children.

A national workshop was held in Delhi in August, 1988 to provide a common forum of exchange of views for NGOs from all over India. Representatives from international organizations and central and state governments attended the workshop so that the awareness created could provide a basis for planning and policy-making at the government level. It was at the end of this workshop that a joint undertaking of the UNICEF and the Social Welfare Ministry, The National Institute of Social Defense emerged to carry out a situational analysis of street children in six major cities in India, with co-operation from voluntary organizations. It was realized that any planning at the national level would necessitate a sound database on the extent of the problem and a better understanding of its causes (Indian Express, August 30, 1988).

In June, 1990 a three-day workshop on 'Children in especially difficult circumstances' was organized by the Delhi Administration's Directorate of Social Welfare and UNICEF to focus on the plight of street children in Delhi. It primarily aimed at evolving strategies to ameliorate the conditions of these children. The workshop also focused on the review of services available to these children (The Hindustan Times, June, 6, 1990).

In order to provide financial assistance of non-statutory voluntary institutions working for destitute neglected and homeless children, the Ministry of Welfare, Govt. of India, started a centrally sponsored scheme in 1975 for the welfare of children in need of care and protection.

A group of 25 children is entrusted to the care of one housemother, who is assisted by another worker. Together they constitute a unit which is housed in a separate cottage. Overall supervision is provided by the Welfare agency which agrees to set up either one cottage or more according to the guidelines of the scheme and in consonance with its philosophy. The Govt. of India provides grants to cover 90% of the expenditure according to a specified schematic pattern and expect the agency to contribute the remaining 10% of the expenditure (Rane, A. & Shroff, N. 1992).

During 1974-75, the Govt. gave grants to 136 Welfare agencies for 173 homes which accommodated 9,281 children all over the country (Deptt. of Social Welfare, 1976). According to data supplied by the Department of Social Welfare, 490 agencies looked after a total of 32,311 children at the end of 1978-79.

In terms of concern for street children, recently there have been two significant developments: first, an awareness of the problems of children in difficult circumstances as a national issue has grown.

Second, the Ministry of Welfare, Govt. of India, has launched a 'Street Children & Juvenile Justice Workplan - 2000' exclusively for the benefit of street children. This Workplan - 2000 has been prepared for implementation of various priority projects of the Ministry with the assistance of UNICEF. The objective is to develop coordinated city level actions to address the rights of street children, including those who come in conflict with the law.

Before introducing this plan, the Ministry of Welfare along with UNICEF in 1988 initiated studies on street children in Mumbai, Kolkata, Delhi, Madras, Hyderabad, Bangalore and Indore. This was a part of the national survey covering selected cities across the country with the objective of creating a sound database on street children which is a prerequisite for formulating and launching of any action plan for the welfare of street children (The Indian Express, March 26, 1992).

The scheme has been included in the eighth Five year plan of the Government of India and aims of protection of street children against abuse and exploitation. The scheme would also cover children who live in slums but spend most of their time on the streets or working in street traders. It provides for integrated, community-based, non-institutional basic services for the care, protection and development of children living on the streets or pavements with or without their families. The scheme expresses concern over the growing magnitude of the problem, the hazardous working and living conditions and exploitation of the children coupled with inaccessibility of basic services to the children.

The work plan has four sub-projects with the objectives:-

* to strengthen family integration for preventing children from working on the streets;

* to demonstrate and replicate workable approaches and actions to protect street children;

* to strengthen development of database and formulation of policy for children affected by armed conflict;

* to promote public awareness of the Juvenile Justice Act.

In order to achieve the above objectives, the activities which are likely to feature prominent in this scheme are in the following categories:

(a) Interventions through NGOs to facilitate access to food, basic education, shelter, health services and other opportunities for working and street children;

(b) Identification of "at-risk" families to prevent destitution of children and this will be achieved through linkages with other programs;

(c) Strengthening children's ties with their families and facilitating their reinstatement in their families;

(d) Suitable arrangements for non-formal education for children who cannot be mainstreamed in the formal education system; and

(e) Undertaking research and dissemination of information about the nature and magnitude of the problems of the street children and the rights of children (The Hindustan Times, April 24, 1993).

In all these spheres of activities, attempts will be made to establish networking and complementarity among government agencies, NGOs and between the government and NGOs. The scheme, to be operated by 40 non-governmental organizations through a network of about 240 centres, will cover initially 24,000 beneficiaries in eleven cities. These cities are Greater Bombay, Calcutta, Delhi. Madras, Hyderabad, Bangalore, Ahmedabad, Pune, Kanpur, Nagpur and Lucknow. The scheme is being co-sponsored by UNICEF which would support and strengthen voluntary organizations already working for the welfare of street children. The scheme has been allocated a sum of Rs. 8 crore. 90% of the cost of the scheme will be borne by the Central Govt. and UNICEF and the remaining 10% by the NGO (The Hindustan Times, May 7, 1993).

Each NGO will implement one project for 300 children. For effective delivery of services, street children have been divided into three categories: those who live on the streets or pavements with or without families; those who live in slums but spend most of their time on the streets engaged in various activities and those who work in street trades like shoe-shining, car washing, rag picking, etc. Of them, priority would be given to those who are destitute. For younger children, priority intervention would be to reinstate them in their families and facilitate their participation in formal primary education. For older children, efforts would be to focus on their education and vocational training.

This programme has spread to 39 cities of the country and has covered around 1,40,000 beneficiaries since its inception. One of the significant features of the scheme is that it emphasized the involvement of local bodies especially city administration and Municipal Corporation in responding to the problems of street children. A city level task force has been constituted for implementing the scheme. It consists of the Secretary and Director, Social Welfare Board, Police Commissioner, Municipal commissioner, representative of the Union Welfare Ministry and UNICEF and convenor of the NGO forum (The Hindustan Times, Aug. 29, 1993).

Few city corporations have made efforts to help street children. The Cochin Municipality was the first to plan welfare programs for street children. The corporation of Cochin and Salesian priests of Don Bosco Society run 'Sneha Bhavan' – a home for street boys. The Corporation has provided the finances, building and other basic amenities to run the home while Don Bosco Society has provided personnel who are responsible for running the programs in the home.

The Children from the streets are the inmates of 'Sneh – Bhavan'. The Corporation staff on the rounds of the city apprehends homeless children and takes them to a Relief Settlement camp. This is entirely run by the Corporation. From here, the boys are taken to 'Sneh Bhavan'. Fr Varghese and Fr. Gaezou brought the first batch of 110 boys from the Relief Settlement on May 31, 1974. At Sneha Bhavan, children who can study are sent to nearby schools. There are sections to impart training in carpentry and tailoring and special classes are conducted for those who cannot go to school.

In the past 15 years over 3,000 boys have stayed in Sneh Bhavan and out of them around 1000 have been rehabilitated. Sneh Bhavan has also introduced employment generation schemes in 1989 including auto rickshaw scheme and rexine bag making scheme. Boys who learn auto rickshaw driving are provided with auto rickshaw on loan basis. Boys are also trained in manufacturing school bags. A "Rubber Wood Turning Unit" is also functioning in Sneh Bhavan (Indian Express, Oct.8, 1992).

The Kochi Corporation also provides night shelter to street children. Children working on the streets stay in the Night Shelter called Sneh Bhavan Annex.

A centrally-aided project has also been drawn by the Bangalore City Corporation to provide educational and vocational training to over 1,000 street children. The project will cost Rs. 15 crores. It was found that the number of street children in the 5-15 age group has increased by 33% in the past decade. The Corporation plans to arrange accommodation and other basic services for these children. Funds from the World Bank loan will be used to provide health care to street children (Indian Express March 26, 1992).

5.6. LIMITATIONS OF GOVERNMENT POLICIES AND PROGRAMS FOR STREET CHILDREN

Among the departments of Government concerned with the Welfare of children, understanding of the subject of street children is inadequate. It is to be noted that in the absence of a proper estimate of the problem and lack of adequate information on the special needs and problems of street children, planning welfare or development programs for them does not hold much relevance. Keeping in mind the growing numbers of street children in India, the problem of so-called "delinquent", "abandoned", or "destitute" children seems to be overwhelming government's capacity to deal effectively with them.

Programs and services offered by the Government usually concentrate on neglected and delinquent children. The emphasis in the approach adopted in these programs is generally on institutionalization. The traditional attitude in govt. – run institutions is to 'reform' the child (Agnelli. S. 1986). Regarding terminology, the names often given to institutions have a negative influence on the child. It jeopardizes the child's future since a child coming out of an institution referred to as an 'Observation Home', 'Remand Home' etc. is stigmatized and practically marked for life. Words such as delinquent, uncontrollable, vagrant and problem children are commonly used for these children. This entirely pejorative language is a reflection of the government's social policy approach which tends to be one of coercive rehabilitation.

Though in certain cases street children may be involved in street crime and violence and at that point institutionalization may be warranted. But imposed, forced institutionalization is a widespread, dominant strategy to deal with street children and it appears to be both short-sighted and often counterproductive. It is now being recognized that no matter how good an institution may be, the institutionalization of street children must always be the last resort.

With respect to social policy, this institutional stance does not appreciate the inherent strengths, adaptability and resilience possessed by these children. For e.g. the term 'vagrant' implies a sense of aimless wandering. However, a look at the daily lives of many street children reflects pattern of organization and goal-directed behaviour (Felsman, J.K. 1988).

Children engaged in street trades are employed, informally or even illegally at times. Many of the strategies of street children to exist and survive on the streets often demonstrate competent, adaptive behaviour and ways to cope with the especially difficult circumstances in which they live. Thus, to describe them as helpless, powerless and pitiable highlights only their vulnerabilities and "at-risk" situations and overlooks their strength and resiliency.

The official attitude towards street children who have severed ties with their families is based on a strong belief also shared by social policy planners which assumes that "street children have nothing while they are on the streets and should be grateful for being rescued from the streets" (Felsman, J.K. 1988). It must however be noted that most of the street children like their lives on the streets. The sense of physical freedom and liberty they possess while being on the streets should not be either overlooked or underestimated.

From having been independent and free on the street, once the child is put in the institution, he finds himself restricted and also has little contact with people outside the institution. He is excluded and segregated from the society and the environment in a typical government run institution is closed, uncaring and rigid (Agnelli. S. 1986).

Infact, it is this closed environment and lack of freedom so characteristic of govt. institutions which is responsible for street children running away from these so-called "protection" or "rehabilitation" homes. Many street children have been in and out of different institutions on several occasions. There have also been frequent reports of street children escaping from these government-run homes. Twenty-four children fled from the children's home at Umerkhadi, Bombay. The children were in the age group of 12-16 years. They had dug a hole in the wall of the main barrack and had camouflaged it well. The boys clambered up a tree to go across the main wall. There were reports that children were starving and not properly cared for but these were refuted by the officials (Indian Express, July 31, 1992).

14 children escaped from the Children's Observation Home at Delhi Gate, run by the Social Welfare Department of the Delhi Administration. These children escaped by removing the iron grill of the main gate. After an enquiry it was fond that the children had escaped because of the negligence of the care-taker and watchman. The inmates of the Home also complained that they were not given desired treatment and good food (The Hindu, Feb.23, 1994).

Institutions like certified schools and Fit Persons Institutions set up under the purview of JJ Act aim at rehabilitation of street children but facilities for education and providing vocational training are often inadequate. Most of the homes run by the govt. are faced with both lack of financial and human resources. "It is in the nature of these institutions to be impersonal, procedure-bound, and they are often dogged by insufficiency of funds for effective implementation of their programs (Misra, S. 1988).

The staff in these institutions are usually underpaid and poorly qualified for their job. They also lack commitment and motivation and rarely make efforts to understand street child's problems and needs. Most of the remand homes do not have proper counseling facilities including services of clinical psychologists and psychiatrists (Rane, Naidu & Kapadia, 1986). On July 28, 1996, the National Human Rights Commission announced that it would begin to investigate the conditions in juvenile homes in several Indian states

(T*imes of India,* Delhi edition, July 29, 1996). Obviously, it is impossible to recreate a family for a child who has lost or run away from his parents, but it is imperative to think about the issues involved in order to make the child feel as happy and secure as possible. This **child-centred** approach helps the children to grow in confidence and feel more protected.

Though there are no readily available reliable statistics on the number of children rehabilitated by the govt. – run institutions, the record of these institutions is most likely to be dismal. The observations and remand homes are not easily accessible for research proposes. However, studies would definitely reveal the adverse and deteriorating effects of such an environment on the child's physical, social, intellectual and emotional development.

PART VI

NON GOVERNMENTAL PROGRAMMES FOR STREET CHILDREN

6.1. RECENT NGO INITIATIVES FOR STREET CHILDREN

More than 150 experts from all regions of the world partcipated in the "Street Children Initiative International Conference" held at the headquarters of the World Bank in Washington in April, 2000. This was the first ever conference of the World Bank dedicated to the growing global phenomenon of street children. The Bank's staff and the global NGO community discussed the issue and the participants of this "Street Children Initiative" suggested that the World Bank develop and approve a specific "Operational Policy and Procedure on Street Children". (2000/04/14 - Global call for World Bank commitment to street children)

Such a Policy (a formal instrument in the Bank) will give the more than 10,000 World Bank staff guidance on how to include specific components for street children in project preparation (including structural adjustment loans) and enable the Bank to supervise implementation of the same.

Such Operational Policies can help street children, who are a vulnerable social group excluded to date from the benefits of the mainstream development projects. The above mentioned proposal has already been endorsed by the leadership of the European Network on Street Children Worldwide - encompassing more than 500 local and international NGOs - and the United Kingdom's Consortium for Street Children, a grouping of 40 NGO members working with street children in 63 countries.

While comparing the efforts made by NGOs for the welfare of street children with existing govt. programs, particularly in the Indian Context, it has been observed that NGOs are more practical in their approach than are govt. programs for street children. Their programmes are also more creative and realistic in functioning. The voluntary sector, having more flexibility and adaptability in it's approach to facilitate interventions for street children, has been more innovative and meaningful in it's solutions.

Some international and national NGOs have pioneered intervention projects for protecting and promoting the interests of street children. Many of the NGOs function as 'multiple service agencies' and work on an integrated approach. Others provide street children with shelter or drop-in centre facilities in addition to health care and recreational facilities. A few organizations provide basic education and skill training which enable street children to find a gainful vocation at a later stage. These programs have a long-term preventive impact.

Some other NGOs which address their services to poor families, particularly in improving their economic condition also play a preventive role. These organisations often define a street child differently, they also differ in their emphasis on children's needs and most significantly, they adopt different approaches and strategies in their programs for street children. Some international and national NGOs have pioneered intervention projects for protecting and promoting the interests of street children.

Intervention approaches

Lusk's (1989) proposes four categories of interventions : correctional (containment, institutionalization), rehabilitative (cure), outreach (street education), and prevention. Correctional measures refer to those which see street children as the problem and remove them from the streets to 'correct' them, usually in institutional settings. The term "correctional" means imprisonment. Measures included in such category illustrate the interventions have been characterized by the attitude of street children as a "public nuisance". Welfare measures such as correction should be used as last resorts.

Rehabilitative approaches regard street children as with special needs and attempt to support them by providing basic services and perhaps counseling. Ortiz et al(1992) conclude, rehabilitative services, while of high short-term value, only serve in the long run to maintain the child's situation, rather than to create better opportunities or to prevent street children in the first place.

Outreach programs, such as street education, find social structures at fault and try, by meeting street children on their home ground, to educate and empower them to find collective solutions to problems.

Finally, preventative approaches, like outreach programs, view social structures and forces as being the main causes of street children and attempt to directly influence social change. This also includes educational programs, which though employed at all levels, tend to have a preventative function. Such programs may be non-traditional and accommodating: adapting to different needs and situations of the child for example nature of child's work and family, and perhaps beginning in the children's environment ("street educators"), aiming at economic self-sufficiency and including vocational components while simultaneously offering preparation for moving into (or returning to) the formal educational system. An underlying guideline is that "the program has to fit the child, not the child the program..." (Foley, 1983)

The increased effectiveness and success of interventions for street children, however, is dependent upon support at national and international policymaking levels.. A key factor in increasing support depends upon redefining public stereotypes that dehumanize street children, perhaps through developing initiatives aimed towards increasing the awareness of the conditions of street children, and ways in which the public can be involved in alleviating them (Hemenway, D.1996). The emergence of policy level legislation and international activities targeting improved and relevant welfare for street children is encouraging.

It is acknowledged that legislation in itself is not the only solution to the complex phenomenon of street children. Where legislation is proposed, its potential to succeed is dependent on two factors: firstly, the nature of services intended for children. In this context it is pertinent to emphasize the multi-sectoral delivery of services to street children and; secondly, legislation's dependency on both available and appropriate human and financial resources and infrastructure. There is need for more co-ordination between the various agencies of government responsible for children.

It is proposed that all levels of government, as well as NGO's and welfare agencies commit themselves to redress to this problem. In order to address to the problem realistically, a census of street children needs to be conducted through city-wide surveys with the assistance of nongovernmental organizations (NGOs). Without an accurate estimate of the population of street children, it is difficult to plan and implement programs for their benefit.

Interventions should be humane, accountable and multi-faceted. Furthermore, there is a need for child care legislation to be drafted, which will protect categories of marginalised children whose special needs are not currently provided for in the existing legislation. All laws relating to child labor and the Juvenile Justice Act need to be reviewed to ensure that the implementation of these laws does not result in criminalizing children who are forced to work. All allegations of custodial abuse and exploitation of children should be investigated thoroughly. Complaints against law enforcement personnel should be promptly and carefully investigated by an independent agency with an adequately trained investigatory staff. This agency should be directly accessible to street children.

More attention must also be paid to the views and feelings of the children involved. In view of frequent reports of abuse and exploitation of street children by the police, it is also important to conduct proper registration of each child taken to a police station, including the time, date, and reason for detention. The government programs for street children in India are also not adequate in number as compared to the scale of problem. The services offered are not comprehensive and also have a very limited coverage given the magnitude of the target population. Therefore, expansion of services and establishing a coordinated network between government and NGOs for delivery of services to street children have been considered essential strategies for responding to the situation.

Based on review of available literature, one of the least explored levels of the phenomenon of street children intervention is that of prevention. Services to street children have tended to focus on protection and rehabilitation rather than the early identification of potential street children and families 'at risk'. This has meant that community-based, preventive projects that deal with contributory factors for children running away are inadequate. Children and young people should be the focus of preventative services and should be viewed within the context of their families, extended families and communities. Programs on parenting skills and child development should be provided to the widest possible range of families. Poverty reduction must be a priority of all of civil society and the state and should be addressed at a macro level. Skills training and the creation of employment opportunities or income-generating activities for families form an integral part of poverty reduction and a valuable part of any preventative street children initiative.

In a consultative paper prepared for the South African Law Commission, Ritchie, M. (1996) proposes a developmental approach while planning intervention services for street children. The significant features of this approach are :

*   focussing on strengths, adaptability and resiliency among street children rather than deviant behavior or pathology;

*   building competency rather than attempting to cure;

*   encouragement of trial and error learning;

* taking context into consideration;

* understanding and responding appropriately to the development tasks and needs of the children;

* working with the total person, not the so called 'pathology' of the problem;

* a strong belief of the potential within each child and family, the aim to maximise potential rather than minimizing the problem;

* an emphasis on most of the 'treatment' taking place in the daily living environment of the child;

* a multi-disciplinary team (not a hierarchy) approach in which the child and family are recognised as members of the team. (Ritchie, M. Inter-Ministerial Committee, IMC, 1998)

For purposes of health promotion and the development of education strategies for street children, it is necessary to understand the circumstances that are responsible for children taking to city streets and ascertain their working and living conditions. If change must occur, it should be within the context of their street experience. Efforts must be made to provide specialist services for children, such as education and vocational training and, in cases of family breakdown, substitute care.

The growing concern, efforts and activities of NGOs have significantly contributed to bringing the issue into a sharp focus of attention of various authorities at national and international level which have the mandate for working for the welfare of children. Besides being instrumental in the delivery of services for improvement in the conditions of street children, the NGOs have also highlighted the weakness of the existing legislative measures and provisions and inadequate enforcement of laws with regard to safeguarding the rights and interest of street children.

Part VII

Street Children : Psychosocial Perspectives

7.1. METHODOLOGICAL CHARACTERISTICS OF THE STUDY

Sondhi, P. (1994) conducted a study on the homeless street children in Delhi to explore describe the phenomenon of street children, its causes and their psychosocial characteristics.

RESEARCH DESIGN

The research design of the study aimed at obtaining valid data pertinent to the problem being researched. To ascertain and delineate the psychosocial characteristics of street children, a descriptive design was considered appropriate. The approach of the study is in-depth, qualitative and descriptive in that it focuses attention on facts relating to :

a) The familial background and composition of street children;

b) Interpersonal relationships with parents, siblings and other caregivers;

c) Experiences of the children at home and reasons for running away from home ;

d) Description and analysis of working and living conditions of children, and

e) Interactions with peers and others in their environment.

OBJECTIVES OF THE STUDY

1. To investigate the socio-economic background of street

children including: demographic characteristics, religion & caste, family income, education and occupation of family members;

2. Identify and analyze the reasons for their leaving home and migration aspects;

3. Describe their working and living conditions;

4. To provide information on the psychosocial health of the children in order to achieve a comprehensive understanding of psychosocial factors affecting their development;

5. To review existing services and programs, both governmental and non-governmental, for street children and suggest modifications to make them more effective.

OPERATIONAL DEFINITION

This study focuses on homeless street children who are working in urban areas. Street children in this study are operationally defined as those children who do not have any contact with their families and are earning income for daily survival. These street children were alone living in the street at the time of the study and were engaged in economically gainful activity. The concept of a 'street child' as used in this study is as follows:

'A street child is any child (below 14 years of age) for whom the street (in the widest sense of the word including pavements, in occupied dwellings, etc.) has become his habitual abode and who is living without any familial contact, support or protection' (NGO, 1987).

IDENTIFICATION AND DESCRIPTION OF THE SAMPLE

The sample of children to be included in the study depended on the definition conceptualized for a 'street child' and the population of street children available. Research on street children in India is relatively new and there is no internationally agreed definition of 'a street child'. Indeed, the criteria for including children in a study are almost as numerous as the studies themselves. For e.g. some studies have included children who work on the streets but return home and maintain contact with their families whereas a few others have included those children who live alone without any familial contact, protection or support whatsoever from their families.

To avoid this problem, a street child was operationally defined as, "any minor child below 14 years of age for whom the street (in the widest sense of the word, including unoccupied dwellings wasteland, etc.) has become his habitual abode, and who is without adequate protection" (NGO, 1987). These children are mostly either orphaned, abandoned or runaways. The criteria chosen for a child to be identified as a street child for the purpose of this study was that the child should have been working and living on the street without any contact or support from his family at least for the last one year, i.e. for at least one year prior to the time when they were interviewed. This made for a more specific identification but it also provided a very limited number of street children.

The research was confined to a study of boys. The reasons for this being:-

a) It was difficult to find street girls as they are more vulnerable and are often picked up by brothel-owners and get sucked into prostitution;

b) Majority of the street children are boys; and

c) A very small number of girls who are found on the streets do not live alone. They either have family contacts or live with other adult females who are homeless and stay on the pavements. Since the study concentrates only on those children who work and live alone without any familial contact, such a group was excluded from the study.

SAMPLE CHARACTERISTICS

A non-random sample of 147 street boys in the age group of

10-14 years constitutes the total sample of the study. The researcher lost 14% (23cases) of her identified sample of 170 street boys. In these twenty-three cases, the researcher was unable to maintain contact with the children as they could not be located and followed up to complete the study.

The present study was conducted at the New Delhi Railway Station and it's adjoining areas like: Paharganj and Ajmeri Gate and the Central Park in Connaught Place, New Delhi. In Delhi, street children are highly concentrated in areas like: main bus depots, commercial centres, railway stations and outside places of workship.

To be included in the sample, the subjects had to meet two criteria:-

a) They had to be street children who worked and lived on the street without any contact with their families. This criterion was used to establish that the sample composed of street children and not street child labor who worked on the street but maintained constant or occasional contacts with their families;

b) Children who were engaged in economically gainful activity and were self-employed were taken in the sample. Children working under supervision, employed by others or found begging were excluded from the study. Street children who work on their own are found to be engaged in various kinds of occupations e.g. shoe shining, rag picking, selling small items on the streets or as porters. In order to maintain uniformity in the nature of their occupation, their working conditions and work-related problems, street children working as porters at the New Delhi Railway Station were selected for the study.

SAMPLING STRATEGY

The scattered nature of the universe, absence of a definite sampling framework and high mobility of the sample posed problems in adopting a probability sampling procedure for the study.

For the purpose of the study, non-probability sampling procedure was used as there were no means of estimating the probability of units being included in the sample. Indeed, there was no guarantee that every unit had a chance of being studied. For selection of subjects, purposive sampling technique was adopted. Jahoda (1962) states that, "the basic assumption behind purposive sampling is that with good judgment and an appropriate strategy one can select the cases to be included in the sample and thus develop samples that are satisfactory in relation to one's need".

According to Garrett (1971), "In purposive sampling technique, a sample may be expressly chosen because in the light of available evidence, it mirrors some larger group with reference to a given characteristic". He states that, "Random sampling formulas apply more or less accurately to purposive samples". This is also referred to as judgmental sampling as the investigator's judgment is involved in sample selection.

RESEARCH STRATEGIES AND INSTRUMENTS

Data for the study came from two main sources: focused (individual and group) observations and in-depth interviews.

1.Focused Observations of individual children and of groups of children while working and living on the station were conducted. The observations made covered a wide spectrum of behavior of the subjects. They included both verbal and non-verbal behavior. Children were also observed in groups in order to gather information about their peer relationships and dynamics.

2.Interview Schedule I: The interview technique as the main instrument in the present study was preferable because children were not sufficiently literate to answer a questionnaire. It was believed that more data can be collected and new insights gained by face-to-face interaction with the children in the field. The Compendium of Research Tools in Social Science Research, Vol. I, Part B, by National Institute of Public Co-operation and Child Development (1986) was consulted for developing the interview schedule. Interview schedules for self-employed children and destitute children were used as reference information. However, considering the difficult circumstances and special needs of children living without families, it was pertinent to design the interview schedule accordingly.

Structured interview with open-ended questions has been used which allows for flexibility in both the number and nature of questions which fall within the limits of the area under study. The interview schedule, however, did not restrict the scope of the study as during the course of study some interesting facts concerning the lives of children became available. The pattern established in the schedule need not be followed rigidly and the sequencing of questions can be changed when required.

The interview schedule- I is a collection of questions which focus on various aspects of the lives of urban working street children. Broadly speaking, it covers the following areas:

i) Respondents' family background;

ii) Demographic characteristics;

iii) Migration aspects and reasons for leaving home;

iv) Working and living conditions on the street;

v) Problems faced during working and living;

vi) Peer life and opportunities for play; and

vii) Future aspirations and expectations.

Interview Schedule II: In order to obtain data about the nature and type of deprivations faced by the subjects, the existing approaches and methodologies employed for assessing deprivation were reviewed. It was found that there is little consensus on what constitutes deprivation and in the specification and determination of its empirical referents. The limitations of the concept of deprivation for contribution to analytic understanding are several and serious.

Over the years various criteria for identification and classification of deprivation have emerged. These include:

- Type of residential area (Gordon, 1968);

-   Membership of some social or cultural or economic group (e.g. Wilcox, R.C. 1971; Goff,   1954; Nurcombe, 1970);

-   Institutionalization (e.g. Sinha & Shukla, 1974; Talmadge, 1969; Langmeier & Matezect 1968, cited in Misra, G. & Tripati, L.B. 1978).

Apart from these, attempts have been made to quantify deprivation and develop its indices (Davis, 1968, Sahu, 1975; Rath & Samant, 1975; Misra, G. & Tripathi, L.B., 1978).

Misra, G. & Tripathi, L.B. (1978) have proposed the concept of 'Prolonged Deprivation'. The underlying assumption made by the authors while referring to prolonged deprivation is that, "the socio- cultural life in any social setting can be conceptualized as a continuum, at one end of which lie those who have all the facilities for fulfillment of their physical as well as social needs, while on the other end lie those who are materialistically, socially and psychologically in a disadvantaged position. In order to measure prolonged deprivation, the authors have developed the Prolonged Deprivation Scale. They suggest that while constructing the Prolonged Deprivation Scale, "the experiential background of the individual can be meaningfully conceptualized as an interrelated continuum along which the life experiences vary both quantitatively and qualitatively".

Fifteen areas of deprivation have been identified which refer to the possible aspects of experimental inputs received by an individual with special reference to life experiences in the Indian context. These areas are: housing conditions, home environment, economic sufficiency, clothing, educational experiences, travel and recreation and miscellaneous socio-cultural experiences.

The scale has been standardized on 471 rural respondents in the age group of 15-25 years. It consists of 96 five-point scale items found to be significant in indicating the degree of prolonged deprivation. The five sub-categories of each item of the scale are ordinal categories denoting various degrees of deprivation ranging from very low (1) to very high (5).

This scale is a marked improvement over other scales and attempts to focus on the global nature of deprivation. However, several factors limit the value of using socio-economic status as a measure of deprivation:

1. Knowledge of an individual's socio-economic status only yields no information on the process through which this aspect of the environment results in deprivation which consequently effects development of an individual.

2. With reference to deprivation, norms or criteria for sufficiency are neither available nor established, especially where psychologically defined variables are concerned. For most of the parameters, which can be specified in different life situations, there is simply no understanding of threshold values below which insufficiency can be defined. (Jessor, R. & Richardson, S. 1968).

3. It is accepted that the conditions of disadvantage can often be characterized just as significantly by the excess of certain kinds of stimulation or environmental attributes as by the absence or limitation of others. Very often, disadvantaged or deprived children are exposed to an excess of certain life situations or conditions, for e.g., excess of stigmatizing experiences, excess of failure in school, etc. In short, the nature of deprivation necessitates a conceptualization of not only what is limited or lacking but also of what can be interpreted as excessive (Jessor, R & Richardson, S. 1968). It should be stressed that both conditions may be present simultaneously in a given situation.

4. A high score on the Prolonged Deprivation Scale is indicative of high degree of deprivation and low score indicates low deprivation. The assumption here is that the greater the value of the parameters, the greater the deprivation. Therefore, the concept of deprivation as used in the scale involves some kind of lack or insufficiency. It overlooks the significance of the presence of excess of certain kinds of environmental

attributes (both adverse and favorable) in the environment as aspects of deprivation.

5. The referents of deprivation used in the scale are given unit value so that all referents are assumed to effect deprivation in an identical manner. But it is the interrelatedness and interplay of these referents which seems to be more crucial to an understanding of their differential effects on the individual's development (Tripathi, R.C. 1982). What is needed is a comprehensive theory of deprivation which can specify relevant variables and delineate the complex nature of their interaction.

6. The scale was pilot-tested on a sample of twelve street children and it was not found appropriate for the sample under study due to the following reasons:

    a) Each item in the scale is divided into five categories ranging from a scale value of one to five. Often the difference between these five categories was not easily discernible to the children who are administered the scale. They were unable to view these categories as mutually exclusive, for e.g., categories like most frequently, frequently, occasionally, infrequently and rarely were often considered overlapping. The respondents were unable to comprehend the underlying differentiation between the categories placed next to each other on the rating scale. This problem is likely to provide inaccurate data and the validity of the responses becomes questionable.

    b) The scale also requires both observations and interview for data collection. Administration of the scale needs to be done at the residence of the subjects and responses obtained should be cross checked with other family members. For the purpose of the present study, this was not feasible.

c) In addition, the scale is limited to the experiences received by the individual at his home. In order to take into account both the street child's experiences at home and on the street, the use of a different tool was necessitated. In view of these limitations inherent both in the nature, structure and administration of the Prolonged Deprivation Scale when used for ascertaining deprivation faced by street children, the Developmental Deprivation Interview Schedule was devised for the purpose.

The rationale for terming the schedule as Developmental Deprivation Interview Schedule was that the schedule incorporates questions which view deprivation faced by the subjects over a period of time. While devising the schedule, special attention was given to ensure that the questions in the schedule were relevant for assessing deprivation faced by the subjects under study. Since children were unable to comprehend the nuances of the items in the Prolonged Deprivation Scale (Misra & Tripathi, 1978), the present interview schedule comprised of open-ended questions which were comparatively easier to understand by the sample.

Care was taken to structure questions in a manner which was comprehensible and direct. This Interview Schedule stresses on the qualitative aspect of deprivation while the Prolonged Deprivation Scale aims primarily at the quantitative assessment of deprivation. In this manner, the present interview schedule was found appropriate and subsequent testing confirmed this aspect.

This schedule aims at examining factors that operate at the family, individual and societal level to cause deprivation among street children. Seifer, R. & Sameroff, A.J. (1987) have argued for the inclusion of variables at different levels of individual, family or societal organization as potential risk factors that affect a child's development process.

Increasing attention is now being given to the multifaceted nature of environment and the correlations that exist among these environmental categories. Jessor, R. & Richardson, S. (1968)

presented a theoretical and research paradigm and the primary conceptual regions of this paradigm are; the environment, the person and behaviour. The Environment is further differentiated into proximal and distal environment. This distinction refers to a dimension of environmental analysis ranging from the proximal or immediate psychologically-defined or experiential variables to the more remote or distal descriptions of the environment (chart 6).

The variables in one column are related to variables in other columns. For e.g. being a street child involves a high probability of being exposed to abusive and stigmatizing environment which often leads to low self-esteem (personal attribute) and this, in turn may lead to social alienation and withdrawal (behavioural attribute).

The Developmental Deprivation interview schedule was designed from the point of view of present study's objective of describing the nature and kind of deprivation faced by the subjects. The schedule is based on the above stated paradigm. The main purpose of introducing the paradigm is to make clear that comprehensive understanding of psychosocial deprivation will require knowledge of all the regions in the paradigm and of their relations over time.

The interview schedule includes variables at different levels of individual, family and society as potential risk factors that are likely to lead to psychosocial deprivation. The term " psychosocial deprivation" will be used in the specific sense of environmental and social conditions that produce stress in the individual and adversely affect his emotional and personality development. The interview schedule concentrates on certain areas of special significance in the lives of street children. It is assumed that these areas refer to psychosocial factors in the child's environment, both while he stayed at home and later on the streets. In order to take into account the ongoing nature of deprivation, the questions in the interview schedule deal not only with the child's environmental conditions at the time of study but also his experiences at home.

Chart 8

Illustrative Scheme for Psychosocial Deprivation and Development
(With special reference to Street Children)

Environment Attributes	Person Attributes	Behaviour Attributes	Symptomatic Behaviour
A	B	C	D
Distal	Proximal		
Social Class practices	Child rearing	Beliefs and values	Aggressiveness & Delinquency
E.g.			
Urban Ecology Phenomenon of Street children	Negative Evaluation (Stigma)	Low Self-esteem	Antisocial behaviour or Social withdrawal

(Adopted from : Jessor, R. & Richardson, S. (1968) Psychosocial Deprivation and Personality Development. In Perspectives on Human Deprivation, U.S. Department of Health, Education and Welfare, 1968).

The phenomenon of psychosocial deprivation as observed in the lives of street children focuses on a specified set of environmental conditions in their lives. It also involves looking not only at insufficiency or lack of certain favorable factors but also at the excess of certain other unfavorable or detrimental factors. Attempts were made to collect information on the general physical health and emotional characteristics of all the subjects by using interview schedules I and the Developmental Deprivation interview schedule.

It must be realized that the domain of psychosocial deprivation is vast and complex and it is possible only to highlight some of its important aspects. Attention was focused on certain situations of psychosocial deprivation in children's lives which included the following significant background variables :

a) **Socio-economic factors:** including housing conditions and home environment, socio-economic condition, educational experiences, leisure and social activities; reasons and consequences of homelessness;

b) **Personal and Social Relations:** including parent-child relationship , interaction with siblings, and other family members, relationships outside the family, especially with peers, relationship with co-workers, opportunities for and kind of interaction with other children and adults in the environment, effects of working and living environment and job satisfaction; and

c) **Health Status:**

(i) General Physical Health; and

(ii) Psychosocial Component of Health.

In addition to obtaining information on the general physical health and emotional characteristics of all the subjects, attempts were made to collect test data on emotional health and functioning of a few subjects. For the purpose, thirty-two boys (which constitutes

22% of the entire sample of 147 boys) were given two psychological tests (Bender Gestalt, 1951and Draw-A-Person Test, 1963) after obtaining data using interview schedules I and II. Attempts were made to connect the test data of the children with data gathered by using both the interview schedules with them.

The tests were exclusively administered to 14 year old children who had been to school and had some level of schooling. Since the Bender Gestalt (BG) required the subjects to copy designs, it was important that the children were acquainted with using paper and pencil, drawing designs or figures and they were able to follow the instructions clearly. Due to the above reasons and in order to maintain uniformity with respect to the educational background of the child, only those children who had been to school were administered the tests. This limited the number of children who could be administered these tests. Care was taken to see that the subject could read and write in Hindi or any other language fluently. One subject was also fluent in Bengali and another in Assamese apart from Hindi. They both were taken as subjects.

The data obtained by administering these tests have been primarily used to supplement information gained through the use of interview schedules I and II. The tests have not been used as a means to make individual diagnosis but only as tools to strengthen the insights gained by using interview schedules I and II and through observations. Aptekar, L. (1988) conducted a study of 56 Colombian street boys using Bender Gestalt and Good-enough Harris Drawing Test. Participant observational data and these tests scoreswere used to describe the neurological and emotional functioning of the boys.

The Bender Gestalt (Bender, 1938) was employed to measure the overall emotional health of the children. The Bender Gestalt (BG) has proved to be a valuable tool in cross-cultural personality research (Goden, 1979; Holtzman, 1980; Hutt, 1985, Tolar, & Brannigan, 1980). Tolar & Brannigan (1980) while reviewing the literature on the use of Bender Gestalt (BG) in cross-cultural contexts concluded that, "the B-G performance is quite unaffected by cultural factors". Holtzman (1980) compared the BG with other cross-cultural personality measures such as Rorschach Inkblot Test, the House-Tree-Person Test, the Thematic apperception Test and the Minnesota Multiphasic Personality Inventory and concluded that "the Bender-Gestalt was found to be second in accuracy of diagnostic judgement. Only the Minnesota Multiphasic inventory was more accurate". Hutt (1985) suggested using the BG in situations where language or culture might bias the results. He reported that the performance on BG was largely independent of these factors.

Goden (1979) is of the opinion that BG "provides a good source of nonverbal material more reliable than many other projective techniques". Many scoring systems have been used for Bender-Gestalt but the Pascal-Suttell (1951) method was chosen for the study. The performance of a subject on the Bender-Gestalt Test was viewed by Pascal & Suttell (1951) as a reflection of his attitude towards reality. The ability of the individual to draw the Bender designs is seen as a function of the individual's integrative capacity or his "ego-strength" and is correlated with the emotional adjustment of the individual. For children under the age of nine years, Pascal & Suttell (1951) do not consider their scoring system very reliable. The present sample was, however, between 10-14 years and Pascal & Suttell's scoring system can be applied reliably to this age group. The Draw-A-Person Test, 1963 (human figure drawing) was used to yield a second measure of the boys emotional health. Important reasons for having used this test are drawings were not mediated by language and the test was easy to administer. Another advantage was that drawing was interesting for the children. Lindzey (1961) quoted Mead, M. who stated that drawings were "an efficient device for the cross-cultural study of children's personality". According to Gardiner (1974) the test "can be used with equal ease in any group without encountering the familiar difficulties of translation or adaptation common to many other research techniques. The task is intrinsically interesting to most children and instructions can be communicated with a minimum of three words - 'draw', 'man' and 'woman'".

Holtzman (1980) believes that the Draw-A- Person Test (DAPT) is 'likely to have a fairly wide range of cross-cultural equivalence, and Koppitz's (1969) Scale of emotional stability looks promising as a quantitative score'. Koppitz, E. (1968) working with children of comparable ages to those in the present study, devised the scoring of emotional indicators (Eis) to "reflect the children's attitudes and concerns of the given moment". The DAPT provides a measure of emotional functioning which reflects the child's current emotional condition whereas the Bender Gestalt yielded information that reflected a more long standing psychological profile. Aptekar, L. (1988) used these two test to evaluate the emotional health and functioning of Colombian street children.

The tests were administered in Hindi and the directions for the test were presented to the children in words which were comparable to the standard procedure in English. The scoring of the BG and DAPT protocols was done by a clinical psychologist with experience in scoring projective test data for children. The psychologist did not have any information about the children and was not aware of their characteristics. The tests were rated separately. The tests were used only as a means to describe the emotional health of these children.

DATA COLLECTION

The amount of data collected in a descriptive study is usually limited by the time and expertise available. The study included children who were working and living on the street without any familial contact or support. To obtain a large number of such children for the sample and maintain sustained contact with them was an extremely difficult task. It was hence considered appropriate to conduct a comprehensive study of a clearly defined sample of street children which would provide better data and also a deeper understanding of the phenomenon of street children. The manageable size of the sample gave the researcher an opportunity for careful study and for intensive work with individual children. This was particularly important in view of the fact that so little was known about street children living without families particularly in the Indian context.

Data were collected in three different locations: The New Delhi Railway Station , the park adjoining it and the Central Park, Connaught Place, New Delhi. All the subjects were identified and selected from the station where they lived and worked as porters. The observations of the children were primarily done at the station. Eventually, after forming a rapport and after gaining their trust it was possible to take them to the park and talk to them individually. Some children were hesitant to reveal information about their families, especially concerning their mother and sister, in the presence of other boys.

The technique of personal, individual interviewing was adopted for the study. Group observations of children were also conducted. The Central Park , Connaught Place is bigger than the park next to the Railway station and the subjects were less distracted by their co – workers or friends as compared to other locations. Care was taken to make sure that the child had finished his work on the station so that he was comfortable during the interview.

A study of this kind is inevitably dependent on the co–operation of the sample group. Irrespective of the size of sample, the confidence that children have in the investigator is of primary importance .It is therefore relevant to consider the attitudes they had towards the researcher at the time of study. Most street children were initially wary of the researcher. They thought that she was from the police and would put them in jail. Though they were willing to talk to her or spend time with her but they were reluctant to talk to her about their families or reasons for leaving home. Thus, it was essential that time was spent explaining that the purpose of the study was to gather information about the lives of street children and problems faced by them. The role of a street child who was already interviewed by the researcher was invaluable when trying to interview boys not known to the researcher. Children, who were already interviewed by the researcher, trusted her and felt comfortable while talking to her. This facilitated interviewing those subjects who were introduced to her by others.

Locating the sample and maintaining contact with them necessitated plenty of time and traveling around the station but the enthusiasm with which many children helped the researcher made it very worthwhile. A pilot study was done as a preliminary exercise to test the effectiveness of the instruments being used and also the handling of the situation by the researcher.

PROBLEMS ENCOUNTERED IN DATA COLLECTION

While collecting data, a major problem faced was losing contact with the subjects. The researcher lost 23 subjects, i.e. 14% of the identified sample of 170 street children. It is also necessary to understand and describe the atmosphere and the settings in which the researcher had to conduct the interviews. It has been widely recognized that data about the situation of working street children and others who live in especially difficult circumstances in cities and urban areas can be difficult to collect. Conducting an interview on the street, where street children are found, also means that background activities divert the attention of both the child and the interviewer. The crowd on the station made interviewing impracticable on the station premises. The atmosphere for the interview was charged with constantly moving crowd and loud noise which acted as sources of disturbance. The idea of a street child being interviewed also aroused the curiosity of passer bys as well as other street children.

In a research done in the Dominican Republic in conjunction with non-governmental organization 'Accion Callejera', close to a hundred working street children was interviewed, using a structured questionnaire (cited in Barker, F. 1993). The following insights and techniques were found useful and these have also been adopted in the present study :

(a) Introducing yourself and stating the purpose of the interview which can be to protect the child, as these children are often approached by adults who abuse or mistreat them or it can be to gather information about the problems faced by them;

(b) Personalizing the interview by using the child's name or nickname. Most street children have a nick-name;

(c) Using the child's street language whenever possible;

(d) Paying the child either in cash or in kind. Sometimes children who had been interviewed asked for some money. They were usually given what they would have earned during that time though care was taken to ensure that the subject had finished his work on the station;

(e) Sometimes the researcher shared tea or eatables with the subjects and it created a bond of friendship and acceptance;

(f) The interview was often made participatory to some extent to break monotony e.g. letting children use paper and pencil or sign the interview schedule. Sometimes children showed lot of enthusiasm in getting their pictures taken by the researcher.

(g) At the end of the interview, the child was given the opportunity to tell anything that might have been on his mind but that might not have been asked.

INTERPRETATION OF DATA

To understand the characteristics of street children, it was considered appropriate to adopt a developmental view-point. This entailed looking at the unfolding life events of the child while he was staying with his family, and later during his stay on the streets. In every case, a series of interrelated social and psychological factors were investigated. Data were organized into categories encompassing various areas relevant to the objectives of the study.

The study involved a number of variables in which some were nominal scales, e.g. religion, native place of the respondents and some were interval scales, e.g. age of the respondents, size of the family, and monthly income of the family. It must be emphasized that data are mostly descriptive and they derive mainly from the observations made by the researcher and both the interview schedules used with subjects. The complex interplay of the psychosocial factors studied is inevitable and it cannot be claimed that areas are discrete in themselves.

Important observations made during the interview were also noted and most of the data is in-depth and descriptive. It was from such detailed descriptions that more information was gathered about their lives and atmosphere in their homes. The following chapter on findings and discussions contains quotations from the children as a record of their feeling and attitudes. The information thus gathered will help to achieve a greater understanding of the lives of street children.

LIMITATIONS OF THE STUDY

1. Data relating to age of the respondents and their family background particularly income of the family, education of the parents, and the general home environment may not be reliable since no records were available and children were the only source of information which had to be relied on.

2. As it was not feasible to obtain female street children for the study, it was decided to include only boys in the sample. This was, therefore, predetermined and the differences in the lives of male and female street children could not be ascertained.

3. Parental characteristics, attitudes and behavior when studied through children's reports should be recognized for what it is, i.e. an account of parental behavior as it is observed by the children. It cannot be assumed that these reports are absolutely reliable or valid indications of underlying parental attitudes. It must be realized that inaccuracies in children's reports due to emotional and attitudinal factors may introduce a source of error. The aim of the study has been to draw as true and detailed a picture as possible of a small number of street children and understand the implications of this phenomenon in the lives of the children.

4. The nature of problems faced by street children point to a constellation of factors and complex interactions of widely diverse kinds of variables. This necessitates a more holistic perspective. The differential effects of various environmental factors on street children cannot be understood by an exclusive consideration of social and psychological factors. Attention must also be paid to differences in physical health, functional impairment (if any) and temperament of the children.

The attempt to systematically explore bio-social or gene-environment interaction in development and deprivation is a major task which would include the synthesis of many factors falling in the domain of different disciplines. However, because of the constraints of time and expertise available, the present study focused on the psychosocial factors of relevance in the lives of street children. The areas included in the study in no sense exhaust the domain of the phenomenon. Rather, they should be taken mainly as representing certain significant factors which affect the psychosocial development of street children.

7.2. FINDINGS AND DISCUSSIONS

Data obtained using the research techniques and instruments selected for the study have been organized into categories relevant to the objective of the study.

The interview schedule-I which will be discussed in the following sections includes data on –

1. Age Distribution of the respondents;
2. Religion and Caste Affiliations;
3. Native Place of the respondents;
4. Family Background -
    (i) Family composition and type,
    (ii) Size of the family,
    (iii)Economic profile of the family, and
    (iv)Literacy level of the parents.

5. Migration Aspects and Reasons for leaving home;

6. Work-life of the children;

7. Problems faced while working on the station:

   (i) Attitude of the police;

   (ii) Institutionalization; and

   (iii) Attitude of other children and adult porters.

8. Peer life and Opportunities for play;

9. Attitudes about life at home vs. street-life;

10. Future plans and aspirations.

1. Age Distribution

The sample in the study was in the age group of 10-14 years (both years inclusive). The age distribution of the boys in the sample is given in Table 1. Only 6% of the sample was 10 years old (9 out 147 boys). 78 (53%) boys were found to be 14 years old. The average age of the children in the study was 12 years. Various studies have indicated that majority of street children belong to the age group of 11-15 years, followed by the age group of 6-10 years. In the cities of Calcutta and Hyderabad, there were more children in the age group of 6-10 years living on the streets while in Bombay and Bangalore the number of children in the age groups of 11-15 was higher (Rane, A. & Shroff, N. 1992).

Table 1. Age Distribution

(N = 147)

Age (in Years)	Numbers	Percentage
10	9	6
11	16	11
12	23	16
13	21	14
14	78	53
Total	147	100

2. Religion and Caste Affiliations

Of the total 147 boys in the sample, a majority of 105 (71%) boys were Hindus and the remaining 42 (29%) were Muslims. 91 (86%) boys were aware of the caste to which they belonged and out of these 12% of the boys belonged to scheduled castes (Table 2a & 2b).

Table 2 (a). Religion

(N = 147)

Religion	Numbers	Percentage
(a) Hindu	105	71
(b) Muslim	42	29
Total	147	100

Table 2 (b). Caste Affiliation

(N = 105)

Caste	Numbers	Percentage
(a) General	78	74
(b) Scheduled Caste	13	12.5
(c) Don't Know	14	13.5
Total	105	100.0

3. Native Place of the respondents

It can be observed from Table 3 that the maximum number of 44 (30%) street children in the sample hailed from Bihar. The second largest number of 37 (25%) boys came from Uttar Pradesh and the third largest number of 16 (11%) children belonged to Madhya Pradesh. Most of the children had migrated from the nearby Hindi-speaking areas. A few boys not hailing from Hindi-speaking states had picked up Hindi language and were able to express themselves in Hindi. Their interactions with other Hindi-speaking boys helped them to a great extent in learning the language. The proportion of children coming from non-Hindi speaking areas like; Assam, Karnataka, Orissa and West-Bengal was low.

Table 3. Native Place of the Respondents

(N = 147)

State/Country	Numbers	Percentage
States:		
Andhra Pradesh	4	3
Assam	2	1
Bihar	44	39
Gujarat	3	2
Haryana	9	6
Karnataka	1	0.5
Madhya Pradesh	16	11
Maharashtra	3	2
Orissa	2	1
Punjab	7	5
Rajasthan	9	6
Uttar Pradesh	37	25
West Bengal	7	5
Countries:		
Nepal	2	1
Bangladesh	1	0.5
Total	147	100.0

4. Family Background

Most of the available studies on street children (Nangia, P. & Pinto, R. 1988; Rane, A. & Shroff, N. 1992) and the series of studies on street children sponsored by Ministry of Welfare and UNICEF in 1989 (Philips, W.S.K., 1989 ; D'lima, H. & Gosalia, R. 1990; Reddy, N. 1989; Ghosh, A. 1989; Arimpoor, J. 1989 and Mallik, B. & Rao, B.V.R., 1989) have included working street children who are living with their families or caretakers. This group of street children forms a major portion of the sample in these studies.

Of the total estimated 4 lakh child workers in Delhi, one-fifth were staying along (Nangia, P. 1988). Similarly, studies of street children of Bombay (D'lima, H. & Gosalia, R. 1990) and street children of Indore (Philips, W.S.K. 1989) indicated that 12% of the total sample of 300 street children in Indore and 30% of the 2,169 sampled street children in Bombay were staying by themselves without their families. The present study deals specially with this special category of street children.

An analysis of the familial situation of these children is of prime importance since the role played by the family is of utmost significance. 116 (79%) boys in the sample belonged to nuclear families, the rest 31 (21 %) came from joint families. This shows that majority of the boys belonged to nuclear families (Table 4)

Table 4. Type of Family

Type of Family	Numbers	Percentage
(a) Nuclear	1·16	79
(b) Joint	31	21
Total	147	100

The home structure of the family has been categorized into two groups:

(a) Complete or normal homes, i.e. homes where both the parents are present (including homes with step- parents);

(b) Incomplete or broken homes- where either both or one parent is missing.

Of the total 147 boys in the sample, 108 (74%) boys came from complete homes (both the parents, including step-parents, were living together). The figures in Table 5 indicate that 78 boys came from families where both the real parents were staying together, 9 boys came from homes with step fathers while 17 boys had step-mothers. In four cases the father had married twice and in three of these homes both the wives stayed separately with the father visiting home occasionally.

In one case both the wives were staying together. This child hailed from Nepal. In the category of broken homes, 20 (14%) boys were without both or either parents i.e., either both the parents were dead or one was dead and the other parent had abandoned the family. Ten homes were without fathers and there were 9 cases where the homes were without mothers.

The data show that majority of the boys (74%) came from normal or complete homes whereas boys from incomplete or broken homes constitute 26% of the sample. This suggests that the factor of broken home per se is not a necessary etiological aspect resulting in juvenile vagrancy or children leaving their homes. It is a widely accepted belief, mostly based on the statistical records of different clinics, which emphasize that majority of problem children come from homes which have been broken because of desertion, delinquency and other manifestations of undesirable behaviour on the part of the parents (Kathleen, E.L. 1932; & Helthy, W.& Bronner, A. 1926).

However, other studies seem to contradict this general impression of the close association between delinquency and broken homes (Shaw, C.R. & Mackay, H.D. 1932; Silverman, B. 1935; Srivastava, S. 1963 & Kapadia, K.M. & Pillai, S.D. 1969). The studies conclude that there is no adequate basis for the belief that the factor of broken home leads to delinquency.

Table 5. Home Structure

(N= 147)

Home Structure	Numbers	Percentage (%)
(a) Complete or Normal homes:		
(i) With both real parents	(78)	
(ii) With step father..	(9)	
(iii) With step mother	(17)	
(iv) father married twice	(4)	
	108	74
Incomplete or Broken homes:		
(i) Without both parents		
— Both Parents dead	(4)	
— Mother dead, father		
— Abandoned the family	(11)	
— Father dead, mother		
abandoned the family	(5)	
(iv) Without Father	(10)	
(v) Without Mother	(9)	
	39	26
Total	147	100

Silverman, B. (1935) asserts that the concept of 'a broken home' can contribute but is insufficient to explain delinquency. "The concept of 'a broken home' is apt to mask the many subtle relationships that may exist in a home which though technically 'not broken is full of internal conflicts existing between various members of the family". It is suggested that the subtler emotional relationships within the family members also need to be examined.

As regards the size of the family, 39 (26%) boys belonged to families with three to five members, 17 (12%) boys had six members in their families while an overwhelming majority of 86 (59%) boys had seven or more than seven members in their family (Table 6). The average size of the families was found to be 5.

Table 6. Size of the Family

(N=147)

No. of family members	Numbers	Percentage
(a) Up to 2	5	3
(b) 3	6	4
(c) 4	9	6
(d) 5	24	16
(e) 6	17	12
(f) 7 and above	86	59
Total	147	100

16 (11%) boys in the sample had no male siblings, 111 (75%) had one to three brothers and 20 (14%) had three or four sisters (Table 7a & 7b). Regarding data on male siblings, in 18 (12%) cases an elder brother in the family had also left the home.

Table 7 (a). Number of Siblings (Brothers)

(N= 147)

No. of brothers	Numbers	Percentage
(a) None	16	11
(b) 1	37	25
(c) 2	40	27
(d) 3	34	23
(e) 4	15	10
(f) 5	3	2
(g) 6 and above	2	2
Total	147	100

Table 7 (b). Number of Siblings (Sisters)

No. of Sisters	Numbers	Percentage
(a) None	28	19
(b) 1	41	28
(c) 2	58	39
(d) 3	12	8
(e) 4	8	6
Total	147	100

The economic profile of the families in Table 8 indicates a poor or marginalized status for majority of the families. 95 (68%) boys reported that the monthly income of their family was extremely insufficient. Out of these, 30 boys came from homes where the father was either dead or missing. 24 boys stated that their father was either unemployed or too old to work or suffered from some kind of chronic illness.

Table 8. Monthly Income of the Family

Income (per month) (in Rs.)	Numbers	Percentage
(a) No income	77	52
(i) Father absent or dead (30)		
(ii) Father unemployed or too old of sick (24)		
(iii) Fathers mostly stays away from home (23)		
(b) Insufficient	18	12
(c) Less than 500	19	13
(d) 500-800	26	18
(e) Don't know	7	5
Total	147	100

23 boys reported that their fathers mostly stayed away from home either because of his work or some unspecified reasons and the family income under such conditions was inadequate. 19 (13%) boys belonged to families with a monthly income of less than Rs. 500 while only 26 (18%) boys came from families earning between Rs. 500- 800 per month. Seven (5%) boys could not provide information on their family's monthly income.

In majority of the cases, the father is the only earning member in the family. In 30 (20%) families, mothers were also found earning and in most of these situations, the fathers were unemployed or the homes were without fathers. The mothers were mostly working on unstable jobs or on daily wage basis. These included: working in fields, breaking stones, selling small items, cleaning soda bottles, stitching clothes and making bangles (Table 9). In 64 (44%) families elder brother of the boys were also earning and supplementing the family income.

Table 9. Occupation of the Mother

(N= 147)

Occupation	Number	Percentage
1. Working :	30	20
(a) Works in the field (6)		
(b) Domestic servant (1)		
(c) Construction Labourer (3)		
(d) Grass cutter (1)		
(e) Vendor (13)		
(f) Runs a tea stall (1)		
(g) Washes soda bottles (1)		
(h) Makes jaggery sweets (1)		
(i) Stitches clothes (2)		

(j) Makes bangles (1)

	Numbers	Percentage
2. Housewife	88	60
3. Not applicable	29	20
Total	147	100

An analysis of the occupation of the fathers as shown in Table 10 revealed that majority of them were employed in the unorganized sector and in low paying occupations, e.g. farm labourer, construction labourer, cart puller and vendor. The income of families in such cases tended to be inconsistent and mostly insufficient. The data reveals that majority of the parents worked as unskilled or casual workers.

Table 10. Occupation of the Father

(N=147)

Occupation	Numbers	Percentage
1. (a) Farmer (owns land) (6)		
(b) Farm Labourer (18)		
(c) Construction Labourer (11)		
(d) Vendor (11)		
(e) Shopkeeper/ Grocer (7)		
(f) Vehicle driver (12) (Tonga/Rikshaw/Truck/Bus/Cartpuller		
(g) Carpenter (4)		
(h) Mason (4)		
(i) Cobbler (3)		
(j) Barber (3)		
(k) Butcher (2)		

(l) Mechanic (2)

(m) Rolls bidis (2)

(n) Potter (2)

(o) Works in a tannery (1)

(p) Works in a factory (1)

(q) Peon (in a school) (1)

(r) Parcel coolie (tailor also) (1)

(s) Watchmen (1)

(t) Painter (Paints hoardings) (1)

	93	63
2. Not Applicable		
(a) Father dead/ missing	30	21
(b) Unemployed	24	16
Total	147	100

Table 8 shows 108 (73%) families had an extremely insufficient monthly income. 98 (67%) boys reported that their families had taken debts. Common reasons for taking debts were: ceremonial occasions like a marriage or a sudden illness in the family. The economic status of the family is often considered a causative factor of various social and individual problems faced by the family. In studies of the families of street children, it has been found that majority of the families are poor and keeping in mind the average size of the family, the economic hardships become more severe (Rane, A. & Shroff, N. 1990)

Data also revealed that literacy levels of both the parents (Table 11a & 11b) and children (Table 12) in the sample were low. 69 (47%) fathers and 63 (43%) mothers could neither read nor write. Of the total 147 boys in the sample only 69 (47%) boys had attended school while the remaining 78 (53%) had never gone to

Table 11(a). Educational Level of the Father

(N=147)

Educational level	Number	Percentage
(a) Primary pass	18	12
(b) Secondary pass	2	1
(c) Can read and write	17	12
(d) Illiterate	69	47
(e) Don't know	11	7
(f) Not applicable	30	21
Total	147	100

Table 11 (b). Educational Level of the Mother

(N = 147)

Educational level	Numbers	Percentage
(a) Primary Pass	3	2
(b) Can read and write	9	6
(c) Illiterate	63	43
(d) Don't know	43	29
(e) Not applicable	29	20
Total	147	100

school. Of those who had attended school., 16 (11%) had studied up to class II, 11 (7%) till class III, 19 (13%) till class V (Table 12). A few Muslim children were able to read and/ or write Urdu. They had attended classes in a "Madrasa" (school for Muslim children). A study of street children of Indore indicates that only 10% of the total 300 children sampled in the study had studied up to middle school, 24% of them had their education up to middle school, 24% of them had their education up to the primary level and less than 1% of the children had reached the higher secondary level. A large majority (65%) of them was illiterate (Philips, W.S.K., 1989).

Table 12. Educational Level of the Child

(N=147)

Educational level	Numbers	Percentage
(a) Never been to school	78	53
(b) Studied till class I	16	11
(c) Studied till class II	21	14
(d) Studied till class III	11	7
(e) Studied till class IV	19	13
(f) Studied till class V	2	·1
Total	147	100

The boys in the sample who had attended school gave different reasons for dropping out of school (Table 13). These included: financial difficulties at home, unwillingness on the part of the parent(s) to send the child to school, excess of work at home with no time to go to school, and in few cases the child's own disinterest or failure at school. Majority of the boys who dropped out of school reported that their parents preferred that the boys should work and earn rather than attend school.

Table 13. Reason for not Attending School or Dropping out
                                                    (N=147)

Reasons		Numbers	Percentage
(a)	Poverty	21	14
(b)	Parents against sending the child to school	28	19
(c)	Excess work at home	14	10
(d)	Run away from home	31	21
(e)	Dislike for school/failure/ illtreatment at school	8	6
(f)	Combinations:		
	(i) b & c	13	9
	(ii) a & b	12	8
(g)	Not applicable (complete orphans)	20	13
Total		147	100

High rate of illiteracy among street children can be attributed to a number of factors:

(a) Majority of the parents were illiterate and they did not consider sending their children to school as important;

(b) The children stated that their parents believed that education does not guarantee employment and that the children of the poor should work rather than attend schools that prepare them for "service" or white- collar occupation;

(c) Very few chidren in the sample were attending school when they were staying at home. Having left their homes, they also had to discontinue their studies.

A look at the literacy rates by age in India shows that the number of illiterates has been increasing and the figure has grown from 222.5 million in 1901 to 424.3 million in 1981.

Chart 9
India Literacy Rates 1951-2001

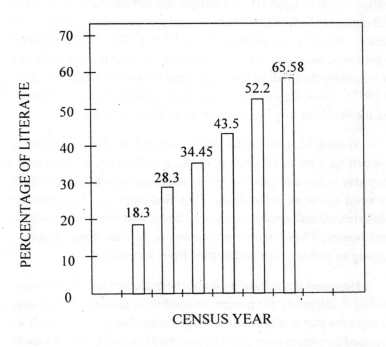

The literacy rates for the country as a whole increased from 18.33 percent in 1951 to 65.38 percent in 2001 (Chart 9). The literacy rate recorded an increase of 13.17 percent from 1991 to 2001, the highest increase in any one decade. The National Literacy Mission (NLM) set up in 1988, seeks to achieve full literacy, i.e. a sustainable threshold level of 75 percent literacy by the end of the year 2005 by imparting functional literacy to the non-literates in literacy to the non-literates in the 15-35 age groups (census of India, 2001).

Regarding the level of education among the child population in India, the 1981 census reported that 82.2 million of India's 158.8 million children aged six to fourteen did not attend school. Only 52.2 million of India's 123.7 million rural children ages six to fourteen were in school (34.4 million boys, 17.8 million girls). Official government estimates also indicate that 60% of children drop out the school by class five and only 23% reach eighth standard (Weiner, M.1991). These figures reflect the poor school attendance figures and the resultant low literacy rate of children in India.

Weiner, M.(1991) states that " less than half of India's children between ages six and fourteen , i.e. 82.2 million are not in school. They stay at home to care for cattle , tend younger children, collect firewood and work in the fields. They find employment in cottage industries, tea stalls, restaurants, or as household workers in middle-class homes. They become prostitutes or live as street children, begging or picking rags and bottles from for resale".

He argues that education should be made free and compulsory, making it obligatory for parents to send their children to schools. He believes that if education is made compulsory it will result in increased enrolment rates and reduced child labour figures. "Modern states regard education as legal duty, not merely a right, parents are required to send their children to school, children are required to attend school, and the state is obligated to enforce compulsory education. Compulsory primary education is the policy instrument by which the state effectively removes children from the labour force" (Weiner, M. 1991)

However, the introduction of compulsory education alone cannot be effective in reducing child labour, particularly the incidence of working street children. These children have to work to fend of themselves or their families. They usually do not stay out of school by an act of choice but due to the especially difficult circumstances in which their families survive.

5.   Migration Aspects and Reasons for Leaving Home:

The distribution of boys according to the age at which they left home given in Table 14 indicates that 68 (46%) boys in the age group of 13-14 had left their homes when they were 12 years old, 25 (17 %) had left home at the age of 11 years, and 26 (18%) boys had left home when they were 10 years old. All the boys in the sample had spent at least one year away from home on the streets.

When asked whether they had left home on earlier occasions also, 16 (11%) boys replied in affirmative. All of them said that they were away from home for a few days and then returned back home. They either went to their relative's place or to a different village or town. 8 (5%) boys in the sample had left home with their friends and one of them had come with his elder brother. However, they lost contact with them after sometime or were deserted by them and were staying alone at the time of the study.

Table 14. Distribution of Children According to the Age at which they left home

Current Age (in years)	Age at leaving Home (in years)						Total	Percentage
	Below 9	9	10	11	12	13		
10	2	7	–	–	–	–	9	6
11	–	4	12	–	–	–	16	11
12	–	–	7	16	–	–	23	16
13	–	–	3	4	14	–	21	14
14	–	–	4	5	54	15	78	53
							147	100

The study investigated the factors that isolate children from their families. Based on the data, these factors can be grouped under the following headings: ill treatment and abuse by parents or caretakers or siblings; economic factors in conjunction with experiences of abuse and neglect; desertion of the child due to ill health or death of either or both the parents; excess work at home (especially in cases where the child was working at home) and discords or conflicts in the family (Table 15). An analysis of the above factors revealed that 65 (44%) boys gave more than reason for leaving home. Maltreatment, gross neglect and abuse suffered by the children at home appear with highest frequency as compared to other factors.

Table 15. Reason For Leaving Home

(N=147)

Reasons	Numbers	Percentage
(a) Il treatment by parents and/or stepparent	51	35
(b) Il treatment by siblings	11	8
(c) Il treatment by parents and Poverty	31	21
(d) Asked to leave home by parent and poverty	17	12
(e) Il treatment by parent and family discord	7	5
(f) Poverty and Family discord	5	3
(g) Complete orphans & abandoned by relatives or caretakers	20	13
(h) Combination:		
(i) a & b & Poverty	3	2
(ii) a & failure at school	2	1
Total	147	100

It has generally been assumed that children are on the street because of economic compulsions. In a study of 1,750 street children of Bangalore, poverty or marginalized status of their families was stated as a major reason for the children being on the street (Reddy, N. 1989). In a study by Nangia, P. & Pinto, R. (1988) 700 street children were surveyed and one-fifth were orphans or runaways who were staying alone in Delhi. The main reasons given by these children for living on the street were: poverty (46%), death of either or both parents (18%), ill treatment by family members (18%) and natural calamities (5%).

Srivastava , S. (1963) studied 300 juvenile vagrants and found that large number of the boys came to cities with the hope of getting employment and majority of them belonged to low- income group families. The study revealed that economic circumstances and familial environment were significant factors responsible for the child leaving his home.

Although boys in the sample were largely from poor families, poverty alone cannot explain their continued presence on the street. Despite the fact that 114 (78%) boys stated that the income of their families was insufficient, economic insufficiency was not the main reason as indicated by most of the children for their leaving the home. In majority of the cases ill treatment, serious neglect, cruelty or abuse by parents/ stepparents/ relatives or sibling, severe and harsh disciplinary measures, and lack of loving nurturing and caring relationship with the parents acted as contributory factors that pushed the child out of home.

20 (14%) boys in the sample were complete orphans, i.e. either both the parents were dead or either parent was dead and other had abandoned the child. In such cases, most of the boys were rejected by their relatives or caretakers and asked to fend for themselves. 17 (12%) boys reported that because of economic difficulties their parents, mostly the father, asked the child to leave the home or they were sent away with some relative and made to work. These boys later ran away. Family discords, poverty and failure at school were other reasons for the child running away from home.

Data revealed that the most significant factor in the present study which is responsible for the child leaving his home is the familial environment and social-emotional atmosphere at home, especially with regard to parent-child relationship. Majority or the boys complained of being maltreated and beaten up by their fathers with bamboo sticks, iron or wooden rods, wooden planks, horse whip or any other object which the father could lay his hands on..

Kapil, age 13, was beaten up by his father whenever he refused to work in the tailor's shop where his father had placed him to work. Kapil liked playing marbles with his friends and whenever his father sighted him playing, Kapil was given a severe thrashing. Kapil said that his father was a 'tonga wallah' and used to beat him with the whip meant for the horse. Kapil sobbed as he said, " If I did not go to the shop or went out to play, I was beaten up with a whip. My father threatened me that he would substitute me for the horse in his tonga. I felt hurt and very often I was denied food "

A few boys hated their fathers to such extent that they used abusive words while talking about them. Shankar, age 14, said, "He is a 'bastard'. He beats so badly that he can almost kill someone. I was fed up of being beaten daily, so I ran away".

Most of the boys reported that their fathers were short-tempered and aggressive. Of the total 110 boys who had fathers, 98 (89%) reported excessive drinking by their fathers while four fathers were reportedly addicted to drugs. Most of these boys said that when their father was drunk he beat the child badly and asked him to leave the home. Raju, age 12 said, " My father was always angry with me. He said that I could never do anything in life. He was very-short tempered. When he drinks, he loses his mind. If I wasn't scared of him, I would have returned home".

"The pandemonium caused by a drunken father and routine quarrels between parents help only to cause the disintegration of children's emotional faculties. In addition, the physical punishment of children amounts to child abuse as it obstructs the free and successful expression of their personalities" (Milton, G. 1992)

Most of the boys who were paternal orphans revealed that they were ill treated by their elder brother. Suresh, age 14 said, " My elder brother beat me often. I was accused of stealing but I had not committed the theft. My brother beat me badly and asked me to leave home. If my brother loved me, I would have never left home".

Children without one or both parents and children with

stepparent complained of excess work at home, differential treatment
meted out to them by the stepparent and obvious rejection or hostility
towards the child. Common forms of maltreatment or punishment
suffered at home included: denial of food and being thrown out of
home (Table 16). As the table indicates, 91 (62%) boys often faced
various forms of physical punishments or abuse, 9 (6%) were denied
food and 22 (15%) boys reported being punished in both the above
ways.

Table 16. Punishment Given to Children

(N=147)

Form of Punishment	Numbers	Percentage
(a) Physical punishment	91	62
(b) Denial of food	9	6
(c) Thrown out of home	7	5
(d) Combination:a & b	22	15
(e) No punishment	18	12
Total	147	100

Apart from being ill treated and punished at home, most of
the boys in the sample also reported lack of warm and loving
relationship with their parents, mostly the father (A detailed analysis
of the parent- child relationship is included later in the section on
Development Deprivation Interview schedule). Parents were not
able to provide a structured, nurturing environment for children. It
is not only the presence of painful punishment that affected the
child but also the lack of a caring, loving relationship with the
parents. Expressions of love and concern by the parents, mostly
the father, for the child were reported to be absent or rare.

In such circumstances of growing up in abusive and neglectful
families, it is not only the experience of being maltreated or punished

but also the inability of the child in getting protection, care and love which loosens the family bonds and makes the child more vulnerable. Such experiences of emotional abuse and lack of empathic understanding along with experiences of painful injury of punishment are determining factors in the phenomenon of children taking to the streets. Among the children interviewed, very few mentioned having positive family environments and bonding. This somewhat low finding was not surprising when one considers that the very reason many street children are out in the streets is their desire to escape their dysfunctional or abusive families

On the basis of data collected in the study, the characteristics frequently found and seeming to contribute to children's problem with their parents and giving rise to an increasing number of street children include: unhappy or violent childhood, regular and/or severe beatings, poor relationship with parents, maltreatment or discrimination by stepparent and family's social and economic circumstances.

In identifying the factors responsible for giving rise to the problem of street children, a few studies emphasize that the dynamics of the family play a crucial role. Bassuk, E.; Rubin, L. & Alison, L. (1986) in their study on homeless children in Philadelphia suggest that, "In addition to external factors, psychosocial factors, particularly family breakdown, play an important role in giving rise to homeless children. There can be little doubt that the constellation of economics, subsistence living, family breakdown, psychosocial deprivation and impoverished self-esteem contribute to the downward cycle of poverty, disruption, stress and violence in the family".

Similar views have been expressed by Agnelli, S. (1986), "All the children on the street can be described as 'victims of the crisis of the family'. This can be attributed at the macro-level to factors like: breakdown of family structure and traditional values, economic deterioration (unemployment or underemployment), and massive immigration while at the micro-level, the child is on the street, typically, because of breakdown in family bonds and relations".

A study by the Child in Need Institute, Calcutta showed that there were around 250 runaway children station and most of them had runaway because they were tortured at home or they belonged to single- parent families which could not support them (cited in Mohan, S. 1990). D'Lima, H. & Gosalia, R. (1989) in their study on street children in Bombay found that the most important factor that influences the decision of the child to leave home is the problems faced in the family due to conflicts and the absence of a supportive and caring parent. The limited or scanty evidence that exists in literature regarding street children and findings of the present study show that majority of the boys were living in a punitive and often hostile environment with poor parent- child relationship.

The time spent by children on the streets showed that 71 (48%) boys had been living on the streets for two years; 64(44%) boys for one year; 8 (5%) boys for three years and 4 (3%) boys had spent four years living on the streets (Table 17). All the boys in the sample had not gone back home during this interval and none of them had any contacts or links with their families.

Table 17. Time Spent Living on the Streets (age wise)

Age (in years)	Time spent on the streets (in years)				Total
	1	2	3	4	
(i) 10	7	2	–	–	9
(ii) 11	12	4	–	–	16
(iii) 12	16	7	–	–	23
(iv) 13	14	4	3	–	21
(v) 14	15	54	5	4	78
Total	64	71	8	4	147
Percentage	44	48	5	3	100

After leaving their homes, only 12(8%) out of 147 boys had come straight to Delhi. 23 (15%) boys had been to one other city before coming to Delhi, 36 (25%) had been two other cities, 41 (28%) had visited three different places and 35 (24%) boys had been to as many as four cities while living on the streets (Table 18).

Table 18. Places Visited While Living on the Streets

(N=147)

Number of places visited		Number of boys	Percentage
(a)	None	12	8
(b)	One	23	15
(c)	Two	36	25
(d)	Three	41	28
(e)	Four	35	24
	Total	147	100

142 (97%) boys had been staying in Delhi for at least one year; only 5(3%) boys had spent less than a year in Delhi. Earlier they had been living in Bombay. This reflects the highly mobile and unstable character of the lives of these children. Most children reported that they moved out of Delhi during the winter as they found the weather here unbearable. They often went to Bombay during this time. Considering the fact that the boys possessed extremely inadequate clothes and slept in the open, the children's move is understandable.

While living in other towns or cities most of the boys were engaged in the following occupations: working in a 'dhaba' or tea stall, ragpicking, working as porter, shoe shining, working in a garage, selling small items on bus stands or railway station. A few street children reported working at marriage parties in Bombay. They used to help in the preparation of food or assist in catering service. This was called 'vadi' work in Bombay. The boys were able to earn about Rs. 15-20 on each occasion in addition to the leftovers which were doled out to them.

6. Work-life of the children:

The following section on work-life of street children includes data on various aspects of their work and the conditions in which they worked, including: the kind of work they were engaged in, duration of work; rest-time, their earnings and savings (if any) and most important, the problems they faced while working.

91 (62%) boys in the sample were working while they stayed at home. In majority of these cases either the father was unemployed, unable to work or away from home most of the time. Most of the children were working in the informal sector being engaged in occupations like: working in the fields, working on shops as an apprentice, working in a beedi/ carpet industry or selling items.

The number of working street children in India is on the rise. Though the estimates of working children vary greatly in India, studies clearly show that these numbers are increasing both in terms of absolute numbers and as a proportion to the total workforce. According to the Asian Labour Monitor, 1990, every third household in India has a working child. It also reveals that in the age group of 5-15 years, every fourth child is employed, 20% of all children in the age group of 10-14 years are employed in one form or the other, and over 20% of the Gross National Product of India is contributed by working children (cited in The Lawyers, Aug.1988)

A number of surveys and studies have shown that most of the street children are working either to support their families or themselves (Nangia, P. 1988; D'Lima, H. & Gosalia, R. 1990; Philips, W.S.K. 1989; Agnelli, S. 1986) Working street children are especially visible on the urban streets mainly in loosely organized economic activities and their work takes many forms. The 1993 Human Development Report of the United Nations Development Programme (UNDP) states that, "Most of the street children are forced to earn their livelihood on the streets in order to survive- collecting rags, shining shoes, selling newspaper, and scavenging on rubbish dumps" (The Hindustan Times, May 22, 1993).

Street children have become an integral part of the urban poor. They are among those thousand of people who labour in the streets at what have often been called 'marginal occupations'. The work of street child takes many forms. Felsman, J.K. (1981) reports in his study on Colombian street children, "In Cali, some waifs (street children) assist the estimated 5,000 ragpickers who pull their carts through the streets, seeking out anything collectable: cloth, cardboard, glass, plastic, wood, etc. Some capital or backing is required for the shoeshine boys as well as for those who sell gum, cigarettes, and newspaper and lottery tickets. Other forms of work include guarding parked cars, cleaning car windshields at a stoplight, or carrying goods in a market place".

After leaving their home and while living on the streets, the boys in the sample had been involved in various kinds of work like: working in a 'dhaba' or teastall, cleaning and guarding parked cars, ragpicking, shoeshine, selling popcorn, peanuts or balloons on the station, pulling a rickshaw, working in a garage as a cleaner and coolie-work. Prior to their present work as a porter, the most common form of occupation found among the boys while living on the street was ragpicking.

97 (66%) boys reported having engaged in ragpicking at some point during their stay on the station. A significant majority of 123 (84%) boys disliked working as ragpicker. It was viewed as a dirty job with little respectability as Vishnu, age 13, remarked, "Rag picking is easy and more lucrative but it is not a respectable job". Another child said, "I don't like ragpicking, it's not a respectable job, others call you a 'kabaadi'(scavenger). As the children grew older, lesser number of them was found to engage in ragpicking. Since children were highly mobile, the nature of their work was unstable and inconsistent. Usually, when they moved from one city to another, they changed their previous occupation also. Other reasons for leaving their previous occupation were: ill treatment

and non-payment of their full wages by the employers (especially when boys were working in a restaurant or garage), excess work without any time for relaxation; disinterest in the work itself and desire to earn more money.

All the boys in the sample were working as unlicensed porters at the New Delhi Railway Station. The New Delhi Railway Station, Paharganj (a main commercial area lined with small restaurants and shops selling different kinds of items) and a few movie houses in the nearby Connaught Place represent the main areas of location where street children were found in large numbers.

Regarding their work of carrying luggage at the station, during the time of study, most of the boys stated that when they arrived on the station they saw other boys working as porters and they also decided to do the same. Other reasons for taking up this work were: firstly, it required no investment to start this work, for e.g. in order to work as shoeshine boy, the child needed to buy a polishing kit which costs between Rs. 50-75 or for selling small items (balloons etc.) or eatables (popcorn or peanuts) on the station the child required to have some money to buy the things. But their work as a porter did not necessitate any such expenditure.

Secondly, most of the boys who had the experience of working in a 'dhaba'(small eating joint), tea stall or restaurant had often been ill treated by their employers and/or co-workers and were denied their full wages. They also complained of being made to work for long hours till late night without any rest interval. These boys thus preferred working as a porter as they were able to avoid these problems. While working as porters they also had the discretion of working when and for how long they wanted to.

For majority of the children who are migrants from other parts of the country, railway stations are their first entrance into a city. Faced with a new and unknown environment, no shelter, and no means of income, children stay in and around the railway station because it is covered shelter, it is perceived as "safe," there are other children there, and they can immediately began earning money as self-employed, unskilled laborers, like railway porters. In this respect, the railway station, especially for unaccompanied migrant or abandoned children, represents an area where they can immediately begin to meet their survival needs.

As stated earlier, all the boys in the sample were working as unlicensed porters and according to the Child Labour (Prohibition & Regulation) Act, 2000, their work is unlawful. Part II, Section 3 of the Act states that 'no child shall be employed or permitted to work in any of the occupations set forth in Part A of the schedule, i.e. any occupation connected with-

1. Transport of passengers, goods or mails by railway;

2. Cinder picking, clearing of an ash pit or building operation in the railway premises;

3. Work in catering establishment at a railway station, involving the movement of a vendor or any other employee of the establishment from one platform to another or into/ out of a moving train;

4. Work relating to the construction of a railway station or with any work where such work is done in close proximity to or between the railway lines;

5. A port authority within the limits of any port'.

Thus, according to the Act, the work that children in the sample were doing can be labeled as 'hazardous' and Part A of the Act forbids the employment of children in this occupation. Further on, Article 24 of the Indian Constitution also prohibits the employment of children in hazardous employment. But despite these provisions most of the street children still work in such occupations.

Since Independence, the Government of India has advocated ending child labour and establishing compulsory, universal, primary education for all children upto the age of 14. The Indian constitution formulated in 1950 declared that "the State shall endeavor to provide, within a period of ten years from the commencement of this constitution, for free and compulsory education for all children until they complete the age of 14 years". (Constitution of Indian, Article 45). The goal was reaffirmed by successive central governments, by the Planning Commission Parliament and state governments.

Legislation restricting the employment of children in mines and factories was introduced early in the century. The Indian constitution contains a number of provisions intended to protect children, including a categorical ban that declares that "no child below the age of 14 years shall be employed to work in any factory or mine or engaged in any other hazardous employment" (Article 24). However, figures on working children are indicative of the government's failure to deal with the problem. It also indicates several inadequacies in the existing administrative setup for the implementation of various laws concerning working children.

In order to gather information about their daily work-life as a porter, the boys were asked to describe their general daily routine and activities. The response obtained in this area did not show much variation. The task of working as a porter involved carrying luggage or other items on their heads and also shouldering one or two bags. The boys carried luggage from outside the station to the desired platform and also from the train compartment or platform to areas outside the station, mainly Paharganj or Ajmeri Gate. While working the children had to climb up and down the stairs of the station bridge with the load placed on their heads. The children were also observed moving in and out of a running train while working.

Working hours of children varied with respect to the time of the day. There were no strictly defined or fixed hours of work and it depended on the arrival and departure of the trains . Most of the boys knew the names of the trains and their timings by heart and they worked accordingly. They were also aware of the change in the train timings in cases of delay of arrival or departure. Usually, it was a little before the arrival or departure of the trains that children could be found on the platform of the station otherwise they mostly sat in the park next to the station, outside the station on the pavement or near the parking places.

The number of hours children worked was also found to be flexible. 86 (59%) boys reported working 5-7 hours on average daily while 37 (25%) boys worked for 7-9 hours a day. 24 (16%) boys said they worked on average for more than 9 hours daily (Table 19). The distribution of hours of work was found to be concentrated during peak hours, i.e. from 5 a.m. to 2 p.m. and 7 p.m. to 11 p.m.

Table 19. Number Of Working Hours (per day)

(N=147)

Hours	Number of Children	Percentage
(a) 5-7	86	59
(b) 7-9	37	25
(c) More than 9	24	16
Total	147	100

With specific reference to the work of children as a porter, the number of hours they work does not necessarily imply that the child is busy carrying luggage during that time. It also involves finding a passenger who allows them to carry their baggage while at the same time escaping police vigilance. This was time- consuming since it involved moving from one platform to another or moving outside the station. Children were also found following passengers requesting them to carry their luggage. This entire exercise of finding a passenger who let them carry his luggage was quite time-consuming, difficult and tiring part of their work. Some boys stated that sometimes they were faced with a situation when they were unable to find enough work on a single day.

A correlation between the number of hours the child worked and the age of the child (Table 20) revealed that of the total 86 boys who worked 5-7 hours on the average daily, 73(85%) of them were 14 years old. In the category of children working 7-9 hours daily, the number of younger boys, i.e. boys in the age group of 10-12 years, was found to be high. 25 (67%) of the total 37 boys working 7-9 hours daily were between 11-12 years of age. Of the total 24 boys working more than 9 hours a day, 21 (88%) boys were between 10-12 years of age.

Table 20. Age Wise Distribution of Hours of Work

Working hours (perday)	Age of children (in years)					Total
	10	11	12	13	14	
(a) 5-7	—	—	2(2%)	11(13%)	73(85%)	86
(b) 7-9	—	12 (32%)	13(35%)	7(19%)	5(14%)	37
(c) More than 9	9(38%)	4 (17%)	8(33%)	3(12%)	—	24
						147

The above analysis shows that younger boys in the sample were, on average, working for longer duration as compared to their older counterparts.

This can be attributed to the comparatively easy availability of work for older boys since they looked stronger and well-built and the passengers also felt that they were capable of lifting their luggage without the danger of damaging it. Younger boys, mainly because of their small body frame, were not trusted and seemed to be incapable of carrying a heavy load.

Children in the age group of 13-14 years stated that they were able to carry a load of 25-30 kg. where as 10-12 year olds preferred carrying less heavier luggage. The younger boys were selective while choosing passengers as they preferred single passengers with fewer luggages both with respect to the weight and the number of items involved. This restricted their chances of getting work and their earnings too. In addition, it also prolonged their working hours.

Data on daily average earnings of the boys (Table 21) shows that 61 (41%) boys in the sample earned between Rs. 50-60 daily, 55 (37%) boys earned between Rs. 30-40 daily while 26 (18%) of the total 147 boys in the sample earned between Rs. 10-20 daily. The daily earnings of the boys can also be correlated with their age (Table 21). All the 9 (6%) ten years old boys in the sample reported earning between Rs. 10-20 daily.

Table 21. Age Wise Daily Average Earnings of the Children

(N = 147)

Daily earning (in Rs.)	Age of children (in years)					Total	Percentage
	10	11	12	13	14		
(a) 10–20	9	7	3	4	3	26	18
(b) 30–40	–	9	19	14	13	55	37
(c) 50–60	–	–	1	3	57	61	41
(d) Above 60	–	–	–	–	5	5	4
Total	9	16	23	21	78	147	100

Of the total 55 (37%) boys earning between Rs.20-30 only 9 boys were 11 years old, 19 were 12 years old and 27 boys were in age group of 13-14 years. In the group of children earning between Rs. 30-40 daily, no child was less than 12 years of age.

Out of the total 61 boys earning Rs. 30-40 daily, 57 boys were 14 years old and only 4 boys were between 12-13 years of age. All the 5 boys who reported earning more than Rs.40 a day, on average, were 14 years old. The above data shows children in the age group of 13-14 years on average earn more than children who are 10-12 years old. Younger boys were working for longer hours as compared to older boys yet the income of the older boys was found higher. This is explainable in terms of the easy availability of work to older boys and the greater number of trips made by them. Younger boys in the sample seemed to be in a disadvantaged position as compared to older boys in terms of their access to opportunities to work, their daily earnings and number of hours spent at work.

A general observation regarding the work- life of children in the sample was that the occupational categories were not well-defined and consistent over a period of time. This is because of the fact that children changed their occupation very frequently or they might be engaged in two different economically gainful activities at a given point of time.

28 (19%) boys in the sample reported being frequently engaged in another occupation in addition to their work as a porter at the New Delhi Railway Station at the time they were interviewed. All these boys were 13-14 years old and were earning more than Rs. 50/- daily. Some of them worked as a porter during day time and at night they worked as a helper in a tea stall, 'dhaba' or restaurant where they washed utensils or served the customers. A few of them reported working for tea stall owners or tea-sellers on the station serving tea to the passengers, collecting empty glasses and money for the stall owner. One boy was working in a juice shop in Paharganj from 4 p.m. to 7 p.m. apart from working as a porter in the morning. Two boys reported that they worked at night for marriage parties carrying petromax lamps on their shoulders or head. This kind of work was reported to be seasonal and fluctuating.

Surinder Singh, age 14, from Gorakhpur, worked as a porter in the mornings and also worked for a marriage party at night whenever such work was available. He used to go to the band-shop in the evening and inquire if his services were needed that they. He was paid Rs. 50-60 for every trip and if the marriage party had to travel long distance he was paid more money. His work involved carrying petromax lamp on his head or shoulder.

The child stated that in addition to his wages he also received free food. Sometimes he was also able to collect coins which were thrown when people dance in a marriage party. He said, "I like working in marriage parties, everyone around is happy, there's music and fun and I also feel happy".

However, it was found that on such occasions the boys were not able to get enough sleep and they complained of frequent headaches. They also said that they slept during the day but the noise, strong lights and activity on the station made it difficult for them to sleep. Vinod Kumar, 14 years old from Bhagalpur, Bihar, worked on a tea stall from 8 p.m. to 5 a.m. Then he slept for a few hours and resumed his work as a porter later in the day. He said, " I will stop working on the tea-stall. My eyes and head ache as I have to keep awake the whole night". His work on the tea stall fetched him Rs. 20-30 a day. The boy reported saving his earning with the tea stall owner.

Ahmed, age 14, from Aligarh, sometimes borrowed a shoe-shining kit from his friend who worked as a shoeshine boy on the station. He used to polish shoes in the evenings and was also carrying luggage on the station during the day. Another boy Nawal, age 14, from Bhagalpur, Bihar worked on a juice shop near the station from 2 p.m. to 5p.m. in addition to lifting luggage on the station. Most of the boys who were engaged in another kind of occupation in addition to their work as a porter reported that they wanted to earn more money and this was responsible for their being engaged in more than one job at the same time. As Nawal said, "I don't get enough money working on the station. If you have to earn more, you have to do some other work".

Some boys had devised other ways of making more money. While working as porters on the station they offered passengers help if they wanted to be taken to a lodge or a hotel. These boys were aware of different hotels or lodges in the vicinity of the station and also their tariff charges. When they escorted the passengers to a hotel or lodge. the boys always asked more money for their services.

In addition to this they were also able to gain tips from the hotel or lodge manager. Dhanbahadur, age 14, from Bhutol, Nepal, said, "It is more profitable if I find a passenger who wants to be taken to a hotel. I can earn around Rs. 50 and the hotel manager also gives me money".

Children who were able to earn more than Rs. 30/- a day had a novel way of adding to their income. They used to lend money to other children in need of money and took back more than what they had lent, for e.g. if a child borrowed Rs. 5/- he was made to pay back Rs. 8 or 10/-.

Savings:

The possession of personal belongings is a basic element of the right to privacy and essential to the psychological well-being of the child. All the boys had no personal stuff since they were homeless and without any space of their own where they could keep their things safely including the money they saved. Out of the total 147 boys, only 24 (16%) of them were able to save their earnings. These boys kept their money with their friends or with the people they knew like: a shopkeeper or tea stall owner. They said that the possibility of being cheated and losing their money was always there. Most of the boys said that the saved money was used when the child was sick and needed medical attention or when he was unable to earn money on a particular day. The amount of money boys were able to save on a single day ranged from Rs. 10 to 15/-.

A study of street children of Bombay also showed that out of the 2,169 sampled street children, 86% of them were unable to save any money, while only 14% saved money. They were able to save amounts ranging from Rs. 10 to Rs. 100. They saved money by keeping it with people in whom they had confidence and with whom they were in daily contact such as their employers or shop-owners (D'Lima, H. & Gosalia, R. 1990)

A few boys in the study (16%) reported that they were unable to earn enough money so that they could save 123 (84%) boys reported being unable to save money though most of them said that they were able to earn enough. The main problem faced by them was the absence of a reliable place or person in whose custody the saved money could be kept. Because of this most of the boys reported spending all their day's earnings before they slept at night. Many boys reported instances when their friends who slept with or near them at night, picked their pocket and even took away their belongings including things like: shoes or chappals, towels, etc.

24 (16%) boys who were saving money were not extending any financial help to their families. Though a few of them (18%) revealed that they were interested in sending part of their income home for their mothers but they avoided doing this because of reasons like:

(a) fear of how their fathers would react to it;

(b) they did not want their family members to know their whereabouts; and

(c) they were unaware of the procedure involved in sending money by post.

As Munnababu, age 14, from Darbangha, Bihar said, "I want to send money for my mother but I am afraid of my father. He will beat my mother and I don't want him to know my whereabouts".

When asked whether they wanted to earn more money, 136 (93%) boys replied in affirmative while the rest 11 (7%) were satisfied with their present earnings. Dendayal, age 14, from Balia, U.P. said, "I don't want more money as there is always the danger of it being stolen. I cannot save it also".

Observations on various aspects of the work-life of street children show that those who live without their families have a pattern of spending their total earnings on the same day because they are often not able to entrust their saving to anyone's custody. The city life offers them enough opportunities of spending money on entertainment in the form of movies, gambling and drugs. Children most often engage themselves in these activities in the company of peer group or sometimes under pressure from grown ups. Gradually, the children get into the habit of gambling, smoking and taking drugs and this reportedly gives rise to various anti-social activities.

7.   Problems faced while working on the stations-

Studies show majority of the street children are working and almost half of them are self-employed as coolies (porters), ragpickers, hawkers, shoeshine boys and are working in other occupations. Almost one- third of street children are working in shops and establishments. These children are not only deprived of their basic rights to health and nutrition, shelter, education and training and recreation but they also have to struggle for survival on a day- to-day basis (Rane, A. & shroff, N. 1990). The kinds of problems they face vary with their age, and the nature of their work but they almost always reflect exploitation, violence and insecurity of street life. "For most of them , life is a hard, unending grind for a pathetically meager return" (Agnelli, S. 1986).

This section of the study includes information on the problems children in the sample faced while working and living on the station. All the boys were working as unlicensed porters. On the basis of observations made during the study, persons working on the station as porters can be grouped in three categories : licensed porters, unlicensed adult porters and unlicensed child porters.

Except for the licensed porters, the work of other two groups of porters is considered illegal by the railway officials and police. Children working as porters, because of their immaturity, seem to be most vulnerable, both physically and psychologically. The government officials and adult porters objected to their working on the station.

Street Children who are self- employed as porters, vendors and shoeshine boys complained of harassment by the police and municipal authorities because they do not have license to work

The police were reported to conduct raids on the station to apprehend children working on the station. Street children reported being subjected to great harassment by the police and municipal authorities. 'Children who live with their families experience much less harassment than those who live alone and have to fend for themselves'(D'Lima, H. & Gosalia, R. 1990)

a) Role of the Police:

31 (21%) of the total 147 boys had been apprehended by the police at some point during their stay on the streets. On days when these 'raids' or search were conducted, the boys avoided working on the station. They mostly stayed outside the station premises on such occasions. Boys who escaped being caught during the raid informed others about it. In this way the word spread and other boys kept away from the station at that time or even for that whole day.

Only a few boys reported returning to the station at night to work for a few hours. Most of the children who had been caught by the police and were later released were ignorant of the reasons why they were caught. A few boys stated that they were caught by the police under charges of vagrancy, gambling or engaging in street brawls or due to some theft on the station. While working on the station the boys were harassed and exploited both by the police and railway officials. They were beaten up by the police when found working on the station. Most of the boys reported that they were forced to part with their earnings or else face the danger of being locked up. Reports of victimization and extortion by the police were frequent, and policemen on the beat were known to relieve street children of their money.

The most common complaint of street children living without families in Bombay was that they were rounded up by the police and put in a lock-up for 2-3 days merely on suspicion. This, they believed, was done to 'fill the quota' which the police are expected to do (D' Lima, H. & Gosalia, R. 1990). Studies by Nangia, P.

(1988) and D' Lima, H. & Gosalia, R. (1990) have also found that policemen extracted money from street children who were living alone. Boys were reported to give 'hafta' (bribe) to them to avoid harassment.

Children in the study also faced extortion by the police and this was another reason why most of the boys were in the habit of spending their earnings on movies or gambling rather than keeping it with them and have it forcibly taken away by the policemen later. A few boys felt that it was better to carry some money in their pockets all the time so that when in danger of being caught by the police, they could bribe them and escape his beatings and harassment.

In a study of street children of Bombay, the children living alone at the railway station revealed that the police themselves were involved in the unlawful activity of selling railway tickets. "They have an understanding with some children who buy and resell tickets at a premium. These children give the police their 'cut' or share. Since these children are in stiff competition with others, the best way of eliminating the others is to frame an offence against these children who do not have any understanding with the police. Either the child bribes the police or he gets locked up and beaten" (D' Lima, H. & Gosalia, R. 1990).

The boys in the sample also faced problems at night when the policemen woke them up and asked them to leave the station. Some children had discovered a place on the roof top of platform No.1 on the station where they could climb easily. This place was rarely checked by the police and thus children used it as a hideout for resting. Whenever a child was sick and unable to move swiftly if sighted by the police, he usually took refuge in this place.

During field visits the researcher on several occasions witnessed children being beaten up by the policemen on duty that time. Usually, whenever a child, while roaming on the station saw a policeman around, he either ran away from that platform or tried his best to stay out of the cop's sight. However, when a child failed to notice a policemen coming close to him, he was mostly beaten up by the cop's 'lathi' and forced to leave the station. The child then stayed away from the station for a few hours and returned to work on some other platform, which he considered safe at that time.

When some property (e.g. a bag) belonging to the public was lost/stolen at the station, these children were the first to be suspected. They are rounded up and some even framed under theft charges. To prove that they were not guilty, the children had to do their best to find the culprit and save themselves or escape. Another form of exploitation by the police which the boys in the sample reported was being sent on errands to get tea, snacks, cigarettes, etc. for the policemen. Children disliked doing such favors since it effected their work but they were compelled to do so. The possibility of getting caught by the police was a constant source of fear and the boys lived in an atmosphere fraught with apprehension and insecurity.

All the boys resented being hit and beaten by the police. Most of the boys reasoned that they were not doing anything unlawful or illegal by working on the station. They pointed out that there were other homeless people living on the station who were engaged boot legging, and pick pocketing and they were allowed to carry on their activities mostly because of the patronage provided to them by the police. However, the boys stated that they were earning money through honest ways and thus, they should be allowed to work.

Suresh, age 14, from Railbareli, U.P., who had been hit by a policemen had a swollen face and a bleeding nose remarked in anguish, "These cops beat us often. We earn money through honest ways. They even take away our earnings. Other boys who are drug peddlers are let –off by them after they take bribes from them. If I become a policeman , I will also hit them the way they hit me". Most of the boys reported many instances when the policemen hit them randomly injuring their arms, back or legs. Because of these injuries, the boys stated that they were unable to work for the next few days.

Three policemen were interviewed while they were on duty on the station. The aim was to elicit their views and attitudes towards these children. All three policemen strongly objected to the children working on the station. They also held views that these boys were 'anti social elements' and that they belonged to 'bad' or 'immoral' homes or families. They strongly believed that the only effective way of 'correcting' them was to institutionalize them. One striking observation was that these policemen did not differentiate between 'neglected juveniles' and 'juvenile delinquents'. For them, all these children working on the station were delinquents and were responsible for cases of the fights and theft occuring on the station.

Brutality against street children by the police has been found to take extreme forms in Brazil where street children have been reported to be murdered. A Brazilian security guard in Central Sao Paulo shot dead a 14 year-old boy who was searching for food in a garbage bag left outside a building (Indian Express, Dec. 20, 1993). Many street children in Brazil depend on petty theft to survive. The quickest and easiest way for them to make money is by picking pockets, shop-lifting, burglarizing stores or homes and even committing hold-ups. " In Rio de Janeiro, investigators have identified around 180 death squads which murder street children living on the streets. Some street kids speculate that drug traffickers were also involved. In the last three years, Brazil has become a major cocaine trans-shipment point en route to North America and Europe. A recent investigation by the Rio de Janeiro state legislature found that drug gangs now account for roughly half the child murders in Rio" (Larmer, B. & Margolia, M. 1993).

The role of the police while dealing with street children, particularly those living alone, is clearly a crucial aspect of the problems faced by these children. "In parts of the world where the incidence of street children is highest, police corruption is a regrettable reality, and may be enormously difficult to control when drugs and huge sums of money that go with them are involved" (Agnelli, S. 1986). A more sensitive positive and preventive role for the police has often been advocated while handling street children but nothing much has been done in this context.

b)   Institutionalization-

13 (9%) boys in the study stated that they had been caught and put in an observation or remand home. Of the 31 children who had been caught by the police at some stage during their stay on the station, 21 of them were let-off after being reprimanded and beaten. They were threatened not to work on the station. Seven boys were put in a lock-up for a day or two and released and three boys were sent to an observation home in Delhi Gate and later to a remand home in Alipur. All these three boys reported having runaway from these homes. The boys called these homes, "chiller (lice-infested) home", and "Killer home".

All the boys were scared of being caught and put in these "jails". Boys reported maltreatment and exploitation during their stay in these homes. They complained of physical punishment, not being fed properly, strict and punitive staff and lack of recreational facilities. They reported that they were often made to work in the kitchen and clean the rooms as a form of punishment. They were not provided adequate medical care and had to work even when they were sick.

In a study of 2,169 street children of Bombay, 126 (6%) boys had been affected by the Juvenile Justice System as they were institutionalized for some period of time. 94 of them had been apprehended on charges of vagrancy or on suspicion and 101 boys reported escaping from a government institution while 51 were released by normal procedures (D' Lima, H. & Gosalia, R. 1990).

The study showed that the impressions children formed about their stay in the institution were mostly pessimistic. "The children were mostly negative about the relations with the staff. Their impressions about the program of education were less negative and least negative about basic necessities. This may indicate the relationships with adults are most important to these children and however protective or well-programmed an institution may seek to be, the warmth of relationships is what creates the sense of security" (D' Lima, H. & Gosalia, R. 1990).

The process of street children being institutionalized has been the subject of debate. "The street child mostly not convicted of any crime finds himself in a cold, impersonal, rigid world of concrete corridors, steel railings and walls tipped with broken glass. In addition to roll-calls and cleaning duties, he will have lessons and manual work, but little contact with the outside world. From having been totally free and independent in the street, youngster is restricted on every side" (Agnelli, S. 1986). In addition to uncongenial environment, the humane approach is missing in the government-run homes. Reports by the children of ill treatment and neglect by the staff were frequent. "Staff in these governmental institutions are mostly poorly qualified, underpaid and poorly motivated. Facilities for vocational training are frequently inadequate" (Misra, S. 1988). Under such conditions many children runaway from these homes.

Misra, S. (1988) describes the environment in a typical government institution as, "It is in the nature of such institutions to be impersonal, procedure-bound, often dogged by lack of funds for proper repairs and maintenance, and plagued by the ills of a poorly paid staff. The problems of staff are often insurmountable. Their workload does not encourage quality, motivation or commitment. The limitations of such institutions are severe and correcting them will require substantial funds and a different kind of approach and will. There have been no instances of a street child walking into such an institution of his own accord."

"Loitering alone is good enough for periodic imprisonment and commitment to closed-door establishment" (Agnelli, S. 1986). The street child not convicted of any crime is a 'neglected juvenile' and qualifies for admission into these government-run homes under the Juvenile Justice Act, 2000.

The proceedings under the Juvenile Justice Act, 2000, are intended largely for the care, protection, treatment, development and rehabilitation of both neglected and delinquent juveniles. Under the scheme of the Act, a neglected child includes a socially maladjusted child such as destitute, a vagrant and a runaway child. According to the Act, the term 'neglected juvenile' can be widely interpreted to include:

(I) a child who is found beginning;

(II) or is found without having any home or settled place of abode or any ostensible mean of subsistence and is a destitute whether an orphan or not;

(III) or has a parent or guardian who is unfit to exercise proper care and control over the child;

(IV) or lives in a brothel or with a prostitute or frequently visits any place used for the purpose or prostitution or is found to associate with any prostitute or any other person who leads an immoral or drunken life;

(V) or who is being or is likely to be used or exploited for immoral or illegal purpose.

The Act also stipulates the establishment of:

(a) juvenile homes (for neglected juveniles, Sec. 9, JJ Act);

(b) special homes (for undertrial juveniles, Sec. 10,JJ Act);

(c) observation homes (for undertrial juveniles, Sec. 11, JJ Act);

(d) After care organizations (Sec. 12, JJ Act).

Under no circumstances should the juvenile be kept in a police-station or detained in a jail pending inquiry against him. However, seven boys in the study reported being locked up by the police for a day or two before being released. Street children in Bombay also complained of being rounded up and locked up by the police for two or three days (D'Lima, H. & Gosalia, R. 1990).

The Juvenile Act also provides that as soon as an officer-in-charge of a police station receives information of any neglected child found within the units of his station, he is required to record the information in a book and take such action as he deems fit (Batra, M. 1990) But, unfortunately, most of the police officers are not well- aware of the provisions in the Act.

Singh, S. & Chauhan, B. (1990) reported that "At present, police officers at police stations are ignorant of their various duties and responsibilities which this Act has given them. For e.g. when a visit to a police station was made and inquiry about the book in which entry of the names of neglected juveniles is made, as is required under Sec. 13(12) of the Act, no policemen could tell anything about it because no such book was being maintained . Police-officers at the station were apparently more concerned about heinous offences and for them care of neglected juveniles was not a matter of priority".

In terms of numbers of street children who can be provided accommodation and other facilities in the homes meant for neglected juveniles, the record of these institutions is extremely poor. For e.g. the state of Maharashtra is reported to have the highest number of juvenile homes (47) and special homes (27) on all India basis (Table 22).

Table 22. Numbe of Juvenile Homes/ Observation Homes/ Special Homes/ After Care Institutions, 1991-92

State/ country	Observation Homes	Juvenile Homes	Special Homes	Aftercare Institution	Total
1. Maharashtra	47	71	27		145
2. Delhi	3	10	2	2	17
India	248	210	71	43	572

(*Source :* Annual Report, Ministry of Welfare, Govt. of India, 1991-92)

A number of surveys have estimated that approximately 25,000 children aged between 6 and 18 live alone in the streets of Bombay (Pestonji, M. 1993). These children coming under the purview of neglected juveniles fall in the category of neglected juveniles. Generally speaking, the capacity of a juvenile home is 150-200 children on average. Keeping this in mind, approximately only half of the Bombay's total population of street children, who are 'neglected juveniles' as defined by the Juvenile Justice Act, 1986, can be accommodated in these homes.

A similar situation holds true for the street children of Delhi which has ten juvenile homes. About 500 children are placed in these homes every year (Kantroo, B.L. 1990) while the number of street children living alone in Delhi far exceeds this number. The Juvenile Justice Act has also empowered the state governments to establish 'after-care institutions' for the purpose of taking care of juveniles after they leave these home. After-care services are a follow –up of the institutional services rendered to a child. However, many states lack such institutions and thereby fail to rehabilitate the juveniles.

A proper implementation of the Juvenile Justice Act necessitates the establishment of elaborate infra-structure to provide services to both neglected and delinquent juveniles as they are perceived as distinct categories. Most of these government-run institutions for do not have separate facilities for the two groups namely neglected children and juvenile delinquents. Many states of the country have not even set up separate institutions for neglected children and juvenile delinquents (Batra, M. 1990). The Act, however, has made it compulsory for every state to set up separate institutions and facilities for both neglected and delinquent juveniles.

A report on street children of Colombia revealed "Every year 7000 children under 12 are tried in Colombia courts. Most serve their sentence in jails meant for adults and usually end up as hardened criminals" (Castellanos, A. 1991).A report on street children of Colombia revealed "Everyday year 7000 children under 12 are tried in Colombian courts. Most serve their sentence in jails meant for adults and usually end up as hardened criminals" (Castellanos, A. 1991).

As Agnelli, S. (1986) puts it, "Imagine the catastrophic effects on a 12 year old of being put in the same cell as hard- core criminals. Physical and mental abuse directed towards children by adult inmates and prison guards is both frequent and severe , various types of sexual abuse appear to be among the most prevalent visited upon the children."

Findings of studies of situation of the children lodged in the government-run homes in different countries are likely to point to delays in physical, emotional and intellectual development of the children. The effects of institutionalization on the psychosocial well-being of children have been a topic of humanitarian concern. It is widely acknowledged that most institutions have deleterious effects on children's behaviour and development caused by the "dehumanizing" and "depersonalizing" characteristics of the institutional environment.'

Children who had been institutionalized reported experiences which can be aptly summarized in Townsend's (1962) words, "In the institution people live communally with a minimum of privacy and yet their relationships with each other are slender...Their mobility is restricted, and they have little access to a general society. Their social experiences are limited, and the staff leads a rather separate existence from them".

Children in the study reported that they had to follow an orderly routine and most of the activities they performed were dull, boring and non-creative. They had little opportunity to engage in activities of their choice. The staff in the institution was also reported to be apathetic to children's needs and lacking motivation.

Most governments have gradually begun to realize the severe limitations of such closed-door residential institutions for street children. Efforts are being made in this direction and programmes of 'deinstitutionalization' have started especially in Latin America. The Indian Government has been slow to respond to this urgent need. The main problem is to devise alternatives, such as home-like family units using the S.O.S. villages model. These are more effective, humane and better equipped to deal with the increasing numbers of street children.

c) Harassment by Co-workers:

Boys in the sample also reported harassment and exploitation by both the licensed and unlicensed porters while working and living on the station. In the area of work, the licensed porter or parcel coolie, as they are called, always got the first opportunity to lift the luggage, next being the unlicensed adult porters while the boys in the sample were the last ones to get a chance to work. The licensed porters often intimidated the boys and threatened to get them caught by the police if they interfered with their work. This was primarily due to the fact that licensed porters charged more money while the boys were willing to do the same work for less money.

The licensed porters also made the children run on errands or work for them, e.g. wash their clothes or even massage them while they rested in the park. All the boys in the sample did not like working for them but said they had no choice. Ramaiya, age 12, from Gonda (U.P.) said, "I was having fever and resting here. One parcel coolie came and started kicking me. He asked me to get him a cake of soap from the market. I had to go as I had no choice. We have to work for them otherwise they create problems for us".

Most boys expressed strong dislike for licensed porters. Pyarelal, age 14, from Sultanpur (U.P.) remarked. "We consider a licensed coolie as a dog". Very few boys said that the licensed porters allowed them to work and that they were not afraid of working on the station. Dhanbahadur age 14, from Butol (Nepal) said, "I am neither afraid of the police nor the licensed porters. I earn my own money".

The children in the sample were also harassed by local 'dadas' or gang leaders. These 'dadas' were mostly older boys or street youth, who also worked and lived on the station. These 'dadas' often forcibly took away younger children's earnings. They were mostly seen gambling and the boys in the sample stated that the 'dadas' usually survived on younger children's earnings or by engaging in gambling.

Though it was difficult to gather data on drug abuse among children , most of the boys in the sample reported that the 'dadas' and other older boys used drugs and were often involved in drug-peddling. The boys called them "charasi." (addicts). A working street child is an easy victim for drug-peddlers. These children earn and can afford to spend money on drugs.

"The peddler's modus operandi is to befriend the children when they seem to be feeling low and unhappy. They persuade them to take drugs telling them that it would make them feel better. Slowly the child gets hooked on the drugs. Consumption of drugs makes the child lethargic and so his earning capacity decreases. Ultimately he is forced to peddle drugs to get his daily quota of smack or ganja" (Nangia, P. 1988). The consumption of drugs by street youngsters also serves as a temporary escape from their daily struggle. As a form of addiction, street children have also been found sniffing glue, shoe polish, paint-thinner of cleaning fluid (Agnelli, S. 1986 ; World Health Organization, 1993)

In this section on harassment and exploitation of street children by co-workers, a comparison between the nature of interactions the boys had with the licensed and unlicensed porters or local 'dadas' was attempted. The boys in the sample felt that unlicensed porters or 'dadas' had a comparatively more positive attitude towards them. Though both the unlicensed and licensed porters were reported to harass and exploit them, there were instances, though occasional, when the unlicensed porters helped the boys.

A small number of 18 (12%) boys in the sample were members of gangs which mainly consisted of boys above 16 years of age (Described later in detail in the section on Peer Life). These older boys sometimes worked as unlicensed porters. When the child needed money or had a fight with another child, he turned to these older boys for help. The younger boys also stated that when they were sick and unable to earn, the unlicensed porters or 'dadas' often came to their rescue and provided them money for their meals. They also took the child to a nearby dispensary when he was seriously ill.

A large number of 129 (88%) boys were not affiliated to any gang or group of older boys. In terms of their interactions with both licensed and unlicensed porters, the boys reported more harsh and bitter experience with the former group.

Five licensed porters were interviewed to elicit their attitudes towards the boys working as unlicensed porters on the station. All the five porters interviewed objected to the children working on the station. They believed that these boys cheat the passengers, steal their belongings and runaway with their luggage. They were of the opinion that all the boys living alone and working on the station should be handed over to the police.

All the five licensed porters who were found to be against the children working on the station, were asked, "If the boys do not work, how will they survive?" The five porters unanimously suggested that the boys should go back or be sent back to their families. They blamed the boys for their present state because they had left their homes, as one of them remarked, "These children deserve these hardships since they have left their families. They bring a bad name to their families". Another licensed porter remarked, "These boys are rogue, ruffians and nuisance who bring the city a bad name. They spoil our work also".

The licensed porters perceived both the unlicensed adult porters and boys working as porters as a threat to their work. It created competition and rivalry and the licensed porters were usually at a disadvantage since the unlicensed porters and the boys working as porters were willing to work for less money. The licensed porters charged a minimum of Rs. 30 to 40 while the boys in the sample were ready to carry the same luggage for Rs.15 to 20. However, it was also observed that most of the boys in the sample, especially those aged 12 and less, preferred carrying lighter luggage while the licensed porters, being adults, managed lifting heavy luggage.

The boys preferred carrying less heavy luggage because in situations when they were chased by the policemen and in the danger of being caught while working, they could move faster and swiftly with less weight on their bodies. It was also observed that the passengers usually paid the licensed porters what they demanded while the boys in the sample were often paid less and thereby exploited.

Most of the boys in the sample reported being cheated by the public. 69 (47%) boys complained that they had sometimes faced situations when they were denied their full wages and were paid less than what they had settled for. The boys said that this enraged them but they felt helpless. Except for arguing with the passenger, they were unable to do anything to get their full wages. They were also afraid of seeking police-assistance when faced with such a situation. They mostly had to be content with whatever was given to them.

Very few boys said they protested when not given their full wages as Suresh Kumar, age 14, from Etawah (U.P.) said, "I throw away the money when I am not paid my full wages. I ask the passenger to keep the money. I am not begging for money".

Regarding the opinion of the public towards the boys, most of them felt that society tends to look down upon them. They are considered as thieves, rogues and pick pockets and the attitude towards street children is prejudiced and often harsh (Nangia, P. 1988; D' Lima, H. & Gosalia, R. 1990).

Agnelli, S. (1986) states that, "It would be wrong to generalize and conclude that outright rejection by the public and repression by officialdom were universal. Within the same country, attitudes to street children, partially or totally abandoned, may be very different. In countries, such as Thailand, the former may be considered essentially as no more than hard-working young citizens and the latter as deserving unfortunates. In sub-Saharan Africa and much of Latin America, both public opinion and government reactions are typically much more negative: apart from those working in the most recognized jobs like shoe-shining, the tendency is either not to see them at all or label them forthwith as undesirables who give the city a bad name".

All the boys in the sample were subjected to a stigmatizing public image. They were viewed as dishonest, illiterate and immoral. The effects of living under such stigmatizing conditions on the social-emotional development of these children need investigation.

In order to analyse the work life of the urban working street children and the problems they face at work, the framework given by UNICEF can be used. UNICEF (1988) has pointed out certain indices of child exploitation which can be applied to working street children. These include:

(a) starting full-time work at an early age:

(b) too many hours spent within or outside the family, so that children are unable to attend   school;

(c) work that results in excessive physical, social and psychological strain upon the child;

(d) work in dangerous situations that cause damage to the health and safety of life;

(e) work and life on the streets in unhealthy and dangerous conditions;

(f) work that does not facilitate the social and psychological development of the child; and

(g) Inhibition of a child's self-confidence and self esteem e.g.

as caused by experiences of sexual exploitation or stigmatizing living conditions.

Apart from the deterioration of the child's heath, the separation of the child from the family has a devastating impact, making the working child highly vulnerable (UNICEF, 1988, cited in The Lawyers, 1988)

Applying the above indices to the working situation of children included in the study, it can be concluded that children's work as a porter reflects both their exploitation and struggle for survival. All the boys had started working at an early age and they were working without any support or protection from their families. All the boys were lifting luggage and their work in accordance with their age, was tiring and strenuous.

As has been observed in a WHO (1987) report, "the skeletal and muscular system of children is not completely developed. Sudden or excessive muscular effort may cause or encourage diseases of the spine. Carrying heavy loads also predisposes to these disorders". In the present study children as young as 10 or 11 years were found lifting 10-15 kg load. The conditions in which children worked were hazardous as accidents occurred while working. The boys often got into and moved out of running trains which sometimes results in loss of a leg or an arm.

Social conditions on the street included elements of deprivation, oppression and hardships. On the street boys were affected by degrading and vicious influences. They were likely to fall prey to habits of gambling, smoking and drug abuse which often leads to a life of crime. The social environment in which children operated was hostile and exploitative which is not conductive to their social-emotional development. While living on the street, the boys were socially isolated since they had no adults with whom they shared nurturing, caring and supportive relationships.

In the area of self-esteem, certain aspects of the street child's reality need to be mentioned. The children were on the streets at a young age without any adult to care for them. The lack of protective and loving relationship with adults (a form of psychosocial deprivation) and the experiences of devaluation and stigmatization all combined to give rise to profoundly lowered self- regard and esteem among the children.

In the long-run , prolonged street existence is likely to leave upon them a stigma which clings to them for years and adversely affects their psychosocial development. The children are excluded from the mainstream or relegated to a realm of marginality which minimizes their interaction with the larger society.

8. Peer Life And Opportunities for Play:

As regards peer relationships, 136 (92%) boys in the sample had friends while 11 (8%) boys stated they had no friends and they stayed alone on the station. A majority of 116 (79%) boys had as friends other boys working as porters on the station. The rest 31 (21%) of them had children working in other occupations (such as shoe shining, rag picking, those selling items) also as their friends. Most of these 31 boys were themselves involved in another job besides lifting luggage on the station. This gave them a wider opportunity to interact and form friends with children other than those working as porters.

The boys in the sample can be grouped into three categories in order to describe their peer relationships. These include:

	Number	%
(a) boys having few and frequently changing friends;	78	53
(b) boys having stable friendships;	51	35
(c) boys associated with a gang as one of its members	18	12
	147	100

None of the boys in the sample reported having girls as their friends. The first category consisted of boys who had few friends, usually 4-5 in number, and the friendships were not intimate and stable. The boys in this category were primarily 'loners'. They stayed with their friends for a purpose e.g. going for a movie, visiting new places or gambling but most of the time they were alone, roaming or resting or sitting alone in the park. These boys reported that they worked and slept alone and preferred to have their meals alone.

The affiliations that the boys in this category formed with others were short-lived, superficial and often broke-up. These boys mostly had friends of their age. Most of the boys stated that they were unable to form stable friendship with other boys as they had been cheated and exploited by their friends on earlier occasions. Some of the boys revealed that they had stable friends earlier but after having bad experiences with them, they preferred being alone instead. Deendyal, age 13, from Mathura (U.P.) said, "I don't have good friends here. Friends take away my money. Only if you have money others are your friends". Laxman Poddar, age 13, from Motihari (Bihar) said, "If you have money, your friend is with you. Once your pocket is empty, friends also desert you".

Akhtar, age 13, from Bhagalpur (Bihar) who had been cheated by his friend narrated his experience, "I do not have any true friend here. They all are cheats. I used to work in a tea-stall in Bombay. A rag picker became friends with me and I trusted him. One day my employer paid me my wages of Rs. 125/-. The boy knew I had money. At night he stole all my money and ran away. I still curse him and do not trust other boys".

Though the boys in this category have a few friends, they have no one with whom they work and stay with over a period of time. Majority of these boys admit to having no one who would qualify as their best friend. 11 boys in this category stated having no friends at all. They reported working and staying alone all the time and very rarely interacting with other boys. These boys appeared more cautious and apprehensive of other children. They stated that for the purpose of eating and sleeping, , they always sought a safer, solitary spot and they never let anyone eat or sleep with them nor did they share food or sleep with other children.

The second category comprised of 51(35%) boys who reported having stable friends. In this category the interactions between friends were more frequent and regular and friends usually acted as constant companions. These boys stayed with their friends for most of the time, they were generally of the same age and sometimes hailed from the same state. As compared to the first category, friendships between boys in this category were more stable and friends were steady for a comparatively longer duration. The boys participated as a group in most of their activities. A group usually consisted of 8-10 members. The common activities included: having meals together, working at the same time, even washing or buying clothes together, watching movies, gambling and often sleeping together.

Out of the total 51 boys in the second category, 16 reported having traveled to and visited other cities together. The boys stated that they enjoyed more with their friends and they also felt secure when traveling in a group, for e.g. Bajrang, age 13, from Madhubani (Bihar) said, "I like staying with my friends. If one is alone, there are greater chances of being caught". Most of the boys in this category formed groups of 8-10 boys and they often had specific hangouts or places where they gathered and could be located easily. These places included: roof top of the platform building, a corner in the park, at the parking place for taxis, or at a particular 'dhaba'. It was found that sharing and lending of money and other belongings (clothes, etc.) was widely prevalent among members of this group.

In comparison with the first category, boys in the second category were apparently more helpful and supportive towards each other. This can be attributed to a great extent, to more frequent and intimate interactions between the boys. Govind, age 14, from Bhagalpur, (Bihar) described his relationship with this peers as, "Amongst friends, two things are important. There are two rules of friendship. First friends will not feel bad about what other friend says or does. Second, whatever we do, we all shall do it together".

There were instances when boys in this group fought and quarreled with each other. Most often the reason of conflict was reported to be money. Gambling also led to ruthless fights between the boys. There were instances when the boys were brutally beaten up or thrashed by their friends. Most boys in this category expressed fear of physical attacks from their friends. Fights between friends in this category often became serious and took an ugly turn. During field visits, the researcher often came across boys with a swollen face, or bruised bodies and on inquiry they revealed that it was due to a fight they had had with their friend(s). One boy reported that when he was unable to pay the money he owed his friend which he lost while gambling, his friend stripped him naked and burnt his clothes.

As compared to the first category, boys in the second category were not only more helpful and supportive towards each other but they were also more likely to fight and have conflicts amongst themselves. This is primarily due to the fact the boys in the first group associated and interacted with each other for a specific and limited purpose. Once their purpose was achieved, the group disintegrated and the boys were themselves again. Children in the second category participated together in wide-ranging activities and for longer durations, thereby increasing chances of conflict among them.

The third category included 18 (12%) boys who associated themselves with a gang. For the purpose of the present study, a gang has been described as a group of boys, mostly of different age groups, (both pre- pubertal & post- pubertal), who live and usually work together on the station. One significant characteristic of this group is that all the boys in this group were above 13-14 years of age.

A gang usually consisted of 10-13 members most of whom are post pubertal boys and one of them is usually considered the leader. Often young boys gain entry into a gang on being introduced by their friend who is already a member of the gang. A gang is characterized by stronger and more stable bonds of friendship and also a sense of belonging to the gang among its members.

The boys in the gang worked individually and the gang was heterogeneous both in terms of the age of its members and their occupations. Children working in different kinds of occupations like : shoeshining, working in a teastall, selling eatables on the station or working as porters, were found to be members of a gang. The boys worked separately but stayed together for the rest of the time. They reported eating, gambling and going for movies together and also sleeping with members of their gang. It was observed that younger boys in the gang (who had not reached puberty) expressed feeling of protection and security in the company of older (post-pubertal) boys. Digvijay, 12, from Chapra, Uttar Pradesh, revealed, " 'Toofan dada'(gang leader) looks after me well. When I don't have any money, he buys me a meal and helps me when older boys trouble me".

A few older (post pubertal) boys acted as benefactors for the younger one. Raju, a 19-20 year old street youth and a leader of one such gang was also a street child. He had been living on the station for the past 6-7 years. He helped younger boys in his gang by buying them food and clothes when they had no money or taking them to a doctor when they took ill. Sandip, 14, from Munger, Bihar said, " Raju takes care of younger boys on the station. He takes us to the doctor. He himself was a street child and he knows how tough life is on the station".

The characteristic feature which differentiates a gang from the second group is that the gang is heterogeneous in nature with respect to both the ages of boys as well as the kind of jobs they do, while the second category is mostly homogenous with regard to these traits. Conflicts and quarrels between members of a gang are also present but they are resolved easily when other members of the gang intervene.

These fights are mainly due to strained relations as a result of cheating, saying something offending or abusive, hurting another's feelings, associating with the rival gang or doing something against the interest of other members. The most common sign of strained relations between two members is ceasing to be on speaking terms and avoiding participative activity. Fights between two gangs were sometimes also involved the use of some lethal weapon like a nail, blade or a knife.

Hostility between gangs was observed as members of one gang held other gangs to be involved in activities like: drug peddling, pick pocketing, stealing and pilfering items for shops. The gang life reportedly provided the boys with the much needed protection and security. The role of gangs in the lives of street children has been appropriately described by Agnelli, S. (1986), "The defense mechanism to ensure survival in such an environment is the street gang. It provides the protection and comradeship of a substitute family, status, excitement and a code of 'honour' or rules to which the youngster can conform. It also meets the need, in particular, for a sense of identity".

Whyte, W.F. (1981) also described the role of the gang in the life of street-corner boys as, "The corner-gang structure arises out the habitual association of the members over a long period of time........ A group once formed is stable for a period, which varies from one group to another. Groups composed of younger children are more unstable. During the stability period, there is a very high rate of social interaction within the group".

Srivastava, S. (1963) in his study of vagrant boys in Kanpur and Lucknow investigated 'forms of companionship and peer life' among the boys. Around 40% of the total 300 boys in his study had no fixed company. Some of these boys stated that they had no friends, the "solitary type" as described by Srivastava, S. (1963). They were most often seen alone but they were not completely devoid of company.

33% of the boys in his study formed temporary gangs with

loose affiliations. The gang membership in this group lacked constancy. These partially- affiliated gangs were homogenous in terms of the age of the members. Nearly 22% of the total sample had active gang-life. The study established a correlation between companionship affiliations and levels of vagrancy in the boys stating, "Boys in higher stages of vagrancy usually have gang or semi-gang affiliations, while most of the early vagrants move in loose company" (Srivastava, S. 1963). In a survey of the peer life of 300 street children of Indore, 51(17%) boys were categorized as 'lonely souls' as they had no friends while the rest of the boys had 1-4 friends. Most of them had friends who were in the age group of 10-12 years (Philips, W.S.K. 1989).

In some cases peer groups among street children exhibit an incredibly sophisticated level of organization and functioning as has been found by Aptekar, L.(1988) in his study of Colombian street children. Boys were engaged in the activities of organized crime like snatching bags or jewellery, stealing bicycles, or the resale or stolen merchandise.

The manner in which the gangs functioned was described as follows, "The ultimate authority of the gallada(gang) resided with the adolescent 'jefe' (boss) who maintained his power and prestige by physical prowess and intelligence. The camadas were composed of two or three preadolescent children who shared the intimacies and camaraderie of being together. These groups were different than the galladas in several ways: they were more like family and friends than business partners and they were composed of fewer children all of whom were preadolescents. There was less hierarchy and formal organization in the camadas as compared with the galladas."

Peer-group influence among street children in certain activities is especially noteworthy. Most of the boys in the study got into the habit of smoking and gambling in the company of their friends while living on the streets. Of the total 147 boys, 101 (69%) boys used to smoke 'bidis' or 'cigarettes'. Most of these boys were in the age-group of 13-14 years and usually smoked 'bidi' as it was cheaper.

Of the 78 boys in the sample, who were 14 years old, 71 were in the habit of smoking. 86 of the total 147 boys reported smoking, on average, less than six 'bidis' a day while day 15 boys smoked at least one bundle of 'bidi' per day. Some boys reported smoking heavily in winters as it made them feel warmer. A few boys (6%) were in the habit of chewing 'paan' (beetal leaf) also.

In the survey of street children of Indore, 20% of the total 300 sampled children were addicted to smoking, 15% were used to tobacco chewing, 4% were in the habit of drinking and 1% each were found addicted to opium, heroin, 'bhang' and 'ganja'. The survey also indicated that children in the age group of 12-14 years and above were most vulnerable to addictions (Philips, W.S.K., 1989).

A large majority of 112 (77%) boys were in the habit of gambling. All the 14 year old boys and 78% of the 13 year olds in the sample were gambling frequently. Most of these boys reported gambling with money while a few used shells, bottle caps, chits of paper, or use platform tickets for gambling. Some boys were found carrying a pack of cards in their pockets most of the time. Many of the boys who gambled could play atleast 2 to 3 card games. Common games played were: 'Rummy',and 'Flash' Younger boys were often found gambling by tossing a coin or a piece of paper in a game which they called (heads or tails).

Sometimes when children did not gamble with money or had lost all their money in gambling, the loser had to buy the rest of the players snacks or ice cream or he was asked to take them for a movie and pay for all the expenses. Used plastic glasses or even pieces of scrap iron collected by the children from the station were also used as stakes which were sold later.

Gambling as an activity has certain elements which a street child expects from play, some thrill excitement, and recreation.

When the children had nothing to do, especially during noon or at night after 9 p.m., when work was slack, most of the boys could be found playing cards. Gambling also acts as a fast and easy way of making money though it frequently led to conflicts and fights between the players. Young children reported being lured into gambling by older boys and they mostly lost while playing with them.

Sometimes boys were found gambling early in the mornings or just after they woke up in the morning because they had spent all their previous day's earning before retiring and they needed money to have a cup of tea. Younger boys had no definite spots for gambling while the street youth reportedly gambled in a place out of sight of the police.

Younger boys were often seen sitting in groups of five to eight boys outside the station on the pavement and gambling. They also used the park or rooftop of the station building as places for gambling. Sometimes when the policemen raided the park in a bid to catch them, the boys scaled the wall dividing the park and the station and jumped on the other side. After a few hours, they were back again in the park and gambling.

Wooden tops were also used for gambling. The boys spun their tops simultaneously and the one who spun his top longest was considered the winner. He either owned the money at stake or got the tops of other players. Children were also found playing 'Gulli Danda'. The preferred place was the park as the game needs to be played in a spacious area.

The most popular and favorite pastime of the boys in the study was watching movies. 83 (56%) boys reported watching at least 3-4 movies a week. The boys sometimes watched a movie more than once. Twelve 14 year old boys in the sample revealed that they sold cinema tickets in black market along with a few older boys. The movie houses most frequented were, 'Plaza', 'Odeon', 'Rivoli', 'Regal', and 'Sheila'. They were close to the station and children did not have to spend money on bus fare.

Most of the boys stated that after strenuous work, it was relaxing and enjoyable to watch a movie and they were able to get rid of their worries and tensions, though temporarily. All the boys who liked watching movies reported having a favorite hero and heroine. They often imitated their style and mannerisms. Sometimes the influence of media on the children was reflected in the language they used or their way of dressing or personal grooming. Majority of the boys watched movies in a group or in company of two or three other boys. They usually bought the cheapest ticket available.

A small number of 13 (9%) boys played videogames in some shops in Paharganj which offered this facility. Only 22 (15%) boys reported having celebrated any festival while staying on the station. They had observed festivals like 'Holi', 'Diwali', and Bakra-Id. The boys used to wok hard the day before the festival and spent their earnings on food and watching movies with friends as celebration of the festival. Boys who did not go for movies spent their free-time roaming around with friends or relaxing in the park. The children had no means to satisfy the needs of his religious life, in particular by attending the services and having possession of the necessary books or items of religious observance and instruction of his denomination.

9.   Future Plans and Aspirations:

Regarding future plans, 63(43%) boys reported that they had plans for their future when they stayed with their families while the rest 84 (57%) boys had no ambition or plans for their future. Of the 63 boys having some plan for themselves, 58 of them had attended school. Most of these boys stated that they had thought of a specific kind of job they wanted to do when they grew up. They wanted a job in a govt. office or a school; a skilled job as a tailor, carpenter, barber, or wanted to carry on their father's occupation. (Table 23).

Table 23. Future Plans & Aspirations

(N= 147)

Future Plans/ Aspiration	Number	Percentage
I. Vague or no plans	81	55
II. Had Plans, these included	66	45
(a) working in a factory/garage (22) or cycle repair shop		
(b) running own business (11)		
(c) working in a hotel or shop (8)		
(d) Vehicle driver (7)		
(e) skilled trade (carpenter, barber, (6) potter, painter etc.)		
(f) wants to be a policeman (4)		
(g) running own stall on the station (3)		
(h) work as domestic help (3)		
(i) government employee (2)		
Total	147	100

Though only 69 (47%) boys had been to school, an overwhelming majority of 131 (89%) boys were interested in studying and wanted to attend school. They also believed that they could have got a better job, both in terms of money and status, had they been educated.

Children's views about education indicate that majority of them wanted to study and they also believed that education and employment were related, and that education guaranteed a lucrative and prestigious job, 16(11%) boys were not interested in studying and they had different views about the value of education. They stated that education did not always help in procuring a 'good' job and that it would be a waste of time for them to study. They reported being interested in earning more than their present income and getting a stable job.

Boys in the study were also asked to evaluate their present work. Out or the total 147 sampled children, 141 (96%) boys wanted to leave their work as a porter. Majority of them felt that being a porter lacked status and respect. This was the primary reason why they wanted to change their work. Most of them stated, "I do coolie work because of compulsions. It is not a respectable job". Another boy expressed his feelings as follows, "Coolie-work is no good a job, and it requires carrying burden like a donkey. You are abused or beaten up. If I get a good job, I will leave this work today".

All the boys in the sample were asked about their plans and expectations for their future while living on the station. It was found that 81 (55%) boys were vague and uncertain about their future plans. Sudhir, age 14 from Nagpur, Madhya Pradesh said, " I am unlucky. At home my parents did not love me. I am living like an orphan 'lawaris'. I don't know what is destined for me." A few boys also stated that they would continue working as a porter at the station till they found another job. Most of them had poorly-defined future plans and when questioned about the nature of work they intended to do, they responded, "I have not thought of the kind of work but I will leave this work and do some other work".

66(45%) boys in the sample aspired to engage in a particular kind of work and their future plans were comparatively clearer. The kind of jobs aspired included: working in a shop or tea stall or in a factory/ garage/ cycle-repair shop; learning to drive and becoming a driver; engaging in skilled trade (carpenter, potter, painter, tailor, barber or in a carpet industry); running own business on a small-scale, or working as a domestic help. Two boys wanted to work as government employees in an office while four wanted to be policemen.

A large number of boys wanted to work as an apprentice in a garage or cycle-repair shop as they believed that after getting trained in this skill they would be able to earn more money. Only eight boys expressed a desire to work in a hotel or shop, the main reason being that they would have safe place to sleep. Most of them, expressed fears that working in a shop entailed a lot of work with hardly any time for rest or recreation.

63 (43%) boys in the study had the experience of working in a hotel/tea stall or restaurant on earlier occasions. Majority of them complained of ill-treatment by their employers or co-workers, non-payment or wages, excess of work and inadequate time for rest or recreation. Mukesh, age 13, from Bhagalpur (Bihar) who had worked in a 'dhaba' said, "I had to work a lot and there was no holiday. I was not paid my salary also". Another child, Dhunia, age 13, from Bhilwara (Rajasthan) had worked in a restaurant in Ajmer for five months. He said he started working there as he got food and a place to sleep.

He narrated his working experience, "I had to work a lot and there was no time to rest or play. I was not paid my full wages. Older boys working in the dhaba bullied me".

Eleven boys wanted to run their own business on a small-scale or start a petty trade e.g. selling small items on the pavement. They planned to earn enough money to be able to start their own business. When they were asked how they would save their earnings, most of them were uncertain and did not give a clear response.

Seven boys wanted to learn driving and later work as an auto rickshaw or taxi driver. Six boys wanted to learn the skilled task of a carpenter, barber, potter or a painter. Six boys wanted to join government service and four of them wanted to be policemen. These four boys stated that they were often harassed and beaten up by the cops on the station and they wanted to avenge them. The policemen were always seen as a source of terror and were feared. Krishan Kumar Banwar, age 11, said, "There are lots of advantages of being a policeman. One can beat the 'dadas' and everyone is afraid of the cops". Three boys intended to run their own stall (tea or book stall) on the station.

The boys in the study were asked whether they were satisfied with their work and their conditions. Only 18 (12%) boys replied in affirmative while the rest 129 (88%) boys stated varied reasons regarding their dissatisfaction about their working and living conditions. These included: harassment by the police, licensed porters and local 'dadas', lack of basic amenities and a resting place, no safe place to keep their belongings or savings and lack of respect and prestige regarding their occupation.

Among the services or facilities desired by street children, employment was the main concern for 112 (76%) boys. They believed that a change in their present occupation and provisions for another job would lead to improvements in their living conditions. However, most of them were unable to specify in clear terms the kind of job they desired. 35(24%) boys stated education as their most important need. The most common reason for giving priority to education was that, at a later stage, education would help them in achieving a better job. Though they described education as their main concern, they nurtured the same ambition of getting the job as the remaining 112 boys who rated employment as more important among the services they desired.

This finding is however in contrast with the needs expressed by the street children of Bangalore (Reddy, N. 1990). The study highlighted that food took priority among 47% of the children which was followed by the needs for shelter, bathing and toilet facilities (29%), then education 13%), clothing (6%) and medical treatment (less than 1%). None of the 1,750 children expressed employment as their need. In a study of street children of Mumbai, it was found that out of 2196 children included in the study, 67% indicated night shelter as their first priority and food as the second priority.

For the boys in the sample food and shelter occupied low priorities as they stated earning enough for having adequate meals and they slept wherever any unoccupied place was available.

10.   Attitude about life at home vs. street life.

The boys in the sample were asked to evaluate their life at home in comparison with their life on the street. This comparison helped in understanding how the child rated his street existence in relation to the time he spent at home with his family. 63 (45%) boys stated that their physical needs (food, clothing and shelter) were better met at home. They stated that they experienced greater physical discomforts and hardships while living on the streets. Most common reasons for stating the time spent at home as more easy and comfortable were: availability of adequate and proper meals, adequate clothing, a place to sleep and sometimes a sense of belonging to their family. Harihar, age 14 said, "I had good food at home and wore nice clothes. On the station food is mostly bad and I have to wear same dirty clothes". Prabhakar, a boy of 13 years used to attend school in his village but he felt bad he had to discontinue his studies while living on the station. Murli, age 13, found life at home better, " Though I was beaten a lot at home I liked it at home. I was among my own relatives but on the station I do not know anyone and friends also cheat you."

The remaining 77 (52%) boys liked street life more as compared to their past life at home. Most of them had experienced severe forms of maltreatment and violence at home. They stated that they had developed a liking for street life. Kapil, age 11, gave two reasons for preferring living on the streets. He said, "I used to break stones at home and earned Rs. 6-7 only. I can earn more here and no one forces me and sends me to work. I find life better in the city than in the village". Shivshankar, age 14, said, "Here, you can work and eat at your own discretion. If someone hits me I also retaliate but at home, I had to suffer all the beatings quietly".

As stated earlier in the section of work-life of these children, 19(62%) boys used to work while they stayed at home. They were working in a field, or in a shop or factory, selling items, making bidis/carpets/paper envelopes/grass mats, or breaking stones or doing most of the domestic chores at home. The children did not find working on the street tough or difficult since they had been working earlier. They reported enjoying their freedom of working when and for how long they wanted to on the station. The children also stated that they could earn more money while working on the streets as compared to the wages they received while they worked when staying with their families. The boys cherished their independent life-style on the streets.

Most of them had been ill treated and were beaten frequently by their parent(s), mostly their fathers, when they were at home. They reported having run away from their homes primarily to escape those beatings and violence. For these children, street life was an alternative to the unpleasant experiences they had with their families. Only seven (5%) boys stated they found no difference in the time spent with their families and on the streets. These boys had been working at home also and they found living on the street equally difficult. Santosh Kaluram Kudawale, age 14, had to work in a tea stall since he was 9 years of age. He said, " It is the same situation at both the places. At home I had to work for long hours and returned late at night. On the station too, I have to work a lot."

While comparing their life at home with their street life, it was found that most of the boys preferred staying on the streets rather than going back home. It was not so much because of the fact that they liked street life more as compared to their life at home but it was primarily due to the absence of experiences of ill treatment, frequent beatings and neglect by parents, step-parent or caretakers at home.

The boys were at times harassed and beaten up by the police, local 'dadas' or even their friends while they lived on the station. Such instances were reported to be less frequent and severe as compared to their experiences at home. It is due to this rather than the presence of any significant favourable experience on the street which is responsible for most of these boys' continued street existence away from their homes.

This finding was confirmed through data obtained by asking the boys whether they wanted to go back to their families (Table 24). An overwhelming majority of 123 (84%) boys did not want to return to their homes while only 24(16%) boys expressed their desire to go back home. Most of the 123 boys who had no desire to

visit or go back to their families confessed that at times they wanted
to leave their street life and go back home but eventually ended up
staying on the station. The most common reason given for changing
their decision of returning back home was experience of abuse,
neglect and harsh treatment faced by these boys at home. Shabbir,
age 14 said, " I used to work more at home. If I go back home, I
will have to work also and suffer the beatings too, why should I
think of going back?"

Table 24. Would Like To Go Back Or Visit Your
Family In The Near Future

Response	Numbers	Percentage
(a) No	123	84
(b) Yes	24	16
(i) go back after earning lot of money	(9)	
(ii) go back after a few years and bring mother along	(1)	
(iii) go back after earning enough money but come backto the city after sometime	(11)	
(iv) same as (iii) but stay at home with the family	(3)	
Total	147	100

A few of them also found city life more attractive and lively.
They liked watching movies and visiting places which was possible
in the city. Thirty –seven boys in the sample reported that they had
no home to which they could return. These boys were either complete
orphans (i.e. both parents dead) or had been abandoned or asked to
leave by their parents or step-parents. They stated that they had no

214 *Street Children*

alternative but to stay on the streets. Prabhu, age 14, from Warangal (A.P.), complete orphan, was rejected by his uncle, "I do not have a home. My parents died and my relatives rejected me. The station is my home now".

Dharmendra, age 14, from Sonepat (Chandigarh) had also lost both his parents and was turned out by his relatives. After his parents' death, his uncle and aunt ill treated him and threatened him that they would send him to an orphanage. He was not allowed to go to school. The child later left his home.

Out of the twenty-four boys who wanted to return to their families, eleven boys wanted to go back after working for a few years and earning enough money. All of them did not want to stay with their families. The children planned to come back to the city. The main reason of going back home was to demonstrate to others, especially their fathers that they were capable of living alone and supporting themselves. Mohd. Tahil, age 12 said, " I will go back home only when I have enough money. I will show my father that I can also do some work." Ratanlal Gupta age 14 also had similar views, " I will go back home after making lot of money but I will not stay at home. I just want to show my father that I have survived without his support."

Nine boys stated specifically that they would go back only after earning enough money. When all these boys were asked how much they wanted to earn, none of them could clearly state the amount. But said they wanted to earn more than what they earned at present. Only three boys wished to go back home and stay with their family. However, they also wanted to have enough money with them before they returned home. In terms of age, all the three boys were below 13 years and wanted to go back home after a couple of years.

All the twenty-four boys who wished to visit or return back to their families were asked whether their families would take them back. Nineteen out of these twenty-four boys said that their mothers would be very glad if they returned home but their father or step – father would not take them back and may ask them to leave.

Veerbahadur, age 13, said, "My mother will be very happy that her son has returned but my father will beat me. He will say that I have brought a bad name to the family by running away from home".

Though a large majority (84%) of the boys in the sample denied any desire to visit or return to their families, an almost equal percentage (77%) of the boys admitted that they missed their families. They stated that when they were alone on the station, they remembered their families. Majority of the boys reported missing their mothers. Suraj, age 12, started weeping while remembering his mother. He said, "I miss my mother a lot. I am worried about her health as she was often sick. She loved me a lot." Vithal kumar, 13 also felt strongly for his mother, " I miss my mother. Whenever my father used to beat me, she always intervened and tried to protect me. In the ensuing melee, she too got beaten up. She has suffered a lot for me."

Some children said that they missed their siblings and a few reported missing their grand parents. However, in most cases the harsh living and working conditions on the street were preferable to the acute deprivations and unhappiness that stalked their homes.

The following section includes description and analysis of the data obtained by using the Developmental Deprivation Interview Schedule. This interview schedule includes data which focuses on the following aspects of the street child's life both at home and on the street:

(1) Home environment and present living conditions;

(2) Economic conditions;

(3) Dietary Pattern;

(4) Clothing needs;

(5) Educational experiences;

(6) Parent-child relationship and emotional atmosphere in the home;

(7) Health status.

(1) Home environment ad present living conditions:

Information on home environment deals with factors like: type of house; whether spacious or not and facilities available for drinking water and lighting. Of the total 147 boys, 102 (69%) had 'Kutcha' homes (temporarily built structures). 12 boys reported that their families stayed in rented houses. Regarding the size of the house, 119 (81%) boys stated that their house was spacious enough for the whole family while only 28(19%) boys found their houses crowded or cramped. A majority of 68% of the children had single-room houses. Keeping in mind the average size of the family and the fact that the majority of the houses had only one room, the children's statement is not very convincing.

Only 21 (14%) houses had taps as sources of water while in the remaining 126 (86%) houses water was collected from wells, ponds and other reservoirs or through hand pumps. In such situations, a large number of boys reported that they were given the task of filling water everyday which often involved walking long distances and also making frequent trips to the source of water. Only 35(24%) homes had a supply of electricity. All these houses were 'pucca' houses. In the remaining 112 (76%) houses, lanterns or lamps were used for lighting.

Regarding their present living conditions, all 147 boys in the sample were homeless and lived on or near the New Delhi Railway Station. An analysis of the lives of children on the station reveals that for the children the station is not just a place, it has complex socio-economic and at times emotional characteristics. The children lived and worked there and engaged in different kinds of activities on the station. A few children had a feeling of belonging to the station, often describing it as their home.

While living on the station, the boys had no proper bathing and toilet facilities. For defecation, most of the boys used services of stationary trains while the younger boys defecate in open spaces across the railway tracks. The public conveniences on the station, according to the children were usually in a bad shape and too unhygienic for use. There were a few municipality-run toilets near the station which charged money for every use. Very few boys used this facility presumably due to the fees charged.

For having a bath, boys made use of washing-lines or pipes which were installed on the railway tracks for the purpose of cleaning the trains. They also made use of this arrangement for washing their clothes. Children had no towels and they either used their shirts or allowed the water to dry on their skins after the bath. Majority of the boys reported taking bath on a week basis while some of them had a bath once in a fortnight or sometimes even after a month. The frequency of bathing dropped appreciably during the winter.

Most of the boys said that it was not easy and even practical to have a bath more frequently. Problems of buying a new soap every time they took a bath, lack of privacy while bathing, lack of a clean set of a clothes to wear after bathing were some reasons cited. The constantly lurking danger of being caught by the police was also responsible for the boys reported reluctance to have a bath frequently. A few children reasoned that it was not logical or even worthwhile to have a daily bath because while working and staying in an unsheltered place, it was certain that they would not be able to keep themselves clean. After the bath the left-over soap was either given away to other children or thrown away as there was no place to keep it for being reused later..

For sleeping, the boys in the sample had no fixed place. Most of them slept either on the pavement, outside the shops near the station, in the park in Ajmeri Gate and sometimes on the stairs, platform or roof of the station building. Platform No.1 of the station was not used for sleeping purpose as it was the main platform with the maximum number of officials and cops present. Most of the boys preferred sleeping outside the station because they were often woken up at night and beaten by the policemen if found sleeping on a platform.

56% of the boys slept in groups of two or three while the

remaining preferred sleeping alone. The boys experienced great difficulty in sleeping when the weather was inclement or it rained at night. Under such conditions, they either took shelter outside a shop or inside the station building at the risk of being apprehended by the police. A few boys reported taking shelter in the telephone booths on the station.

The children were asked about the arrangements they made for sleeping during winters. 63 (43%) boys said they took a quilt on hire every day. There were two or three shops near the station (in Paharganj market) where quilts were available on hire at the rate of Rs.4 to Rs.5 per night. Children collected their quilts after 8 p.m. and returned them back before 10 a.m. the next day. 79 (54%) boys stated that they usually shared a quilt with their friends or even other boys sleeping on the station. 5 (3%) boys had come to Delhi recently and had not experienced winters in Delhi. Most of the boys reported that initially they found it difficult to get a good sleep on the station because of the loud noise made by the trains, strong lights, and the hustle- bustle on the station. Gradually the boys got accustomed to such an environment.

A few younger boys, mostly pre pubertal, indirectly revealed that they were sexually abused, mostly by older boys while sleeping with them at night. They said the older boys often slept with them on the pretext that they did not have a quilt or they quietly slipped into their quilt late at night and later exploited the child sexually. The children were, however unable to express their experiences explicitly as, probably the presence of female researcher made them feel uncomfortable. Most of them who had faced sexual exploitation often described their experience as, "At night, the older boys sleep with us and later on, abuse us sexually. Sometime they even take off our clothes". (Ratilal, age 12).

Data about sexual exploitation of street children was difficult to obtain which is suggestive of the extremely sensitive nature of the topic. The gender of the investigator also made it difficult to obtain such data. However, important insights can be gained by exploring this area.

(2)   Economic Conditions:

108(73%) boys stated that their family income was not sufficient to meet the entire family's expenditure   98(66%) boys reported that the family needed to borrow money on interest and was under debts most of the time. This can be related to the fact that of the total 147 families, 77 (52%) families can be characterized as very low income families. This group includes families where either the father or both the parents were dead or cases where the father was sick/too old/unemployed or he mostly stayed out of town without extending any financial help to the family or the income was highly irregular and inadequate.

96 (65%) boys stated that there were frequent quarrels or conflicts in their homes due to economic insufficiency. In families where the elder brother was earning, the child was often ill treated or discriminated against. Ramdulara , age 14, reported that his father is very old and unable to earn. His elder brother was a farm laborer. The child said that everyone in the family favored his elder brother and listened to him. All the boys who were complete orphans and most children with step-parents also experienced frequent quarrels in their families as the boy were considered a burden on the family.

Regarding their present income, 121 (82%) boys stated that it was insufficient and they wanted to earn more. Most of them admitted that the money they earned was usually enough to meet their daily expenses on food and they were also able to buy clothes for themselves. The boys ran short of money and needed to borrow from others when they gambled with money and lost the game. It was mostly on such occasions that they found their earnings insufficient. 122 (77%) boys were in the habit of gambling.

Most of the 26 (18%) boys who found their daily income sufficient were often engaged in another task apart from lifting luggage on the station. These boys reported that they earned more than what they needed for their daily expenditure on meals and they also lent money to other boys.

Around 75% of the boys reported that they needed to borrow money from others and 60% of them did so frequently, i.e. twice or thrice a week. The rest 25% of the boys reported reluctance in borrowing money from other boys because most of the time their friends did not oblige them, or they had to pay interest on the borrowed money. If a child borrowed Rs.5/- he was asked to pay back Rs.7 or 8. This was a common practice of making fast money among some street children.

(3) Dietary Pattern

It is essential that every child receives food that is suitably prepared and available at normal meal times and of a quality and quantity to satisfy the standards of dietetics, hygiene and health and, as far as possible. Information on the dietary pattern of the children was also gathered. Two important variables influencing the dietary pattern were considered. These included:

(a) The number of meals, and

(b) The quality of food as based on the child's report and experience.

89 (61%) boys said that they had adequate two square meals a day at home while 58 (39%) felt that food at home was inadequate. A large number of boys reported that at home they were often denied food as a form of punishment and had to starve. While living on the station, 116 (79%) boys reported having adequate meals. Only 31 (21%) boys sometimes missed a meal because of shortage of money. Sometimes they were unable to earn because of sickness or presence of a large number of policemen on the station on a particular day. These boys also hesitated in borrowing money from other boys and at times they had to skip a meal. On such occasions they either had a cup of tea or only a plate of rice instead of a complete meal. As Sandip, age 13, said, " When one is

hungry, one needs food even if it is stale, and when one is sleepy, one needs a bed even if it is broken."

Regarding the source of food on the station, 109 (74%) boys had their meals from 'dhabas' or restaurants. There were a number of 'dhabas' near the station, in Paharganj area, which offered food at cheap rates. The remaining 38 (26%) boys had their food from hawkers/vendors. These hawkers usually sat on the pavements in a corner and cooked there. They mostly offered chapatti and a vegetable and their rates were cheaper than a 'dhaba' or restaurant. The children squatted on the pavement and had their meal in the open. One meal in a 'dhaba' or small restaurant usually cost the child between Rs.5 to Rs.8. When the child ate from a hawker or vendor, he spend Rs.3 to Rs.5 on a meal.

Majority of the boys preferred having food in a 'dhaba' or restaurant. One 'dhaba' owner was reported to provide his clients which chilled water from his refrigerator and boys said they preferred eating at his dhaba. Most of these 'dhabas' or restaurants also provided children the facility of having non-vegetarian dishes in the price range of Rs. 7 to Rs. 11. Very few boys said they had non-vegetarian food mostly because they found it expensive. Eating in a 'dhaba' or restaurant also provided the child a safe and secure place to eat. The boys reported that they were also served onion and 'chutney' with their meals which served as attractions. It follows that not only have the children developed casual eating habits, they are also exposed to health hazards associated with food sold under unhygienic conditions.

Children were sometimes able to procure food through other means for e.g. left-over food found in the train, food given by passengers or the left-over from the pantry-cars of a few long-distance trains. Some children reported that they were able to get food from the 'Shatabadi' and 'Rajdhani Express' on various occasions. Boys also said that sometimes railway cooks, who prepared food to be served in trains, could be found sitting on a not – so – frequently used platform. These people often took pity on the children, especially the younger ones and gave them raw vegetables or sandwiches. Children were sometimes seen scavenging the trains and collecting edible stuff.

The boys were asked to compare their dietary pattern at home with their present dietary intake. 98 (66%) boys felt that the quality of food they had at home was better as compared to the food they had on the station. Some boys felt that food in the 'dhabas' or restaurants was not cooked well (mostly undercooked) or the food contained both excess or very little spices and fat. Some boys did not like the environment in which they had their meal. Dilip, age 12, revealed, " I always eat alone. At home, mother used to feed me with love. I don't like the food here. I am losing weight because of tension and worries." A few boys said they felt hungry most of the time while working on the station. Dhanbahadur, 14 years old used to drink 5-6 cups of tea daily. He said, "Drinking tea reduces the appetite for food and even if I have no money to buy myself a meal, I drink a cup of tea and do not feel hungry." Another boy Santram said, "I rest after finishing my work. I do not roam around as it makes me feel hungry."

(4) Clothing needs :

All children need to have personal clothing suitable for the climate in which they live and which is adequate to ensure good health among them. All the 147 boys that they had enough clothes at home which was more than two sets. But while living on the station, 144 (98%) boys had insufficient clothing. They possessed only a set of clothes worn all the time. After having a bath, they had to wear the same dirty pair of clothes. A few boys washed and dried them and wrapped a towel on their bodies till the clothes dried.

Only 3 (2%) boys had another set of clothes. They kept this pair with a shopkeeper or a pan wallah (one who sells betel leaf) whom they knew. The boys mostly bought new clothes from Sadar Bazar, Delhi. There were a number of people selling old or second-hand clothes on the pavements in Sadar Bazar. Every Wednesday, there was a 'Wednesday market' when a large number of people sold clothes at cheap rates. Children were able to buy a shirt for Rs. 10 to Rs. 20 while a pair of trousers was available for Rs. 20 onwards. During winters, children bought sweaters and woolen garments from the same market which cost them Rs. 20- 30. These were mostly second- hand or defective clothes.

(5) Educational Experiences:

69 (47%) boys in the sample had some level of schooling while 78 (53%) boys had never attended school. All the 69 boys had dropped out of school at some stage. 16 boys had studied till class I, 7 boys till class II, 11 till class III, 27 till class IV and 8 boys had left school when they were studying in class V. Out of 69 boys who had been to school, 61 of them liked going to school while 8 boys disliked studies because of failure at school or bad treatment meted to them by the teachers at school.

When the boys were asked if they were interested in studying, only 16 (11%) boys replied in negative while a majority of 131 (89%) boys were keen on studying. These boys said that if facilities were made available to them, they would like to study while earning at the same time to support themselves. Every street child of compulsory school age has the right to education suited to his or her needs and abilities and designed to prepare him or her for return to the society. Street children who are illiterate or have cognitive or learning difficulties should have the right to special education. Sadly, there are no initiatives by the government in this regard.

(6) Parent-Child Relationship and Emotional Atmosphere in the Home:

An important segment of the Developmental Deprivation Interview Schedule was focused on certain factors that make up the general emotional atmosphere in the home as perceived by the children. This section describes the child's experiences and perceptions of his problems regarding family-life, their views about their parents and their relationship with them. It was these questions about interactions with their parents which enabled the children who had problems in relationships with their parents to describe their experiences and difficulties.

The discussion is presented in three general headings:

(a) Parental Affection and Identification;

(b) Parent-Child Interaction; and

(c) Home Climate

(a) Parental Affection and Identification: This presents findings regarding which parent the child felt gave him the most affection, which is one of the significant factors in this study. It also provides data on which parent the child identified with, and the child's perception of parental neglect and hostility.

(b) Parent-Child Communication and Interaction: This presents data on the kind and degree of interaction the child had with his parents. It also provides information on which parent the child felt understood him and which parent he turned to when he was in trouble.

(c) Home Climate: This section includes data on whether there were quarrels or conflicts at home, whether the child felt free to express his opinion and whether he liked staying at home.

It must, be emphasized that the multifarious factors considered in this section form a complex, interacting whole and it is difficult to separate them. The factors studied in the above three headings are central to the present study's objective of ascertaining the affective roles of both parents and examining the psychosocial deprivation faced by the children at home. For validity of the responses the answers to the questions in the above three sections pertain only to children who had both parents living, i.e. 108 (74%) boys of the total children.

Apart from the statistical evidence given, it is worthwhile

reporting some of the statements that reflect qualitative differences between the child's relationships with his parents. These statements, in verbatim form, have been included in the following sections.

(a) Parental Affection and Identification: This focuses on the child's perceptions of his parents' affection and love for him and also with a view to establishing, if any differences exist between both the parents. The role of both parents needed investigation, especially the role of the father. A study on street children by Sondhi, P. (1994) had provided insights on the prime significance of the role of fathers and their relationship with the children. Information was collected by asking simple questions like, "Which parent do you think loves you most?" and "Which parent nagged or punished you most?"

The answers to the questions in the section on parental affection showed that 88 (81%) boys, of the total 108 boys who had both parents living, felt more loved by their mothers than by their fathers. 18 boys felt that none of their parents loved them while one child who had a stepmother, stated that his father loved him more.

The question, "Which parent nagged or punished you a lot?" showed the degree of parental hostility towards the child. Data revealed that only 15 (14%) boys felt that their mothers nagged them more, while the bulk of 74 (69%) boys reported that their fathers nagged or punished them more. 19 (17%) boys stated that they were equally punished or nagged by both parents. All the nine boys in the sample who had stepfathers reported being punished and often beaten by them while 15 out of 17 boys with stepmothers were nagged or punished by them.

The following statements clearly express parental (mostly paternal) hostility felt by the children: "My elder brother was sick and he passed away. When my father was angry, he used say it would be good if I too die. Which father would wish so for his child?"(Sohan Kumar, age 14)

Shailesh, age 14, narrated his experiences. "I used to earn at home by working in a near by shop. One day I did not go to work. My father learnt about this. He beat me badly, then stripped me naked and threw me out of the house. I swore that day not to ever go back home." Dharmender, age 13, was hit by his father with a saw in a fit of rage. The scar on his leg was a testimony to the abuse he had suffered.

On occasions some fathers beat their wives when the latter intervened to protect the child from being beaten up by the father. This also made the child more hostile towards the father. Pappu, age 14, said, "My father is very short-tempered. If he was angry with me, he abused my mother also." Some boys expressed anger towards their father when he ill treated their mother. Murli, age 14, revealed that when his father quarreled with his mother and got physically aggressive with her, he felt like hitting him but he was helpless.

Identification of the child with his parents was ascertained by asking the children which parent they resembled in their behaviour and temperament. Such identification provided information on whether the child had positive or negative identification with one or both the parents. Also, keeping in mind the responses to earlier questions in this section, the children were asked if they would like to be the kind of person their father is?

64 (59%) boys out of 108 boys felt that they resembled their mothers more in their temperament. The responses support the warm relationship the children shared with their mother who was also found to be the most affectionate parent for majority of the boys. When the boys were asked if they wanted to be like their fathers, only 8 (7%) boys replied in affirmative. 100 (93%) boys expressed a strong dislike for their fathers. A few of them stated that they wanted to adopt their father's occupation but they did not want to be like them as a human being.

Negative identification with fathers was expressed in statements like: "My father almost strangled me once. Why should I be like him? He is a butcher". Shabbir, age 14, said, that he did not want to grow up like his father as his father was a drunkard and beats him a lot. Mohd. Akhtar, age 14, was often beaten by his father with bamboo sticks. He said, "He gambles, drinks and is addicted to drugs. I do not want to get in to these habits". Pankaj, age 14, was maltreated by his father and he said, "If I treat my kids in the manner in which my father treated me, they will suffer like me."

In this section certain aspects of the general affective relationship between each parent and the child were studied. The study of this aspect of the child's experiences at home is central to the study psycho social perspectives in the lives of street children. Loving, nurturing and caring parent-child relationships are a basic prerequisite for emotional health and vital determinant of the adequacy of the parental role. The findings of this section can be summarized as follows:

(i) Majority (81%) of the street children tended to feel that their mothers loved them more ;

(ii) Majority of the boys (69%) experienced paternal (fatherly) hostility towards them in terms of nagging and beatings;

(iii) Majority of the boys (93%) whose fathers were living showed negative identification with their fathers.

(b) Parent-child communication and interaction : The concept of parent-child communication is an important aspect of family's emotional harmony, and reflects interactions between parent and child. Emphasis was placed on two important characteristics of parent-child communication: the adequacy of communication between the child and the parent and the emotional content of communication. The adequacy of parent-child communication was assessed by whether the child spent enough time with his parents. The emotional component of parent-child communication focused on quality of parent-child interaction. It was ascertained by whether or not the child felt understood by his parents and turned to them when in trouble or for advice.

It was found that majority of the boys spent most of their time with their mothers or siblings when at home. 30 (20%) boys whose mothers were working reported that they spent most of their time outdoors when the mother was not at home. In 23 (16%) cases, the fathers usually stayed in a different village or town and visited home irregularly. These boys said they hardly had an opportunity to interact with their fathers or spend enough time with them. It can be inferred that majority of the boys experienced less contacts or interaction with their fathers.

The quality of contacts between father and son was found to be poor. 83 (77%) boys revealed that they felt more understood by their mothers while 23 (21%) boys said that none of their parents understood them. Only two boys felt more understood by their fathers. The responses revealed that for majority of the boys being understood implied an understanding and awareness of the child's feelings, actions and emotions.

Majority of the boys whose father mostly stayed away from home said they rarely saw their father at home. They felt their father never showed any understanding of their feelings. Naresh's (age 14) father was a truck-driver and he visited home occasionally. Naresh said, "He never stayed at home. I heard he had a mistress. If he cared for us, would he have done this?" Karmakar, age 14, said, "My father was very money-minded. He told me that I would get food only if I brought home some money. He treated me like an animal."

84 (78%) boys reported that when in trouble they felt confident of turning to their mothers for advice and support. The fact that only 3 out of 108 boys felt that they could turn to their fathers when in a difficulty, was another indication of the inadequate paternal-child communication. Most of the boys who did not seek help from their fathers said that they first turned to their mothers and sometimes tried to solve their problems themselves instead of turning to their fathers for help.

Responses indicated that when the boys were in trouble or

in need of advice, majority of them turned to their mothers who also happed to be the most affectionate parent. This shows that these boys had better emotional relationships with their mothers than with their fathers and the boys consequently felt closer to their mothers. For most of the boys, the father did not appear to be adequately affectionate. In fact, he was found to be hostile and harsh and under such conditions it is not surprising that the mother-child communication was more adequate and satisfactory than the reported father-child communication.

(c) Home Climate : This section is concerned with factors that can be related to the general realm of emotional atmosphere of the family. It includes information on whether or not there was marital disharmony or family conflicts in the home; whether or not the child expressed his opinion freely and whether or not the child felt neglected or unwanted at home. Of the total 147 boys, 124 (84%) boys stated that there was frequent quarrel or discord in their families. These were mostly between the parents or between the child and the parent. In the case of children who were orphans or abandoned by their parent (s), conflicts were reported to be frequent between the child and his relatives or caretakers or siblings (mostly elder brother).

Most of the boys reported getting upset or tense in such situations. Disagreement between parents was also frequent and often violent in a number of cases resulting in battering and physical assault on the mother by the father. A large number of boys reported that they were afraid of speaking up or expressing their thoughts in presence of their fathers. As Bhagat, age 14, said, "I could never speak in front of my father". When he was at home, the child said he used to sit quietly or else got beaten up. Most of the boys also said that their fathers were short-tempered and when angry, he often became physically and verbally aggressive.

131 (89%) boys stated that they often felt neglected and unwanted at home. They said they mostly experienced such feelings when they faced ill-treatment or beatings at home. Shafiq, age 14,

said, "No body cared for me at home. We are four brothers and five sisters. It will not make a difference if I am not there". Banwari, age 13, said, that his father asked him to work in a relative's shop. The employer used to beat him if the child refused to work and also complained to his father. He said, "I was getting beaten from both sides. No one needed me at home". Children who were ill treated by their caretakers or siblings also expressed feelings of being unwanted at home. Aslam, age 14, complained that his brother never intervened when his father beat him up. The brother used to provoke the father by saying that the child had loitered around and played the whole day.

Information was also collected on the number of boys who had indulged in truanting. 16 (11%) boys stated they had left home sometime earlier also and the reasons given for truanting were similar to the reasons when they last left their homes. Majority of the boys stated that they did not intend to go back home this time.

Findings on home climate suggest that for most of the boys the home was a tense, unpleasant place characterized by stress and discord. Boys with step-parents mostly felt that they were discriminated against by them. The home atmosphere was perceived as characterized by frequent parental dissensions and strife. Two features indicative of domestic tensions among the boys were fear of being beaten up by the fathers and violent quarrels among parents or other family members.

(7) Health Status:

Information on the health status of the boys was primarily based on observations made during the course of study. Data on the health conditions particularly psycho social health of working street children is limited and difficult to obtain. A study of 2,301 street children of Calcutta by Ghosh, A. (1992) assessed the degree of nourishment of street children and found that 90% of them were under nourished, while 3% were severely undernourished. The age-height ratio for 61% of the children was found unsatisfactory and

91% of the boys did not have access to any medical facility when they were ill.

68% of the 2000 street children of Chennai, India were undernourished and 67.8% were affected by moderate protein deficiency (Arimpoor, J. 1989). Information on the proportion of street children in Indore, India, who were below normal with respect to height and weight, was collected by Philips W.S.K. (1989). Majority of these 300 cases were found to be below normal, both with respect to height and weight The Lions Club of Vishakapatnam, 'Taruni', conducted a health camp for street children and majority of the boys were found suffering from frequent gastro-intestinal, respiratory and skin problems (Indian Express, Oct.11, 1993).

The general health status of majority of the street boys in the sample was adversely affected by the environmental hazards linked with their working and living conditions, their nutritional status and lack of medical facilities. Most of the health problems faced by the children can be directly related to the kind of work they performed and the circumstances in which they were living. Most prominent among these are: being constantly, dust, dirt, smoke and unhygienic conditions, lack of proper bathing and toilet facilities, exposure to the vagaries of weather and factors associated with their work environment.

Outwardly, children were generally alert, agile and quick in their movements and most often were cheerful, lively and outgoing. In the area of physical safety, they seemed to lack a sense of self-protection, being careless with the use of their bodies and getting injured frequently. Accidents, injuries and even sickness were usually not accompanied by expressions of appropriate concern and affect. It was believed that there was no need to seek any help as the pain would pass away with time. Medical aid was rarely sought especially by older boys, even after a severe fall or deep wound. The children either were not aware of the hospital where they could go or they felt cut off from the mainstream health services. A list of common diseases suffered by most of the children includes: head ache, fever, bodily pains, stomach problems, skin problems, eye complaints and toothache. Exposure to the vagaries of weather also acted as contributory factors for their poor health.

Most of the boys complained of frequent backache, neck ache, headache, muscular pain (mostly in arms & legs) and sprains and abrasions. This can be linked to the strain of the work they performed and also the posture they were required to maintain while lifting luggage. Studies have established that urban environment can be particular hostile to street children. Poor housing, malnutrition, acute respiratory infections and high environmental risks are endemic and contribute to the ill-health of young children (Shah, P.M. 1987). High level of air-pollution in their working and living environment is very likely to harm their respiratory system. A large number of boys in the sample were observed spitting frequently and many complained of chronic cough and pain in their chests.

The boys used coal powder or sometimes bought neem-stick (branches of a medicinal plant) for brushing their teeth. During observations and interviews a large numbers of boys were found to have dental problems like: bad breath, dental cavities and infected gums. There were instances when three boys all aged 13 years, lost a tooth. Two of them had been experiencing pain and swelling in their gums and one child fell down from the stairs and lost a tooth.

A majority of 132 boys were barefoot and never used any footwear. The common reasons given were that wearing shoes or ' chappals' obstructed their movements while carrying luggage and also the fear of losing them. A few older boys possessed a pair of canvas shoes. Many children who worked and roamed around without any footwear were found to have bruised or ulcerated heels and soles. All the boys used shaving blades to clip their nails and at times they had bleeding fingers or toes.

Because of unhygienic living conditions and poor personal hygiene, most of the boys were observed to have lice on their bodies and hair. The researcher often came across boys helping each other get rid of the lice. A few boys reported that they got their heads shaved off when it became unbearable for them because of acute lice-infestation in their hair. Sleeping with other children who had lice on their bodies or hair or using lice- infested quilts during winter gave rise to this problem. Due to lack of personal care and hygiene, the children reported respiratory problems and skin rashes. Many children had also suffered due to violent attacks on them or physical accidents.

A few example indicate the abysmally poor health status of the boys in the sample:

(a) Shashank, age 11, had a worm-infested leg. He had a deep wound on his right leg, just below the knee, which was left uncovered and it attracted flies and other insects. The child said that the wound itched most of the time and it led to bleeding. He used to limp as he had difficulty in walking for even short distances. He complained of constant pain and said that he used a stick to pull out worms when he could not tolerate the pain. Asked why he did not see a doctor, he said,

"Medical treatment requires money. It will heal up on it's own".

(b) Ram Mistry, age 14, said he had a severe gripe in his stomach every time he ate something. His hands used to tremble and he was often unable to work because of this problem. He seemed to be very upset about it because his friends made fun of him and started calling him handicapped.

(c)Sharvan, age 13, (child on the cover page of the book but not included in the sample since he was not working)was a cheerful boy who lost his leg in a train accident eight months back while working as a porter on the station. There was a wound on the part of his leg where it was amputated. The child was not taking any treatment for this. He had a pair of crutches but the padding had worn out and it hurt his arms and hands. Because he lost his leg and was alone most of the time, he sometimes had bouts of severe depression. He reported that at times, in sheer desperation he started hitting himself not knowing what to do.

Majority of the boys felt that living on the station had affected their health adversely. Puran Singh, age 13, said, "I have lost weight and have not gained height. If I lift such heavy loads, how will I grow tall?" It was also observed that while working chidren not only transported heavy loads to the station but also got into or out of a moving train in a bid to find work. They were also seen sitting on or between the railway tracks while gambling.

Regarding availability of medical facilities to the children, very few, only 11(7%) boys stated that they went to a doctor when they were sick. There were a few small clinics in Paharganj and the boys usually availed of these facilities. They, however, stated that it was very expensive to get treatment at these shops. The rest 136 (93%) boys said that they had never gone to a doctor. A few of them went to a nearby medical store and asked the chemist to help them. Rest said they stopped working when they were unwell.

(b) Information on Psychosocial health of the children:

In the following section, attempts have been made to summarize the understanding of children's psychosocial characteristics in relation to their environmental influences. Comparable studies and research done exclusively with street children living without families were not available in the Indian literature. The present writings on street children in India deal mostly with street children living with families and working children. The available literature can only provide gross analogies, similarities and differences. In the Indian context, literature on psychosocial health of children living on the street without any familial contact and protection is extremely inadequate hence the present study assumes significance.

In view of the above limitations, the views and generalizations to be found in this section are suggestive in nature. Having acknowledged these limitations, what follows is a discussion of the distinctive qualities of the children from a psychosocial viewpoint. Observations and personal individual interviewing helped the researcher in gaining insights about their psychosocial health.

The data are descriptive and derive mainly from the observations made during the study by using interview schedules I and the Developmental Deprivation Interview Schedule. In addition, thirty two boys in the sample were administered two psychological tests (the Draw-A-Person Test and the Bender Gestalt test) to gather more information on how they were functioning emotionally. The Bender-Gestalt test assessed the children's current "ego-strength", a term used by Pascal & Suttell (1951) who gave cut off scores for different ego functioning abilities. They suggested that 'children with a score of 50 and below were free of pathology, scores between 50 and 70 were in a transitional zone and those with scores above 70 were in need of psychiatric help" (Pascal & Suttell, 1951). The sample was grouped according to the above three categories and 21 out of 32 (66%) boys scored in the pathological range and 11 (34%) boys were found to be in the transitional category. None of the boys scored in the healthy range of emotional functioning.

The Draw-A-Person (Human Figure Drawing Test) was used to obtain a second measure of the children's emotional functioning. In accordance with the procedure of the test, children were asked draw both a man and a woman. Koppitz, E. (1968) devised the scoring or 'emotional indicators' (EIs) to reflect the child's attitudes and concerns of the given moment. Thus, this measure of emotional functioning was an assessment of the child's current emotional condition, whereas the Bender-Gestalt Test yielded information that reflected a more long-standing psychological profile of the child.

In differentiation between children with and without emotional problems according to the Draw-A-Person Test, there are potentially 30 emotional indicators (EIs). A score without any or with one EI was indicative of good emotional health. Two EIs were suggestive of psychopathology and three or more EIs were indicative of emotional problems and unsatisfactory interpersonal relationships (Koppitz, 1968). 5 (16%) boys in the test sample had none or one emotional indicator, 9 (28%) had two emotional indicators and 18 (56%) boys had three or more emotional indicators. The test results on both the tests (Bender-Gestalt and Draw-A-Person Test) indicated poor emotional functioning in majority of the children administered the test.

Another qualification that needs to be emphasized is that the researcher is generalizing about trends which appeared in the children as a group. Among the children, there are variations in the degree to which these general observations are true. Despite divergent individual histories and family backgrounds, the group of street boys in the sample shared most of the observed traits and characteristics.

In a study of Colombian street children, Aptekar, L.(1989) also used Bender-Gestalt and Human Figure Drawing Test to assess the emotional functioning of the children. Of the 56 boys in his sample, half of the boys on the human-figure-drawing test and three-quarters of the boys on the Bender-Gestalt did not score in the pathological range. In another study of street children that looked at the emotional health of street boys, Felsmen, J.K. (1981) noted that he, "witnessed no cases of overt psychotic behaviour within the population" and most of the boys in the sample appeared to enjoy sound emotional health.

The test results in the above two studies (Aptekar, L.1989; Felsman, J.K. 1981) indicated that the children were functioning much better than was commonly believed. The observations suggested two reasons for this, "once the children were on the streets, almost all of them had a series of benefactors. Second, by the time they were ten or twelve, they had developed intense "chumships" with other children of their own age" (Aptekar, L. 1989). Both these factors were responsible in alleviating the negative factors associated with living on the street.

These children were often in contact with their families (i.e.

mostly their mothers), and rather than being entirely on their own and being 'children of the street' they could be described as children on the street with occasional or irregular links with their families. Almost 75% of the children in the sample were in contact with at least one parent at one point or another. Most children also came in contact with programmes for street children where they received food and companionship (Aptekar, L. 1989). The factors of social support and assistance they received from their peers and benefactors on the streets played a significant role in the area of emotional health of the boys.

However, the emotional health of the children in the present study should be viewed from the perspective of the high-risk environment from which the boys came and the neglectful and abusive conditions in which they worked and lived on the station.

The children in the present study differed from the Colombian street subjects in a number of important ways. Firstly, all the children in the sample were living on the streets, without any contact, whatsoever, with their families for at least one year. Most of them had been actively rejected or abandoned by their parents or step-parents.

Secondly, half the boys (53%) reported having few friends and no stable company. Boys, especially younger ones, complained of being cheated or exploited frequently by their friends. A small number (only 12%) of them said they had a stable group of friends who helped them when they were in trouble. Strong and stable peer relationships on the street were missing for majority of the boys. Children in the sample were very rarely helped by any adult on the station. They had no adults who acted as their benefactors, and they were viewed with suspicion and mistrust. They were perceived as potential sources of threat and competition by the adult porters. The children were living in an environment in which they were neglected or rejected hence, they mistrusted and feared other. The pain of rejection and ill treatment by their parents led them never to trust those in authority.

All the above factors contributed to the deterioration in the general emotional health of children. Some behavioral indicators of poor emotional health among the boys were: feelings of inadequacy and pessimism, inability to relate or trust other children, fatigue and lethargy and self-deprecating remarks about themselves like: no good, 'sadak-chap'. While living on the station, many factors influenced their psychosocial health and among these deprivations, presence of threat and anger and attitudes towards self appeared highly significant.

As stated earlier, the definition and conceptualization of deprivation is not so clear-cut, consequently the role of this factor and it's relationship to other gross influences on a street child's development and behaviour is complicated and indistinct. The characteristics of the children's environment namely: deprivation, presence of threat and danger and attitudes towards self played an instrumental role in the children's daily lives and relations with others on the station.

In the face of stressful situations, it has been observed that many children develop behavioural and psychological difficulties. In recent years, a great deal of empirical work has focused on resilience and vulnerability. In research on stress resistance, the shift toward focusing on competence rather than on maladjustment is laudable, representing a more positive outlook on development and adjustment.

There is, however, a major drawback in endorsing this approach. It does not allow for the fact that despite competence on behavioral indices, individuals may have a variety of other difficulties, particularly psychological, such as emotional maladjustment, depression or anxiety. This needs to be emphasized while planning research with street chidren. It has been found, and is also indicated by the present study, that in spite of their impressive competence and 'street-smart, characteristics, street children are vulnerable to problems in the area of emotional health and functioning.

(I) Deprivation:

Life on the station can be described as a mixed picture or deprivation and stimulation (at times excessive and age-inappropriate, for e.g. exposure to deviant role models on the station). In relation to deprivation, what was particularly lacking were the many varied physical and emotional stimulations that are ordinarily essential for forming warm, nurturing relationship. Most children were deprived of loving, caring relations with adults or had only occasional and shallow contacts with them. Bonds of friendship for majority of the boys were often weak and limited. Opportunities for play were at a minimum.

Very often the child's presence in a group or being with other children was a dominant factor in providing them feelings of security. Growing up in a noisy, hectic, unpredictable environment, and being constantly overwhelmed by the manifold burdens of everyday living, the children were missing out the experiences and pleasure of childhood. The lives of these children were a picture of severe neglect and deprivation. The boys seemed to grow up in an environment in which lack of consistent care and protection also added up to considerable personal, social and emotional deprivation.

(ii) Presence of external dangers and threat : Children were constantly exposed to real dangers in their environment. At home, the kind of danger which they faced involved experiences of harsh punishment and abuse. They were often scolded and beaten frequently. Most of them had witnessed parental drunken inebriation and dissensions between parents or other family members which sometimes became violent. Because of the fear of being beaten up, many boys reported being afraid of their fathers.

On the station, danger and survival considerations appeared to influence their daily lives significantly. All the boys exhibited a strong sense of alertness and guardedness. The boys' mistrustful attitude towards others seemed more than just the absence of trust. It was also accompanied by a vigilant watchfulness to avoid threats either from friends, adults or the police.

"In their unstable, insecure world, physical danger was all too real. Visibility implied not protection but vulnerability. The possibility of violence in the form of stabbings and beatings was ever present. Street youngsters experienced the fear of brutality at the hands of others, fear of disease and disablement, fear of police, fear of prison or being 'put away'. The street youngsters 'violence was a part of the language of deprivation and perhaps no more than a logical consequence of violence of which he was victim in his family" (Agnelli, S. 1986).

(iii) Attitude towards self: This section provides information on children's attitudes towards self and their self-esteem and how they are affected by psychosocial deprivation faced by the children. Self esteem can be defined as, "the individual's evaluative attitude toward himself" (Coopersmith, S. 1967).

As observed in children in the present study, this attitude ranged from extremely positive to extremely negative. There were children in the sample who had a positive self-image. These children felt, at least to some degree, worthy, capable and successful. There were others who predominantly thought poorly of themselves, who considered themselves incompetent and a failure. Data seemed to indicate that 68% of the boys had poorly developed self image. Their evaluative attitude towards themselves showed a repeated mention of the children's poor self-image.

Derogatory comments about themselves and their work were common, for e.g. Pitambar, age 14, said, "I feel worthless and incompetent, it is better to die than work as a porter". Bhagwandas, age 14, remarked, "The life of all unlicensed porters is hopeless and without any respect. They roam around like vagabonds" (Unlicensed porter)

Lack of pleasure or satisfaction with their present conditions or with future possibilities was a shared characteristic for majority of the boys. Most of the boys were pessimistic or fatalistic in their attitude towards their future and there was no discernible motivation toward a goal or any future plan. The boys seemed uncertain of achieving something of their own. To the question, "How do you think can your present situation be improved?", most of them were of the opinion that external sources in their environment, e.g. government, institutions or organizations and interested individuals could only help them.

Studies of individuals with low self-esteem report that they are desirous of success but, given their background and present situation, they find it hard to believe that they will actually succeed. These persons do not believe that they have the capacities or resources that lead to successful social acceptance. They anticipate that their goals will remain unfulfilled and their ambitions frustrated. This pessimism is likely to lower their confidence. This explains the vague goals of disadvantaged youth and their expectations have the unhappy effect of reducing motivation and available energy, it should be noted that they are generally a realistic response to the facts of rejection, poverty and failure" (Coopersmith, S. 1967).

Information on the children's work-life and future aspirations indicated that 141 (96%) boys were not satisfied with their present work. Most of them wanted a secure and permanent employment. These boys revealed persistent feelings of personal inadequacy regarding their work-life and living conditions. At times, the boys were overwhelmed with feelings of helplessness and hopelessness. "Conditions that reduce feelings of worthiness, competence and power include both the absence of favourable influences and the presence of harsh, rejecting and destructive factors" (Coopersmith, S. 1967).

While living on the station, children were growing up in an environment in which they experienced profound feeling of neglect and despair. Instances of exploitation and harassment by the police and others on the station contributed to or were responsible for such feelings. In addition, the boys felt being devalued by the society. They were looked upon as a nuisance or as thieves, rogues and ruffians. This negative response of devalued status in the eyes of

8

of the boys.

They experienced resentment in the manner in which they
were treated and were often the objects of suspicion and hostility
by both the police and public, in general. They were, to a great
extent, alienated from the society and lacked various important
opportunities for their optimal development. Apart from being
deprived and disadvantaged, the boys in the sample also faced
rejection. Isolation from the society and social disapproval are
conditions which are likely to adversely affect their social, emotional
and vocational development.

A few children showed some degree of positive self-image
and many had started enjoying life on the streets. As described by
Agnelli, S. (1986) , "Harsh though his sufferings are, it would be
wrong to think of the street child as invariably miserable. Despite
conditions which outsiders would consider intolerable, they accept
their street existence as no more than normal. Even those who live
entirely alone can think of it as one step up from their previous
sufferings within the family. With it's dizzying thrills, spills and
variety, street life can exert an undeniable fascination. Those who
learn to ride it's unpredictable changes of fortune can need a lot of
convincing before they try any alternative which may be offered".

While the vast majority of studies about street children have
concentrated on the problems children faced, the fact that many of
them preferred street existence in spite of their difficult circumstances
opens up another area of research, which centers around the study
of resiliency in children (Aptekar, L. 1989). The development of
street children cannot be completely ascribed to, nor fully understood,
in terms of deprivation alone. This leads to consideration of other
formative influences in their environment. In this context, certain
qualities of children need a reconsideration and emphasis. The
children's skills in coping with daily living, their orientation and
adaptation to danger in spite of the risks in their environment and

reflections of autonomy and early independence need to be commended.

Many of the daily survival strategies of these children demonstrated healthy, competent and adaptive behaviour. To view them as helpless, powerless and 'at-risk' emphasizes only their vulnerabilities. Most of the work with regard to street children has focused on and highlighted their weakness and pathology instead of recognizing their coping skills and signs of strength and resiliency these children also display. The children demonstrated 'street survival skills' that enable them to live in the street and survive. Many street children in general had learnt a number of survival skills. They knew how to beg, steal, lie, cheat, evade arrest, fight, or use drugs to forget their hunger or feel good momentarily in order to survive in the streets. Although these types of behavior are anti-social by the usual social norms, they have survival value for street children who resort to them at different times in their lives. The children grew up prematurely in the face of harsh economic compulsions. The need to fend for themselves leads to a certain kind of independence.

Engaging in economically gainful activity was one the areas of ability which were beyond the children's years and gave the impression of independence. Most of the children, in spite of their histories and past experiences, expressed satisfaction with their ability to earn and fend for themselves. They cherished their independence and freedom from parental authority and harsh discipline. Donald & Swart-Kruger (1994) emphasize that in the overall development of street children freedom, sense of autonomy and self-reliance may be extremely important attributes. Most of the boys placed a high value on the freedom they enjoyed living alone on the street.

While the survival consideration stimulated by their living conditions, assisted the boys in adapting to their especially difficult circumstances, they also contributed to their premature entry into adulthood, social isolation and alienation. Some illustrations clarify this point. These children were **not withdrawn** and were desirous of making contracts with people. **They coped** by not investing too much or counting too much on **people and relationships.** They were wary of forming close, intimate **bonds with** others.

This suggests that in the **process of managing** to accommodate and adapt to their environment, and **learning** to carry burdens beyond their years, these children attained **an early** independence which was not age-appropriate for them. **Data** suggest that because of economic reason and in the **absence of parental** support, guidance and care, the children grew up **in to adults** prematurely, took on adult tasks and thereby relinquished **their childhood** too early. Many children in the study who were **able to abstain** from drugs or keep themselves away from street fights **and gambling** showed self-control. An illustrative case is **Manoj. 12 years old** Manoj was introduced to the use of 'charas' (marijuana) **by the** older boys he worked with in a market place. When told **by the** owner of the place where he ate food, of the harmful **effects of the substance,** Manoj decided to stop using it. He left his **work in order** to get away from the temptation and company of the **addicts.** He came to the station to get another job.

These children often **appeared as** strong, independent and experienced, their struggle for **survival having** provided them with skills and knowledge far **beyond their age,** yet they too seemed to show desperate need for love, **affection,** support and security, "The gamins (street children) deserve **respect** for their ability to survive, with so little help, against overwhelming odds. But their lives remain filled with pain and suffering" (Felsman, J.K. 1984).

Advances in developmental **psychology** have helped us realize that the child's mind is not the **'tabula rasa'** (blank slate) that Locke (1693) postulated. Piaget's (1952) **work** on cognitive-development describes the child as an active **agent in** the world seeking out interaction, accommodating **and assimilating** elements in the environment. Similarly, theorists of ego- psychology such as Erikson, E. (1950) and White, R. (1959) **have helped** us appreciate important sources of the child's **internal** motivation. The need and the ability of the street children to **engage in** competent, industrious engagement with their environment **and their innate** strivings for increased control over their environment **and autonomy** require careful observation and consideration. An **analysis of these** may help in understanding the intrinsic factors of **character, personality** and individual differences these children bring **into the street** with them.

In the light of **information** gleaned from the data it is clear that homeless street **children are** living in conditions which deny them their rights under **the Convention** on the Rights of the Child to special protection, **adequate** housing, protection from neglect, abuse and exploitation; **to grow up** healthy, to benefit from social security and to support **through their** families (Future, 1987-88). India has ratified the **Convention** on the Rights of the Child. Legislation and the ratification of international standards are however, not enough by themselves **to end** exploitation of children. What is needed above all is the **effective implementation** of both international and national legislation **and practices** through the provision of adequate resources.

A number of **Articles** (Articles 3,6,18,19,24,27) included in the convention on **the Rights of** the Child require that the Government undertakes **all appropriate** legislative and administrative measures to ensure the **child all** necessary protection and care. The Govt. is required to **take measures** to ensure both, the child's survival and development. **However, homelessness** threatens the survival and development of **innumerable** street children in India. Street children, being homeless, **lack protection** and the inputs for optimal growth and development. **The legal** and welfare systems have failed to address the needs **of homeless** street children effectively.

The Convention **(Articles** 32 & 36) emphasizes the child's right to be protected from **work that** threatens his/her health, education or development. Many **street** children are engaged in occupations which are hazardous. **These** children are often exploited due to economic reasons and **they perform** work that interferes with their healthy development. According to Articles 40 of the Convention, judicial proceedings and institutional placements of children shall be avoided. This provision has particular importance for homeless street children as they frequently come in contact with the legal and child welfare systems. In practice, government-run institutions are frequently used and other alternative services are inadequate. Rehabilitative care and support services for mainstreaming street children into the larger society are poor.

In India, the implementation of the rights of the child as expressed in the UN Declaration of the Rights of the Child seems tedious as it is closely tied to the state ideology and it's welfare approach. It is necessary that child welfare policies and programs should be contextualized in relation to particular social systems. To a very large extent, the Indian legal system guarantees the rights and the entitlements of the child as envisaged by the UN Convention on the Rights of the Child. But despite extensive legislature to protect children from abuse and exploitation, the role of the state and welfare agencies is inadequate and ineffective.

7.3.   SUGGESTIONS FOR FUTURE ACTION

While developing effective programs for street children, strategies need to be devised by the govt. to solve two most basic policy issues. These are, first, the identification of a suitable model to follow while planning welfare measures for street children and choice of effective programs. The second is the development and utilization of efficient channels for delivering these services (Myers, W. 1988). The programs devised for street children else where must be adapted to Indian socio-cultural realities.

The strategy for tackling the problems of street children involves action at different levels: involving improvement in basic social services, the humanizing of institutions, economic and legal measures and a greater degree of participation of the community. Various forms of intervention are necessary, both short-term and long-term, for the child, his family and his community (Agnelli, S. 1986)

At the macro level, social policy and development programs can make significant preventive efforts to deal with this problem. Effective implementation of the national policy for children and welfare services constituted to safeguard the interests of children is one such measure. Priority should be given to families facing economic destitution. Rural employment promotion (e.g. Training of Rural Youth for Self-Employment (TRYSEM) and poverty alleviation programs, which enjoy high priority in the national development plans should make a positive impact in this regard. Projects which focus on urban poverty alleviation through integration of basic services like shelter, health care, education, employment and recreation should be given priority in urban development plans.

There is growing incidence of children of poor families, both in rural and urban areas, taking to streets. Recognition of the family as an integral and pivotal component of society for development of children is imperative by the government. Family 'at-risk', or in a state of crisis like those facing chronic illness, unemployment or extreme poverty can be identified and supported. Economic deprivation results large in a number of rural poor moving to urban areas. Policy measures to contain rural to urban migration can be formulated. This will entail creating employment opportunities for livelihood in the rural sector.

Utilization of available resources of government and Municipal Corporation can be stressed. In this context, the role of city administration or Municipal Corporation assumes significance. In the city, main areas of location where street children are commonly found or engaged should be identified. Welfare measures developed by the urban local bodies for urban poor such as community centers, night shelters, school premises, health care and recreational facilities should be made easily accessible to street children. The scope of the services provided through the Metropolitan Development Authority and the Urban Basic Services Program can be expanded to reach street children to cover the above mentioned needs. Government municipal school buildings can be used to conduct classes for street children. It has been found that some street children are school dropouts and keen on studying. Mobile Health Units can extend medical facilities which can be coupled with referral services.

The legislative measures set up for the welfare of children should be made more effective. The role of the police is of crucial importance. It is necessary to change the punitive attitude that influences current social policy addressing the issue of street children. Emphasis should be on non-institutional services e.g. foster care, sponsorship programs and adoption. The atmosphere of the state-run institutions should be improved to allow opportunities for integral personal development. Coercive rehabilitation of street children should be avoided. The institutions can be run by staff trained in working with children facing stress and deprivation. These services can be made more humane and creative and this does not always necessitate increase in finance. The programs can be stimulating and innovative and the atmosphere in the children's home run by government should be made liberating and informal.

At present, most of the programs available for street children are those run by non-governmental organizations. Instances where Municipal Corporations have initiated any interventions for street children are very few. The government should actively strive for a more constructive partnership with NGOs already in this field. While developing policies and programs for street children, the experiences and insights of the NGOs can also be utilized.

A list of working principles has been given by Myers, W. (1988) which can be considered while developing model programs for street children. These principles have been derived from observation and analysis of programs for street children. According to Myers, W. (1988) the model program for street children is based on two premises. The first is the move away from the traditional institutionalization approach, and the second need to focus on the holistic development of children.

I.   The objectives of services for children should be to promote their integrated physical, intellectual and social development.

The program should be comprehensive, attempting to meet the varying needs of children. Attention to the physical health of the children should include provisions for adequate nutritional and medical care. This can be done by providing daily meals, access to medical assistance and referral services.

II. Schooling should be adapted to meet the practical needs of children by providing meaningful and relevant educational opportunities. Schools should have flexible hours to accommodate children's work schedules. Institute of Psychological & Educational Research (IPER), Calcutta has developed a model for providing educational services to street children . Classes are held at places where street children are found. A similar program was started in Bangkok in 1979. It utilizes the services of street educators who identify street children interested in education. The formal education lessons are adapted to street child's level of understanding.

III. Condition of work of working street children can be improved. Appropriate vocational training and secure and protected employment alternatives can be provided. Various programs provide employment alternatives so that street children do not depend on street work for earning their income e.g. SKI Courier Services, Canada and 'Meals of Wheels' run by Butterflies- an NGO in Delhi. The above programs help preparation of children for self-support as an adult and also aim a protecting working street children from marginalisation.

IV. For children who cannot be reintegrated in their families, provision of alternative rehabilitative care either foster care of group living projects should be emphasized.

The S.O.S. Children' villages in India and 'Snehsadan' in Bombay have evolved 'group home models' (Rane, A. & Shroff, N. 1992). A few organizations have also devised a 'half-way home approach' (Misra, S. 1988). These organizations maintain an open house for street children where street children can come on certain days and use facilities offered at these drop-in centers. They are free to return to the street later.

It is not necessary and often not possible for any one program to provide all the services needed, although there are a few instances of this being done. For a model program to succeed, it is imperative that the community be involved in it's activities. UNICEF's Regional Programs on Abandoned People from the community work in collaboration with state and municipal authorities to provide street children education, recreation, nutrition and health care, and vocational training.

The advantages of community-based programs are widely acknowledged. Community-based alternative services have been found to be more effective and creative in helping street children. They have also been more innovative and practical in the kind of services offered to children. Very often this has been achieved through less expensive way as compared to services provided by government-run institutions. Considering the growing numbers of street children, the government alone cannot realistically reach a significant proportion of street children using it's own resources. Community-based strategy employing community resources will have to be relied on. The government can also support NGOs by providing financial and technical support.

7.4. SUMMARY AND CONCLUSION

Data reveal that the problem of street children is complex in nature. It's causes, implications and solution are multi-dimensional. The children in the sample were literally homeless and isolated from their families. One-fourth of them came from incomplete or broken homes where both or either parent was dead or absent. Most of them had surviving parents or relatives but none of them maintained even minimal contact with them. Majority of them families were poor, large and with high level of illiteracy. Almost half of the total sampled children were illiterate and the rest who had been to school had dropped out of school at some stage.

Studies by Srivastava, S. (1963), Nangia, P. & Pinto, R. (1988) and Reddy, N. (1992) have indicated that economic compulsion was the primary factor for children leaving their homes. The present study revealed that majority of children had left their homes because of maltreatment, cruelty and abuse they had faced at home. Analyses of the present findings show that conditions of poverty were contributory to the tension and violence in their homes. Most of the children attributed running away from home to escape from physical and/or psychological circumstances which were intolerable to them. These children mentioned that they 'ran away from their parent(s)'. It emerged that most of these parent-related factors involved cold, unsupportive and neglectful families. A 14-year-old street boy summed it up: I was going to school. My father left my mother and my sister and myself. My mother married again but my stepfather never liked me and he often used to hit me. My mother used to take good care of me but always the way my father treated me made me feel too bad so I ran away from home".

Some of the children were on the streets because their parents had died and there was nobody to take care of them. Such cases reflected a breakdown of the traditional extended family system. This is a major factor in the increase of children in the streets. In the past, extended families could be depended upon to help families who could not adequately care for their children, but now this is not so because of the decline in economic conditions and increase in poverty. The communal spirit of neighborhood groups has also suffered for similar reasons. The idea that children run into the street to escape domestic crisis is further reinforced by their decision making process. None of them said they discussed their decision to leave home with their parents. Presence of conflict and aggression (verbal and physical) and absence of warmth and support at home lead to a deterioration in the family relationships.

The children felt alienated psychologically and eventually removed themselves physically from the distributing and destructive home environment. The phenomenon of running away from home seemed to involve a constellation of certain factors the most important of these being the 'social-emotional' environmental of the family, especially with regard to parent-child relationship. This was followed by the factor of acute poverty and it's concomitant strain on the family.

The family has been perceived as a universal social institution and an integral component of human society. Parsons, T. (1965) states that the family performs the primary socialization of children in a warm, secure and mutually supportive environment. Functionalists (Murdock, G.P. 1949; Parsons, T. 1965) have concentrated solely on the positive aspects of the family. They have idealized the family with a description of well-adjusted children and sympathetic spouses providing care and emotional security to each other. This conceptualization of the family has been questioned by some family theorists.

Laing, R.D. (1976) views the family in terms of sets of interactions and concentrates on the exploitative aspects of family relationships. He argues that many children are subjected to gross forms of violation of their rights within their families. Like Laing, Cooper, D. (1972) regards the family as 'a stultifying institution which stunts the individual members'. The close supportive relationships and warmth between family members may be missing. In the case of street children, the family's failure in providing the children nurturing, stable and supportive relationships with their parents reflects the dysfunctional nature of the families.

Vogel, E.F. & Bell, N.W. (cited in Haralambos, M.1980) believe that the tension and hostility of unresolved conflicts between the parents are projected on to the child. The child is thus used as an emotional scapegoat by the parents to relieve their tension. The process of scapegoating is dysfunctional for the child and is likely to disturb him emotionally. Abuse and neglect of children are also more likely to occur when parents are overwhelmed by financial problems. Anger and frustration, in such situations, are directed toward the spouse or children and family stress has been found to be closely linked with child abuse (Helfer & Kempe, 1980). Large number of children in the study had lived in conditions of physical and emotional stress with poverty aggravating the family's problems.

It is generally assumed that where community and family structure are intact, the welfare of chidren is protected. The family is the single institution that can respond to the basic needs of children on a long term basis. It exerts the most powerful influence over the child's emotional, social, psychological, and physical development. Whether it is a two-parent, single parent, adoptive or foster family, it normally provides significant protective factors that help build resiliency in the individual. In some instances, as in a dysfunctional family, it may be a source of significant risk. There are many circumstances in which it is the practices, attitudes and values of the family, community and society which give rise to some of the most serious child welfare problems (MacPherson, S. 1987). Among the street children interviewed, very few mentioned having positive family environments and bandings. This was not surprising when one considers that the very reason many street children are out in the streets is their desire to escape their dysfunctional families. The present study highlighted that in some circumstances children are neglected and abused within the family and they do not receive the love and care that they need. Children's family ties were tenuous, stormy and weak and the family did not provide affection, security and support which is imperative for a child. An analysis of the parent-child relationship showed that most of the boys lacked a satisfactory relationship with their fathers who were mostly reported to be harsh, punitive and aggressive.

The present study supports Parsons (1955) position regarding father's role in the family. He considers father as the primary family executive providing discipline, authority and objective judgment. Fathers in the study were found to exercise considerable authority in the family. They were the decision-makers and had more power over the children. Fathers were also viewed as less affectionate and nurturing than mothers. The mothers in the study played roles which were predominantly of a caregiver and homemaker. They provided emotional support and often functioned as mediator of the father child relationship. This suggests that Parsons, T. (1955) theory of the "instrumental" role of the father and the mother's "expressive role" in the family is relevant to this study. Role differentiation in terms of mother as "socio emotional leader and father as the breadwinner "instrumental leader" is also evidenced.

Parent-child communication and interaction, as perceived by the child, indicated that both in terms of quantity and quality, most of the boys in the sample had poor interpersonal contacts with their fathers than with their mothers. This was more pronounced in the case of those twenty-three boys in the sample whose fathers mostly stayed out of home. Sharing of recreational or leisure-time activities between father and child was absent or severely inadequate. The emotional aspect of parent-child communication revealed that most of the boys tended to turn to their mothers for help or advice. They also perceived mothers as being able to understand their feelings and indicated a marked maternal preference.

Personality development and psychosocial health of a child is to a large extent dependent on whether father-child relationships have or have not been established satisfactorily. This is not surprising in view of the fact that Freudians have always attached great significance to the role of the father (Freud, S. 1949; Hall, C.S. 1956). For most boys, it was the father's affective role that was consistently less satisfactory than the mother's. It seems that faulty or inadequate paternal relationships rather than faulty or inadequate maternal relationships primarily occurred for most of the sampled children. Many children verbalized strong dislike for their fathers, very often deep feelings were expressed by some children who cried or were almost in tears while they narrated how their fathers beat them up and were punitive towards them. It was thus observed that in most cases the problematic affective relationships between the child and the father not only implied lack of emotional warmth, but was also associated with concomitant parental aggression and punitive behaviour.

Analysis of parent-child relationship revealed that fathers

did not serve as adequate role models. As suggested by Lynn, D.B. (1974), in such situations the boys would experience frustration from his father's punishment and rejection and would perceive the father as a model of aggression. Boys in the study saw their fathers as neglecting, unprotective and offering little direction. The fathers did not share in their son's activities, plans and interests. Most of the boys did not want to be like their fathers when they grew up which shows negative identification with the father.

The findings presented in the study are also meaningful if viewed from the perspective of Learning Theory and Behaviourism. A child who perceives his father in a negative way may gradually develop hostility towards the father. It was found that most boys perceived their fathers as being unsatisfactory not only in the affective dimension but also in other aspects of father-child relationship such as communication, guidance and nurturance. 'Where a father shows inadequacy primarily in the area of affection and other related area, it would be difficult for a boy to identify himself positively with his father' (Andry, R.G. 1971). The results provide strong indications that the role of father is of great significance and reaffirm the relevance of father's contribution for a boy's psychosocial well being and development.

Studies have been conducted to address the issue of the social behavior and social standing of children living in homes with high levels of conflict and aggression. Results show that those living with hostile and aggressive parents had fewer of the positive skills that facilitate successful interactions with peers (Crockenberg & Lourie, 1996; Pettit et al., 1988) or were more likely to behave in an aggressive or antisocial manner (Hart et al., 1998).

Poverty, landlessness and unemployment are responsible for families and children moving to urban centers. Rapid industrialization and urbanization are responsible for large number of rural poor migrating to cities (Agnelli, S. 1986; Nangia, P. 1988; Singh, R.R. 1989; Kanbargi, R. 1992). This also gives rise to street children who form a segment of the urban poor. The broad category of street children living without familial contact can be distinguished in two subgroups. One comprises of children who had been orphaned or abandoned. The second subgroup includes children who are abandoning, who have taken a decision to leave their homes due to varied reasons (Felseman, J.K. 1981). The sample in the study comprised of both these groups.

After leaving their homes, the boys in the sample were earning their livelihood by engaging in economic activities in the unorganized sector. High mobility and instability characterized the work-life of these children with most of them showing strong preference for self-employment. Living in the streets was harsh, unstructured, unstable and fraught with insecurity. The boys slept either on the pavement, outside closed shops or any other unoccupied place. While living on the station, they had no access to proper toilet and bathing facilities.

The children had no place to keep their belongings and meager savings. They were mostly in the habit of spending their complete earnings on the same days as they were unable to entrust their savings to anyone's custody. The behaviour of spending all the money can also be viewed as a situational response. Leibow, E. (1967) also reported similar finding in his study of black American street corner men in a low income area. He suggests that such behaviour can be considered as a direct and indeed rational reaction to situational constraints of their environment.

In the domain of peer relations, most of the boys had few friends and no stable companionships. Friends played a crucial role in the lives of few boys and provided emotional and material support. Very few boys in the sample associated themselves with gangs. Whyte, W. (1981) has also described the role of gang in the life of street corner boys. He reported that "social interaction within the gang give rise to a system of mutual obligations which is fundamental to group cohesion. If the children are to carry on their activities as a unit, there are many occasions when they must do favours for one another. The code requires the child to help his friends when he can and to refrain from doing anything to harm them". In the present study, the gang reportedly played a dominant role in the lives of a few street children providing them protection, security and support. On the street, the children's relationships to other people were mostly need-oriented, mistrustful and superficial. They had no opportunity for developing intimate and affectionate ties with adults in their environment.

Nobel Laureate William Golding (1954) in 'Lord of the Flies' describes the course of events among a group of preadolescent boys marooned on an island, living without any contact with adults. Golding describes the consequence of absence of adult participation on the lives of these children as, "Patterns of civilized human relationships are too shallowly rooted, and are soon destroyed by the quickly rising sadism of peer power". The book delineates the adverse and tragic eventuality of such a situation.

While living on the station most of the boys were deprived of adult interaction, guidance and support. Relationships with peers were also not trusting or mutually- satisfying. Fear and mistrust and frequent instances of being cheated by friends characterized peer relations. "In human terms, moving about makes it difficult for them to form lasting human relationships. Consequently, may are emotionally immature, and have a desperate need for affection" (Agnelli, S. 1986).

Conflicts between friends were frequent with aggression manifested both verbally, in the form of abusive language, and in a physical manner. Only a few boys in the sample had cohesive and stable relationships with their friends. The children's mode of relating to others reflects their coping strategy to deal with their situation. The element of mistrust and fear in their behaviour while interacting with others, and the prevalence of predominantly need-oriented relationships represent a reaction and pattern of adaptation to their unstable and insecure life experiences on the street. The basic trust which is an essential prerequisite in the course of development of close and reciprocal relationships was conspicuously missing. This can be understood keeping in mind the fact that all the boys reported having bitter experiences at home and with other boys. They had been cheated or exploited by them and this made them hostile or averse to trusting other children.

The precarious living and working conditions and the hazards of their work added to the vulnerability and insecurity of their street existence. While working on the station, the boys were harassed by the police, the licensed porters and 'dadas'. There were frequent reports of victimization and extortion by the police. Street existence resulted in cumulative damage to the children's health and well being. This was evident at the physical level (under nutrition, illness and disease); social level (alienation and marginalization); and psychological level (adverse effects on self-esteem and emotional deprivation). Thus, children's living and working conditions had deep social and psychological implications for them.

It is widely accepted that homeless children are in poorer health than children who are not homeless. Unhygienic living conditions of poverty result in nutritional deficiencies. This may also result as a 'secondary' response to illness, either physical or psychological, which diminishes the child's appetite (Davis, K. & Schoen, C. 1978). Although homeless street children are more in need of health and care services than other children, their access to such facilities is almost absent.

The children lacked basic health services and had no source of continuing health care. The lack of ongoing care also implies that medical problems which could have been treated were otherwise were overlooked. The boys in the sample tended to seek help only when they had severe problems. The problems of living on the street were marked by poor-quality diet, overcrowding and in sanitary conditions which resulted in frequent gastro-intestinal, respiratory and skin problems, as reported by the boys. The lure or necessity of eating thrown away or leftover food is likely to lead to digestive disorders and food poisoning. Scavenging is one example of the extreme risks children face in street work. Sometimes children picked up used paper, plastics, rags, bottles, tin and metal pieces from the street, train compartments, railway tracks, garbage dumps or waste bins, and sold them to retailers for recycling. The nature of their work is most unhygienic, dangerous, debasing. Most children reported facing humiliation by others when they were rag-picking. Apart from this, they develop several kinds of skin diseases like ulcers, scabies, etc. While collecting rusted iron or other metal pieces, they usually receive cuts on their hands and become prone to tetanus. While collecting broken glass pieces, which can be sold later, they injure their bare feet.

The children's work of carrying load is also likely to affect their physical development. Research has shown that carrying loads by children loads by children can cause deformity, particularly of the bones and the spine. Lifting heavy weight or engaging in jobs requiring an abnormal posture, can result in permanent deformities (Challis, J. & Elliman, D. 1979). Carrying heavy loads under the arms, on the shoulders or on their back adversely affects the height, weight and stamina of the growing bodies. It seems that poor nutrition and sanitation, homelessness and physical and psychological stress of children's work all interacted to intensify their health problems. While the streets presented opportunities for work and freedom, they also infringed on children's dignity and adversely affect their physical, emotional, and overall well-being.

The child's presence on the street carries many implications. Research suggests that homeless children are highly vulnerable to developmental delays and emotional disturbances. Such problems in children appear to have their roots in the stress related to their home-life and their present homelessness (Fox, E. & Roth, L. 1989). Data indicated that emotional health was poor in most of the children. On the station, the environmental factors predisposing the children to psychosocial problems were multiple. Conditions of deprivation, unpredictability of their lives and low-esteem presumably led to deterioration in the general emotional health of children. The boys also expressed persistent feelings of personal inadequacy and dissatisfaction regarding their work.

None of the children in the sample was attending school. Majority of the boys were keen on studying. They believed that education guaranteed a well-paid and prestigious job. Studies in different countries show that a large proportion of working children do not go to school. "Lack of schooling perpetuates a bleak and hopeless status quo, barring the way to any advancement or a better life" (Dogramaci, I. 1981). However, the introduction of compulsory primary education, as advocated by Weiner, M. (1991), will not be effective in reducing the incidence of working children, particularly homeless street children.

The phenomenon of children living and working on the street should not be considered exclusively as an education or child labour issue. Compulsory education or prohibition of employment of these children would be meaningless. Compulsory education cannot be implemented effectively if other problems are not addressed. There can be no radical improvement in the situation or working children without associated social and economic changes directed at eradicating poverty. (Subrahmanyam, S. 1992 ; Reddy, N, 1992) . Education policies can be made more flexible in order to allow a combination of school attendance with part-time work (MacPherson, S. 1987). It is important to acknowledge the realities of social and economic lives of urban, homeless working children and to find holistic solutions to improve their conditions.

As regards their leisure-time activities, most boys were in the habit of watching movies frequently and gambling. They had no opportunity or facility to play. "Leisure, recreation and chance to play are absolute essentials for normal healthy development of children. Long hours of work or lack of opportunities for play have a stultifying effect on the child's social, intellectual and emotional development" (Dogramaci, I. 1981). The repercussions of lack of education and socialization by parents and other caregivers have not been quantified but are undoubtedly immense.

The absence of responsible adult involvement, supervision and guidance in the children's lives is likely to lead to children drifting into anti-social activities. Emphasizing the role of the family, Bronfenbrenner, U. (1974) asserts that inadequate participation of adult leads to 'increased alienation' indifference, antagonism, and violence on the part of the younger generation in all segments of the society'. He further argues that if children have contact only with their own age-mates (as in the case of street children), there is no possibility for learning culturally established patterns of cooperation, mutual concern and social responsibility.

Children in the study were living in extremely difficult circumstances, working under hazardous conditions and deprived of their rights to optimal development, education, and protection from abuse. In India, there is a plethora of laws which, in principle, both guard chidren from abuse and ensure their welfare and development. In reality, the rights and needs of street children are neglected.

The scenario of the children's street lives illustrated the variations in the manner in which they managed and adapted to their circumstances. Most of the boys did not want to return to their families. They preferred the harsh working and living conditions on the street to the neglecting and abusive environment in their homes. Street life also offered them sense of autonomy and freedom which they highly valued and cherished. The children's problems and coping mechanism cannot be considered identical. However, what particularly characterizes this diverse group of chidren is that they live outside the parameters that society has allocated to the stage of childhood. The children's apparent liberty and independence from adult supervision, guidance and protection created an image of these children which contradicted the characteristics associated with their developmental state.

The adult's concept of a child as vulnerable and in need of family to provide him protection and a child who was earning and living alone were contrasting and incongruent. The present study, in addition to increasing knowledge about street children, also brings to attention the 'relativity of child development'. "Childhood is not a consistent phenomenon, untouched by societal or personal circumstances" (Aptekar, L. 1988). This study offers insights in the context of homeless street children, highlighting both their adaptive behaviour and vulnerabilities.

Several implications emerge clearly from the present research. On is that in the long-run, prevention or intervention efforts have little prospect of significant success unless they include a major emphasis on changing the child's home environment. Existing patterns of parent-child (especially paternal-child) relationships, particularly in low income group families are problematic. Another important point is that in most instances, efforts to help the street children directly need to be concerned with improving or enhancing his social and vocational competence, rather than trying to prevent delinquent behaviour.

'To be of genuine help to these children, social policy must respect and foster their strengths, providing greater opportunity of the expression of the demonstrated competence' (Felsman, J.K. 1984). Further more, such efforts have their best chance of success if they are part of a large programme of comprehensive psychological and physical care, education and training directed towards their optimal growth and development.

Future Research

The phenomenon of urban, homeless, working street children is much in need of careful investigation and more comprehensive social action. An understanding of the complexity and diversity in the lives of these children will need to draw upon the interrelated fields of sociology, psychology and cultural anthropology. Felsman, J.K. (1988) in his work with Colombian street children found that they lacked any signs of overt psychopathology. However, he believes that there are street children who are deeply disturbed, or show deviant behaviour. It has also been reported frequently that street children are poorly nourished and also use drugs. Studies can be conducted in order to understand the degree to which their health is affected due to poor nutrition and their alleged drug abuse.

In the perspective on the current state of knowledge in the field of street children, the issue of psychosocial deprivation appears to be significant. To increase our understanding of psychosocial deprivation, a major research impetus with homeless street children should involve more empirial research in their natural settings. There is also a need for longitudinal studies, particularly those formulated to asses the long-term effects of street existence on the child and also the effectiveness of intervention programmes.

7.5.   CASE PROFILES

Krishan Kumar Banwar, age 14, hails from Balia (Uttar Pradesh). His father worked as a construction labourer and sometimes also worked as a helper at a grocer's shop. Krishan left home a year ago and has since never gone back. His father used to beat him frequently, especially when the child refused to work. Whenever, Krishan did not work he was denied food that day. One day Krishan decided to leave his home as he recalls, "I decided to leave home. I thought I will die if I take such beatings everyday".

At home, Krishan always felt closer to his mother. He says he always turned to his mother whenever he needed help or advice. Krishan was afraid of his father as he says, "I was scared of my father. When he was at home, I preferred staying out."

After leaving his home Krishan went to Gorakpur and then came to Delhi. He worked in a hotel in Paharganj but left that work after a week. He says he was made to do a lot of work and whenever he took rest, he was abused or beaten up by his co-workers or employer. He saw other boys working as porters at the New Delhi Railway Station and decided to take up the same work. He worked for 7-8 hours daily and earned Rs. 20-25 per facility for doing so. Regarding his work he said, "I am able to earn enough money but it is a tough job and one gets beaten up also".

Krishan wanted to change his present work but he was vague about the kind of work he is interested in. He expressed his wish to be a policemen as he thinks that a policemen can beat 'dadas' and he has immense power. Krishan missed his family. He admitted, "I remember my mother and younger sister". But he said he did not intend returning home, "If I return home, I will again face those beatings and conflicts. I will stay here and work".

3.   Ram Ratan, age 14, comes from Bhagalpur, Bihar. His father worked in the fields as a labourer but was mostly without work. Ram's mother and elder sister also worked in the fields as the family income was extremely inadequate. The family was facing

acute financial problems and was under heavy debts.. Ram's father was a drunkard as he reported, "The family income was insufficient. My father's drinking habit reduced the income and debts also had to be repaid".

Two years back, Ram's father met with an accident and lost his leg. It involved a lot of expenditure on his treatment. Being disabled, it was difficult for his father to get a job. The family having five children was facing acute financial crisis. Because of poverty, there were frequent discords and conflicts in the family. As Ram puts it, "There were frequent fights in our family because of economic insufficiency. My father was always angry and frustrated. He asked me to leave home and earn money".

The child left home almost a year back. He came to Delhi and started working. He worked as a porter and earned Rs. 20-25 daily. He expressed anger at the treatment meted out to him by the policemen on the station. He complained that the policemen took bribe from drug-peddlers or others engaged in anti-social activities. He said "We are not thieves, we earn out money. The policemen take bribe from those who steal and let them off but we are beaten by them".

Ram wanted to earn more and save money. He said he liked living on the station, "I like living here. If I go back home, there will be fights and quarrels. I will go back only after earning enough money".

4.Mahusudan is 14 year old and hails form Sultanpur, Uttar Pradesh. His mother died when he was10 years old and his father married again. Madhusudan's stepmother started illtreating him. Things became worse for Madhusudan after his stepsister's birth. He was made to do the entire household chores as he says, "My step mother was always angry with me. She made me do the entire household chores. When my father came back after work, she complained to him about me. Then, my father used to beat me".

One day the child left home without telling his parent. He

has been to various places like Lucknow, Jhansi, Nagpur and Banaras. He came to Delhi last year and started ragpicking and did not like the task. A few months back he started working as a porter. He works for 8-10 hours daily and sleeps on the pavement outside the station. He spends his entire day's earnings on food, movies and smoking.

On the station, Madhuban has a few friends and Pappu is his best friend. He helps Madhusudan whenever he is in trouble or needs money. They have their meals together and often watch together. He says most of the boys are selfish and exploit other children. He reported that fights between friends were common on the station.

The child does not wish to return home as he says "I have vowed that I will never go back home. He has studied till class II and is keen on going to school and studying futher. Regarding his future plans, Madhusudan was vague and uncertain, he said, "I don not know what I will do in the future. I want to do some good work but I do not know what is destined for me".

5. Naseem Ahmed, age 13 years, belongs to Banaras, Uttar Pradesh. His stepfather worked as a rickshaw-puller and mother did embroidery on sarees. Nasim was the eldest child in the family with four siblings. Because of economic compulsions Nasim also had to work in a handloom factory since he was 7 years old. He reported "I had a step father. My real father deserted my mother. My stepfather gave me a lot of trouble. I had to work a lot. I used to work in a handloom factory since I was very young".

Nasim's employer illtreated him and used to beat him if the child took some rest while working, he says, "One day my employer beat me black and blue. Then I decided not to work for him. My father wanted me to work the whole day and learn the skill".

The child said he often felt unwanted and neglected at home. His stepfather often threatened him that he would leave Nasim in an orphanage. He was also never allowed to go to school. Nasim left home last year. He has visited Bombay also. He was working at the New Delhi Railway Station as a porter. He was able to lift 25-30 Kg. and worked for 8-9 hours on average. He had his daily meals from a 'dhaba' near the station. He spent Rs. 3-5 per meal which included chapaties and curry. He did not like the food but at the same time he was free to eat as much as he wanted, " I earn my money and eat as much as I want. In the village, I was denied food often".Nasim enjoyed watching movies and smoked a bundle of bidi everyday. He also gambled in company of his friends. He was interested in learning tailoring or working in a garage.

BIBLIOGRAPHY

Agnelli, S. (1986) Street children – A growing urban tragedy, London Weidenfeld & Nicolson.

Anarfi,J K.1997 Vulnerability to STD: street children in Accra 303Supplement to Health Transition Review Volume 7

Andry, R.B. (1971) Delinquency and Parental Pathology, London, Staples Press.

Annual Report (1991-92), Ministry of Welfare, Government of India, New Delhi.

Aptekar, L. (1988) 'Street Children of Colombia', Journal of Early Adolescence, Vol 8, No. 3.

Aptekar, L. (1988) 'Colombian street children – their mental health and how they can be served', International Journal of Mental Health, Vol 17, No.3.

Aptekar, L. (1990) 'How ethnic differences within a culture influence child rearing: The case of Colombian Street Children' Journal of Comparative Family Studies.

Arimpoor, J. (1992) Street children of Madras – A Situational Analysis, Noida, National Labour Institute.

Ausbel, D. (1952) Ego-development and Personality Disorders, New York, Grune & Stratton.

Bagwell, C. L., Newcomb, A. F., & Bukowski, W. M. (1998). Preadolescent friendship and peer rejection as predictors of adult adjustment. Child Development, 69

Barker, F.K. (1993) 'How to interview children who live or work in the streets', In First Call for Children – A UNICEF Quarterly, No. 1, Jan.- March, 1993, UNICEF.

Barker, G. 1993. Research on AIDS: knowledge, attitudes and practices among street youth. *Children Worldwide* 20,2-3:41-42.

Barrera, M., Chassin, L., & Rogosch, F. (1993). Effects of social support and conflict on adolescent children of alcoholic and non-alcoholic fathers. Journal of Personality and Social Psychology, 64

Bassuk, E.; Rubin, L. & Alison, L. (1986) 'Characteristics of sheltered homeless families', American Journal of Public Health, 76 (9).

Batra, M. (1990) The Law and the Indian Child, New Delhi, Y.W.C.A. (India).

Bernstein, A., & Gray, M. (1991). Khaya Lethu-An abortive attempt at dealing with street children. Social Work, 27(1), 50-58.

Blanc, C. (1994). Urban Children in Distress: Global Predicaments and Innovative Strategies. Gordon and Breach

Bose, M. (1988) 'Child Labour Legislation in India', The Lawyers, Vol. 3, No. 7 Bombay.

Braden, A. (1981) 'Adopting the abused child: Love is not enough', Social case work, Vol. 62, No. 6.

Brody, G. H., & Flor, D. L. (1998). Maternal resources, parenting practices, and child competence in rural, single-parent African-American families. Child Development, 69

Bowlby, J. (1952) Maternal Care and Mental Health, World Health Organisation, Geneva.

Boyden, J. 1991. *Children of the Cities*. London: Zed Books Ltd.

Boyden, J. & W. Myers, *Exploring Alternative Approaches to Combating Child Labour: Case Studies from Developing Countries*, Florence: UNICEF

Bready, J. (1935) Doctor Barnardo, London, Allen & Unwin Ltd.

Bronfenbrenner, U. (1974) Two worlds of childhood, Harmondsworth Penguin Education.

Campo, A. T., & Rohner, R. P. (1992). Relationships between perceived parental acceptance-rejection, psychological adjustment, and substance abuse among young adults. Child Abuse & Neglect, 16

Cantwell, N. (1979) 'Parental Physical Violence towards Children', Assignment Children, Vol. 47.

CASA Alianza, 1995, Report to the United Nations Committee Against Torture on the Torture of Guatemalan Street Children. New York: Casa Alianza.

Castellanos, A. (1991), 'Swimming in Sewers', Sunday Mail, October 6, 1991.

Challis, J. & Elliman, D. (1979) Child workers' Today, Anti-Slavery Society', United Kingdom.

Child Workers in Asia, July-December, 1991, Street education for street children in Bangkok, Vol. 7, Nos. 3-4.

Claire O'Kane Street and Working Children's Participation in Programming for their Rights, Children, Youth and Environments 13(1), Spring 2003

Cockburn, A. (1990). From concern to concrete action: The story of the Homestead. In Centre for Intergroup Studies, The influence of violence on children. Cape Town: Centre for Intergroup Studies.

Cockburn, A. (1991). Street children: An overview of the extent, causes, characteristics and dynamics of the problem. The Child Care Worker, 9(1), 12-13.

Connolly, M. (1990). Adrift in the city: A comparative study of street children in Bogota, Colombia, and Guatemala City. In N. Boxhill (Ed.), Homeless children: The watchers and the waiters (pp. 129-149). New York: Haworth Press.

Cronje, G., Van der Wait, P. J., Retief, G. M., & Naude, C. M. B. (1976). The juvenile delinquent in society. Pretoria: University of South Africa.

Connolly, M. & Ennew, J. (eds.) Children out of Place: Special issue on street and working children , Childhood, Vol. 3, No. 2, London: Sage Publications, May 1996

Cooper, D. (1972) The Death of the Family, Harmondsworth, Penguin Books.

Coopersmith, S. (1967) The Antecedents of self-esteem, San Francisco, W.H. Freeman.

Coopersmith, S. (1968) Psychosocial Deprivation and the development of self-esteem. In Perspectives on Human Deprivation: Biological, Psychological and Social, Washington, D.C., U.S. Department of Health, Education and Welfare.

Country Reports on Human Rights Practices for 2000—India (Washington, D.C.: U.S. Department of State, 2001), Section 6d.

Davis, A. (1968) Social class influences upon learning, Cambridge, Harvard University Press.

Davis, K. & Schoen, C. (1978) Health and War on Poverty, Washington, D.C., Brookings.

Dawes, A. (1994). The emotional impact of violence. In A. Dawes & D. Donald (Eds.), Childhood and adversity: Psychological perspectives from South African research. Cape Town: David Philip.

Denton, R. E., & Kampfe, C. M. (1994). The relationship between family variables and adolescent substance abuse: A literature review. Adolescence, 29(114)

de Oliveira, W., Baizerman, M., Pellet, L. (1992). Street children in Brazil and their helpers: Comparative views on aspirations and the future. International Social Work, 35

Derek Hemenway, December 1996, Street children and education: Cross-cultural comparisons and program implications Florida State University.

Diggory, J.C. (1966) Self-evaluation, New York, Wiley.

D'Lima, H. & Gosalia, R. (1992) Street Children of Bombay A situational Analysis. Noida, National Labour Institute.

Dogramaci, I. Child labour: an overview. In Pitt, D.; Shah, OP\\P.M.; Sterky,G. & Williams, A. (eds.) (1981) child labour: A threat to health & development, S.H.O., Geneva.

Donald & Swart-Kruger. (1994). The South African Street Child: development implications. South African Journal of Psychology. 24(4)

D. P. Chaudhri, *A Dynamic Profile of Child Labour in India* , as cited in UNICEF press release, "Child Labour in India" (New Delhi: UNICEF Information Service, 1996

Duncan, N., & Rock, B. (1994). Inquiry into the effects of public violence on children (Preliminary Report). Commission of Inquiry Regarding the Prevention of Public Violence and Intimidation.

Dunford, M. (1996). Occasional papers no. 58. Tackling the symptoms or the causes? An examination of Programmes by NGOs for Street Children in Nairobi, Kenya. Centre of African studies, Edinburgh University

Easton, P., Klees, S., Milton, S., **Papagiannis, G.,** Clawson, A., DeWees, T., Hobson, H., Lyons, **B., Munter, J.** (1994). Asserting the Educational Rights of Street **and Working** Children: Lessons from the Field. Report submitted to UNICEF, Urban Section: New York

Economic Survey 2000-2001 (India: **Ministry** of Finance, February 2001

Emery, R. E., & Laumann-Billings, L. **(1998).** An overview of the nature, causes, and consequences of abusive family relationships. American Psychologist, 53

Ennew, J. (1987) Children of the **Street, Internation** Catholic Child Bureau, Vol.14, No.1.

Ennew, J. & Milne, B. **(1989) The Next Generation** – Lives of Third World Children, London, **Zed Books Ltd.**

Ennew, J. & Young, P. (1981) **Child Labour in** Jamaica, London, Anti-Slavery Society .

Erikson, E. (1950) Childhood and **Society, New York,** Nortion.

Felsman, J.K. (1981) 'Street Urchins of Colombia', Natural Histories (41-48), New York, American **Museum** of Natural History.

Felsman, J.K. (1984) 'Abandoned Children – A reconsideration', Children Today, May-June, 1984.

Fieldman, H. L. 1994. Reproductive health in adolescence. *World Health Statistics Quarterly* 47,1:31-35.

Fox. E. & Roth, L. "Homeless **Children: Philadelphia** as a case study. In Lambert, R. (ed.) **(1989) The Annals** of the American Academy of Political and Social Sciences, Vol. 506, Newbury Park, Sage Publications.

Freeman, M.D. (1979) Violence in the home, England, Saxon House.

Freud, S. (1949) An outline of Psychoanalysis, London, Hograth Press.

Freud, S. (1964) New Introductory Lectures in Psychoanalysis, New York, Norton.

Garbarino, J., & Sherman, D. (1980). High-risk neighborhoods and high-risk families: The human ecology of child maltreatment. Child Development, 51.

Gardiner, H. (1974) Human Figure Drawings as indicators of value development among Thia Children, Journal of Cross-cultural Psychology, (5).

Garmezy, N. (1983). Stressors of childhood. In M. Rutter & N. Garmezy (Eds.), Stress, coping and development in children. New York: McGraw-Hill

Ghosh, A (1992) Street Children of Calcutta A situational Analysis, Noida, National, Labour Institute
Gil, D. (1971) 'Violence Against Chidren', Journal of Marriage & Familay, Vol. 33.

Gil, D. (1971) 'Violence Against Chidren', Journal of Marriage & Familay, Vol. 33.

Gil, D. (1973) Violence against children: Physical child abuse in the United States, Cambridge, Harvard University Press.

Gil, D. (1975) 'Unravelling Child Abuse', Americal Journal of Orthopasychiatry, Vol. 45.

Giovannoni, J.M. (1988) 'Parental mistreatment: Perpetrators and victims', Journal of Marriage and Family, Vol.33.

Giovannonj, J.M. & Becerra, R.M. (1979) Defining child abuse, New York, The Free Press.

Goffman, E. (1963) Stigma – Notes on the management of strained identity, New Jersey, Prentice Hall.

Golding, W. (1954) Lord of the Flies, London, Penguin.

Gordon, E.A. (1965) Review of Compensatory Education, American Journal of Orthopsychiatry, (35).

Gordon, J. S. (1979). Running away: Reaction or revolution. Adolescent Psychiatry, Developmental and Clinical Studies, 7, 52-61.

Hall, C.S. (1956) A Primer of Freudian Psychology, London, Allen & Unwin.

Haralambos, M. Heald, R. (1980) Sociology : Themes & Perspectives, Delhi, Oxford University Press.

Healy, W. & Bronner, A. (1926 Delinquents and Criminals, New York, MacMillan Company.

Helfer, E.R.: Kempe, H. Mondale, W. (1976) Child Abuse & Neglect: The Family and the Community, New York, Ballinger Company.

Heredia, R.c. & Kaul, K. (1987) 'Children off the Streets an evaluation on Sneh-Sadan, Bombay' Social Science Centre, St. Xavier's College.

Hodge, W. 'Bogota School Reclaims Waifs from the streets', cited in Felsman, J.K. (1984) 'Abandoned Children – A Reconsideration', Children Today, May-June, 1984

Houston, B. K., & Vavak, C. R. (1991). Cynical hostility: Developmental factors, psychological correlates, and health behaviors. Health Psychology, 10

Human Rights Watch, 2000 Promises Broken: Police Abuse and Arbitrary Detention of Street Children World Report 2000 Section on Children's Rights: Police Abuse and Arbitrary Detention of Street Children HRW Publications.

Ideas Forum (1984/3) Abandoned & Street Children, Issue No. 8 Geneva, UNICEF.

Ideas Forum (1984/3) Mexico- Pictures of another reality in Acapulco, Issue No. 18, Geneva, UNICEF.

Ifthekar, J.S., Under the sheltering sky, The Indian Express, December 6, 1992, Kochi.

Indian Express, 5 February 2000 Street Children - The Law Minister said that the country has 2 million street children. ("Laws alone cannot tackle child labour", New Delhi.)

Inter-Ministerial committee (IMC) on Young People at Risk. (1998). Minimum Standards. South African Child and Youth Care System International Catholic Child Bureau (1987), 'International Action for street children and street youth: an overview', Vol 14, No.1.

International Labour Organisation (1986) Child labour: A briefing manual, Geneva, International Labour Office.

International Labor Organization (2000), Yearbook of Labour Statistics (Geneva: ILO, 2000).

International Labour Organisation, 2002, *Every Child Counts: New Global Estimates on Child Labour* (Geneva, Switzerland: International Labour Office), 15

International Labor Organisation,"Preventing and Eliminating Child Labour in Identified Hazardous Sectors" (Geneva: ILO-IPEC, September 2001).

Jahoda, M. (1955) Research methods in social relations, New York, The Dryden Press.

Janus, M. D. et al 1987. *Adolescent Runaways*. Toronto: Lexington Books.

Jones, D.N. (1982) Understanding Child Abuse, Great Britain, Hodder & Stoughton.

Kaime - Atterhog, W. 1996. Street children and prostitution: the situation in Kenya. *News on Health Care in Developing Countries*, 10

Kakar, S. (1978) The Inner World – A Psychoanalytic study of society in India, Delhi, Oxford University Press.

Kalu, W. J. 1986. Emotional abuse and neglect in contemporary Nigerian family: a reassessment of parenthood skills. In *Child Labour in Africa. Proceedings of the First International Workshop on Child Abuse in Africa, Enugu, Nigeria, April*. UNICEF.

Kamerman, S. 'Eight Countries: Cross-national Perspective on child abuse and neglect, children Today, 1975, Vol.4.

Kanbargi, R. (1991) Child Labour in the Indian Sub-continent – It's Dimensions & Implications, New Delhi, Sage Publications.

Kantroo, B.K. "Role of Juvenile Welfare Board in Juvenile Justice Act', Paper presented at the state level of workshop for children in especially difficult circumstances, New Delhi, 6-8 June, 1990.

Kapadia, K.M. & Pillai, S. (1969) Home desertion by Juveniles, Bombay, Bombay University.

Kathleen, E. 'Broken Homes. & Juvenile Delinquency', Social Forces, May, 1932 (1).

Kempe, H.C. & Helfer, R.E. (eds.) (1980) The battered child, Chicago, University of Chicago Press.

Kerns, K. A., Klepac, L., & Cole. A. K. (1996). Peer relationships and preadolescents' perceptions of security in the child-mother relationship. Developmental Psychology, 32

Kessler, J. (1988) Psychopathology of childhood, New Jersey, Englewood Cliff.

Klair, M. A rag-tag table, The Hindustan Times, January 10, 1993, New Delhi.

Kleck, R. (1968) The Role of Stigma as a factor in social interaction. In Perspectives in Human Deprivation, Washington, D.C., U.S. Department of Health, Education and Welfare.

Knutsson, E.K. (1991) First Call for Children. In Bhatia, S.C. (ed.) (1991) The Citizen Child: Socio-cultural Perspectives, Delhi Department of Adult Continuing Education & Extension, University of Delhi.

Korbin, J. (ed.) (1981) Child abuse and neglect: Cross-cultural perspectives, Berkeley, University of California Press.

Korbin, J.E. 1983. Introduction. In *Child Abuse and Neglect, Cross Cultural Perspectives*, ed. J.E. Korbin. Berkeley: University of California Press.

Kufeldt, K. and M. Nimmo. 1987. Kids on the street, they have something to say: survey of runaway and homeless youth. *Journal of Child Care* 3,2:53-61.

Kumar, K. (1993). "Study of Childhood and Family." In Saraswati, T. S. and B. Kaur, eds. *Human Development and Family Studies*. New Delhi: Sage.

Laing, R.D. (1976) The Politics of the Family, Harmondsworth, Penguin Books.

Landry, S. H., Smith, K. E., Miller-Loncar, C. L., & Swank, P. R. (1998). The relation of change in maternal interactive styles to the developing social competence of full-term and preterm children. Child Development, 69(1).

Leibow, E. (1967) Tally's Corner, Boston, Little Brown.

Levine, S. & Levine, R. (1981) Child abuse and neglect in sub-saharan Africa. In Korbin, J. (ed.) (1981) Child abuse and neglect: Cross-cultural Perspectives, Kerkeley, University of California Press.

Liyanara, L., 'Training of social workers dealing with street children – Remedial Programmes, Paper present at the South – Asian Workshop on street children organised by Tata Institute of Social Sciences. Bombay, in collaboration with International Association of School of Social Work, Bombay, April 22-25, 1992.

Lominitz, (1977) Organization of a Mexican shanty town, In Lornelius, W. & Trueblood, F. (eds.) Latins American urban Research, New York, Sage Publication.

Lusk, M. (1989). Street children programs in Latin America. Journal of Sociology and Social Welfare, 16 (1).

Lynn, D.B. (1974) The Father – His Role in Child Development, California, Brooks Company.

MacPherson, S. (1987) Five hundred million children, Poverty and child welfare in the third world, New York, St. Martin Press.

MacPherson, S. & Midgley, J. (1987) Comparative social policy and the Third World, Bighton, Wheatsheaf Book.

Mallik, B., 'The Freedom School: The street child's own school', paper presented at the South-Asian workshop on street children oganised by Tata Institute of Social Sciences. Bombay, in collaboration with International School of Social Work, Bombay, April 22-25, 1992.

Marfatia, M., Innocence on the run, The Times of India, May 23, 1992, Bombay.

Martin, E. "Bogota's Waifs live in their own world stealing and drifting", Wall Street Journal, Jan. 8, 1979.

Mayhall, P.d. & Norgardm N.E. 1983 Child Abuse & Neglect: A sharing Responsibility, New York, Macmillan Company.

McLeod, J. D., & Shanahan, M. J. (1996). Trajectories of poverty and children's mental health. Journal of Health and Social Behavior, 37.

McLoyd, V. C. (1998). Socioeconomic disadvantage and child development. American Psychologist, 53.

Mead, M. (1949) Male & Female, New York, William Morrow.

Mendelievich, E. (ed.) (1979) Children at work, Geneva, International Labour Organisation.

Meunier, J. (1977) The gamins of Bogota, Paris, J.C. Lattes.

Milton, D. Saving the world's children, The Indian Express, July 14, 1992, Kochi.

Ministry of Education and Social Welfare (1976) Handbook of Social Welfare Statistics, Department of Social Welfare, New Delhi.

Ministry of Human Resources Development, Education for All (EFA) 2000 [online], Country Report, India, Section 2

Misra, G. & Tripathi, L.B. 'Prolonged Deprivation Scale', Indian Journal of Psychology, 53 (2).

Misra, S. 'Street Children – A strategy for an institutional plus programme, paper read at the National workshop on street children organised by the Ministry of Welfare, Government of India, National Institute of Social Defence and UNICEF, August 29 & 30, 1988.

Mohan. S., Children of the mean streets, The Times of India, September 2, 1990, New Delhi.

Mukherjee, S. 'Onto Streets and back home – Issues of street children in a conundrum', Paper presented at the 2nd National Seminar on child abuse and Neglet: Social and Legal Protection, organised by socio-legal aid Research & Training Centre, Calcutta, New Delhi, August, 1990.
Mukherjee, S. The Status Report on Street Children by the Social Welfare Directorate, Govt. of West Bengal, cited in Mukherjee, S. 'Abuse of Street Children and the riddle and rigmorale of the stable society heading for nemesis', Paper present on the international conference on education for street children, Bombay, 1992.

Mumba, F. 'Adoption in Zambia', Child Abuse and Neglect, 1981 (5).

Munoz, V.C. & Palacios, M.V. (1980) The Child Worker of Bogota Colombia, Carlos Valencia.

Murdock, G.P. (1949) Social Structure, New York MacMillan.

Mussen, P.H.; Conger, J.J. & Kagan, J. (1974) Child Development and Personality, New York, Harper & Row.

Myles Ritchie ,February 1999 'Children in ('Especially difficult Circumstances') Children living on the streets. Can Their Special Needs Be Met Through Specific Legal Provisioning? Consultative Paper prepared for the South African Law Commission.

Nandana Reddy, *Street Children of Bangalore: A Situational Analysis* (NOIDA: National Labour Institute, 1992)

Nangia, P, 'Impact of urbanization on street urhcins: A focus on Delhi', Paper presented at the National Workshop on street children, organised by Ministry of Welfare, Government of India, National Institute of Social Defence and UNICEF, New Delhi, August 29-30, 1988.

Nangia, P., 'Children at risk in Delhi – Struggle for Survival', Paper presented at the state level workshop on children in especially difficult cjrcumstances, orgnaised by Delhi Administration and UNICEF, June 6-8, 1990.

Nangia, S., 'Strategies for strengthening and extending services for children in especially difficult circumstance', Paper presented at the State level workshop on children in especially circumstances organised by Department of Social Welfare, New Delhi, June 6-8, 1990.

Nangia, P. & Pinto, R. Situational Analysis of Children in especially difficult circumstances in the U.T. of Delhi with special focus on working and street children, Report prepare for UNICEF, Mid-North India Office, 1988, UNICEF.

National AIDS Control Organization: www.naco.nic.in/

National Institute of Public Cooperation and Child Development, Introduction. In Report on the National Seminar on Child Abuse in India, June 22 & 23, 1988, New Delhi.

Neron, G. (1953) The Child vagabond cites in Aptekar, L. Street Children of Colombia, Journal of Early Adolescence, 1988, Vol. 8, No.3.

Nicolo, J. (1981) The Vermins, Bogota, Servico Juvenile.

Noble, C., Coram, R. (1994). Nobody's Child: A Woman's Abusive Past and the Inspiring Dream that Led Her to Rescue the Street Children of Saigon. New York: Grove Press.

Nurcombe, B. Deprivation: An essay in definition with special consideration of the Australians aboriginals, Medical Journal of Australia (2), 1970

Obikeze, D.ssss. Perspectives on child abuse in Nigeria, International Child Welfare Review, 63, 1984.

Okeahialam, T. 'Child Abuse in Nigeria', Child Abuse and Neglect, 5, 1984.

Ortiz de Carrizosa, S., Poertner, J. (1992). Latin American street children: Problem, programmes, and critique. International Social Work, 35.

O'Sullivan,C.M. (1991). "The relationship between childhood mentors and resiliency in adult children of alcoholics." Family Dynamics of Addiction Quarterly, 1(4), December

PANGAEA. (1995). Street Children: Russia. PANGAEA [On-line].

arker, J. G., & Asher, S. R. (1987). Peer relations and later personal adjustment: Are low-accepted children at risk? Psychological Bulletin, 102

Parsons, T. 'The Normal American Family' In Faber, S.M. (ed.) (1965) Man and Civilization: The Family's Search For Survival, New York. McGraw Hill.

Parsons, T. & Bales, R.F. (1955) Family, Socialization and Interaction Process, Glencose, Illinois, Free Press.

Patino, N.O. (1983) 600 out of thousand children consumer basuko, cited in Aptekar, L. Street Children of Colombia, Journal of Early Adolescence, 1988, Vol.8, No.3.

Pestonji, M. 'A Strange Sort of Childhood', The illustrated Weely, Vol.XIII, 43, Oct. 23-29, 1993.

Piaget, J. (1952) The origins of intelligence in children. New York, Norton.

Pinto. R. & Nangia, P. (1992) Working and Street Children of Delhi, Noida, National Labour Institute.

Pilling, D. & Pringle, M.K. (1978) Controversial issues in child development, London, Paul Elek Lts.

Power, C., & Hertzman, C. (1997). Social and biological pathways linking early life and adult disease. British Medical Bulletin, 53

Raffaelli, M., E. Siqueira, A. Payne-Merritt, et al. 1995. HIV-related knowledge and risk behaviours of street youth in Belo Horizonte, Brazil. *AIDS Education and Prevention* 7,4.

Raman, V. (2000). *Childhood-Western and Indian, an Exploratory Essay*. New Delhi: Women's Development Studies.

Rane, A.; Naidu, U.S. & Kapadia, K. (1986) Children in Difficult situations in India, Bombay, Tata Institute of Social Sciences.

Rane, A. & Shroff, N., 'Street children in India, Emerging need for social work intervention', Paper present at the South-Asian workshop on street children organised by Tata Institute of Social Sciences in collaboration with International Association of Social Work, Bombay, April 22-25, 1992.

Rao, B.V.R. & Mallik, B. (1992) Street Children of Hyderabad - A Situational Analysis, Noida, National Labour Institute.

Rasario, A., 'Ragpickers' Education & Development Scheme – A programme in Bangalore city', Paper presented at the NGO workshop on street and working children in the U.T. of Delhi, organised by Indian Council of Child Welfare and UNICEF, July 16-17, 1987.

Reddy, N. 'Education and the Working Child', Molake, Vol.2, No.2, 1992.

Reddy, N. (1992) Street Children at Bangalore. A Situational Analysis, Noida, National Labour Insitute.

Reeta Dutta Gupta, "Juvenile homes are like jails," *Times of India* (Delhi edition), January 11, 1996.

Reid, J., Macchetto, P., & Foster, S. (1999, January). No safe haven: Children of substance-abusing parents. Report from the Center on Addiction and Substance Abuse, Columbia University. New York: CASA Publications.

Rena L. Repetti, Shelley E. Taylor and Teresa E. Seeman University of California, Los Angeles Risky Families: Family Social Environments and the Mental and Physical Health of Offspring Psychological Bulletin, 128(2)

Reubens, E.P. (1967) Planning for children and youth within national development planning, Geneva, United Nations Research Institute for Social Development.

Ritchie, J.W. & Ritchie, J. Child rearing and child abuse. In Korbin, J, (ed.) (1981) Child abuse and neglect: Cross-cultural Perspectives, Berkeley, University of California Press.

Romero, F. Children of the Streets, UNESCO Courier, Oct. 17 1991, UNCESCO, France.

Ruiz, J. 1994. Street youth in Colombia: lifestyle, attitudes and knowledge. *AIDS Health PromotionExchange* 1.

Scaria, J.J., 'Coordination Committee for vulnerable children: A model on networking', Paper presented at the South-Asian workshop on street children organised by Tata Institute of Social Sciences, Bombay, in collaboration with International Association of Social Work, Bombay, April, 22-25, 199

Schmitt, D. Battered child syndrome. In Kempe, H.C. & Helfer, R.E. (eds.) (1980) The battered child, Chicago University of Chicago Press.

Segal, U. Child Abuse in India: A Theoretical Overview, The Indian Journal of Social Work. Vol. L.11 No.3, July, 1991, Bombay, Tata Institute of Social Sciences.

Seifer, R. & Sameroff, A.J. (1987) Multiple determinants of risk & invulnerability. In Anthony, E.J. & Cohler, B.J. (eds.) The Invulnerable Child, New York, Guilford Press.

Shah, P.M. (1987) Health Status of Working and Street Children and Alternative Approaches to their Health Care. In Advances in International Maternal and Child Health, Vol.7.

Sharda, N.K. (1988) The Legal, Economic and Social Status of the Indian Child, New Delhi, National Book Organisation.

Shaw, C.R. & Mackay, H.D. 'Are Broken Homes a Causative Factor in Juvenile Delinquency', Social Force, May, 1932 (1).

Silverman, B. (1935) The Behaviour of Children From Broken Homes, American Journal of Orthopsychiatry, 5, 11.

Singh, H., 'Juvenile Justice Act – Implementing mechanism,' Paper presented at the State level workshop for children in especially difficult circumstances, New Delhi, June 6-8, 1990.

Singh, R.R., 'Rights of street children: their Welfare and Developmental Dimensions' Paper presented at the National Symposium on Rights of the child: Socio-Legal Perspectives, New Delhi, September 15 & 16, 1990.

Singh, S. & Chauhan, B., 'Juvenile Justice in India', Paper presented at the National Symposium on Rights of the child: Socio-Legal Perspectives, New Delhi, September 15 & 16, 1990.

Sinha, D. & Shuka, P. Deprivation and development of skill for pictorial depth perception, Journal of Cross-cultural psychology, 1974, 5,4.

Srivastava, S. (1963) Juvenile Vagrancy, Bombay, Asia Publishing House.

Steele B. & Pollock, C. A Psychiatric Study of Parents who abuse Infants and small Children, In Halfer, R. & Kemper, H. (eds.) (1980) The Battered Child, Chicago, University of Chicago Press.

Subrahmanyam, S. Book Review In Contributions to Indian sociology, 26 (2), 1992, New Delhi, Sage Publications.

Supplement to Health Transition Review Volume 7, 1997 Vulnerability to STD: street children in Accra 283

Sweet, J.J. & Resick. A. (1979) The Maltreatment of Children of Journal of Social Issues, 32 (2).

Tacon, P. Greatest wishes of winged street creatures, Ideas Forum, Issue No.18, 1984/3, Geneva, UNICEF.

Tacon, P. (1981) 'My Child now: An Action Plan on behalf of children without families', UNICEF, New York.

Tacon, P. (1983) Regional Programmes for Latin America & Caribbean, UNICEF, New York.

Tacon, P. & Morch, J. Surviving Together, Suffering alone, Series of articles on Street and Abandoned Children, Ideas Forum, Issue No. 18, 1984/3, Geneva, UNICEF.
Thaiparambil, A., 'Ashalayam – At a Glance', Paper presented at the 2nd National Seminar on Child Abuse & Neglect: Social & Legal Protection, organised by Socio-Legal Aid Research & Training Centre, New Delhi, August, 1990.

The Hindustan Times, Focus on plight of street children, June 6, 1989, New Delhi.

The Hindustan Times, Urban World Population 2234 b, June 8, 1990.

The Hindustan Times, Plan to rehabilitate street children, September 18, 1992, New Delhi.

The Hindustan Times, Teresa likely to launch scheme for street kids, November 15, 1992, New Delhi.

The Hindustan Times, Welfare Plan for street children, April 24, 1993, New Delhi.

The Hindustan Times, Welfare Scheme for Kids, May 7, 1993, New Delhi.

The Hindustan Times, India Tops in street children, May 22, 1993, New Delhi.

The Hindustan Times, Street Children Exploited, July 30, 1993, New Delhi.

The Hindustan Times, When death squads meet street children, August 8, 1993, New Delhi.

The Hindustan Times, Task Force to aid Street Children, August 29, 1993, New Delhi.

The Indian Express, Tackling problem of street children, August 30, 1988, New Delhi.

The Indian Express, India tops in child labour, April 23, 1989, New Delhi.

The Indian Express, Rs. 1.5 crore scheme for street kids; March 26, 1992, New Delhi.

The Indian Express, 24 children escape from children's home, July 31, 1992, Kochi.

The Indian Express, From ragpickers to respectable youth, October 8, 1992, Kochi.

The Indian Express Health camp for urchins, October 11. 1993, Vishakapatnam.

The Indian Express, Street boy shot in Sao Paulo, December 20, 1993, Vishakapatnam

The Lawyers, Child Labour – The UNICEF Approach, Vol.3, No.7. Bombay, Aug. 1988.

The Lawyers, Child Labour in India: An overview, vol.3, No. 7, Bombay, Aug. 1988.

Thomas, V.S., Helping street kids be normal, The Indian Express, August 25, 1992, Kochi.

Townsend, P. (1962) The last Refuge, London, Routledge & Kagan Paul.

Turner,S.,Norman,E.,& Zunz,S. (1993). "From risk to resiliency, a paradigm shift, a literature review and annotated bibliography". Fordham University Graduate School of Social Sciences

UNAIDS Epidemiological Fact Sheets on HIV/AIDS and Sexually Transmitted Infections, India: www.unaids.org/hivaidsinfo/statistics/fact_sheets/ pdfs/India_en.pdf

UNESCO Courier, 'Africa's Lost Generations', Oct. 1991, UNCESCO, France.

UNESCO/UNAIDS International Seminar " Protecting street children's rights : combating HIV/AIDS and Discrimination" (Bamako, 3rd- 5th December 2003)

UNICEF. 1986. Child abuse and neglect in a global perspective. Paper presented to the 1986 Executive Board, New York

UNICEF. (1996). About the Convention. UNICEF [On-line] http/
/www.unicef.org/crc/conven.htm

UNICEF (1998). Rights and Opportunities: The Situation of Children and Women in
India.

UNICEF,2000, The State of the World's Children 2001 (New York:
UNICEF)

UNICEF. (1987). New alternatives for care of children in and on
the street of Mexico. Bogota: Editorial Gente Nueva.

UNICEF (1987) Convention on the rights of the child, New Delhi,
UNICEF.

(US Dept of State, Country Reports on Human Rights Practices -
1999, 25 February 2000) Street Children - Child welfare
organisations estimate that there are 500,000 street children nation-wide.

Wahler, R. G. (1990). Some perceptual functions of social networks in coercive mother-child interactions. Journal of Social
and Clinical Psychology, 9

Walters, M. The Homeless Street children of Latin America,
Reader's Digest, Vol. 135, Aug. 1989.

Weiner, M. (1991) The Child and the State in India, New Delhi,
Oxford University Press.

White, R.W. Motivation Reconsidered: The concept of Competence, Psychological Review,1959, Vol. 66, No. 5.

Whyte, R.W. (1981) Street Corner Society, Chicago, University
of Chicago Press.

Wilcox, R.C. (1971) The psychological consequences of being
Black American, New York, Wiley.

Williams, P. & Clare, A. (1979) Psychosocial disorders in General Practice, New York, Grune & Stratton.

Woodall, K. L., & Matthews, K. A. (1993). Changes in and stability of hostile characteristics: Results from a 4-year longitudinal study of children. Journal of Personality and Social Psychology, 64

World Bank (2000), World Development Indicators 2000, The World Bank: Washington, D.C.

World Health Organisation, 1979, The Child and the Adolescent in Society, Report on a WHO Conference, Copenhagen, WHO.

World Health Organisation, 1982, Manual on Child Mental Health & Psychosocial Development, (I-IV), Geneva, WHO.

World Health Organisation, 1987, Children at Work, Geneva, WHO.

World Health Organisation 1993 STREET CHILDREN Worldwide World Health Organization Programme on Substance Abuse, Jul 93. " A One-Way StreetWORLD HEALTH ORGANIZATION Programme on Substance Abuse July 1993
Young, R.L., et al. 1983. Runaways: a review of negative consequences. Family Relations 32:275-281.

USED URLs:

www.childabuse.org

"Census of India," Registrar General and Census Commissioner, India (www.censusindia.net/)
http://www.casa-alianza.org/EN/street-children/

www.cairotimes.com/content/archiv06/streetchildren0619.html
www.eurekalert.org/pub_releases/2002-04/uab
http://www.indianembassy.org/index.html

http://www.indiabudget.nic.in/es2001-02/chapt2002

www.ilo.org/public/english/standards/ipec/ simpoc/index.htm).

(www.ilo.org/public/english/standards/ipec/simpoc/stats/child/ stats.htm); cited October 24, 2001.

www.mentorfoundation.org Cornelio G. Banaag, Resiliency, Street Children, and Substance Abuse Prevention, PERSPECTIVES, Nov. 2002, Vol 3.